pollock

twentieth-century masters

pollock

Alberto Busignani

Hamlyn
London New York Sydney Toronto

twentieth-century masters
General editors: H. L. Jaffé and A. Busignani

London · New York · Sydney · Toronto
Hamlyn House, Feltham, Middlesex, England
ISBN 0 600 36914 5

Distributed in the United States of America by Crown Publishers Inc.

Printed in Italy by: Industria Grafica L'Impronta, Scandicci, Florence
Bound in Italy by: Poligrafici il Resto del Carlino, Bologna

contents

List of colour illustrations

List of black-and-white illustrations

Jackson Pollock and American romanticism

We may perceive in contemporary art that eternal contrast in human activity between spirit and matter, reason and sensation, rational abstraction and sentimental immediacy. On the one hand there is Mondrian, with his hypothesis of human history as a supreme balance in which the emotions are refined in the absolute morality of reason. On the other hand there is the American painter Jackson Pollock, engaged in a pure emotional activity, the activity of the 'gesture'. Action-painting (the phrase was coined by Harold Rosenberg), or painting-as-the-equivalent-of-action was a total liberation of the emotions.

To reduce these two sides of human activity to terms that are thoroughly familiar, we may speak of classicism and romanticism. In classicism, we see a utopia of forms disciplined in relation to an absolute concept of beauty which, moreover, is somehow identified with morality. In romanticism, we see the driving force of the existential condition, the *Sturm und Drang* within us which binds us to the earth and to an autochthonous tradition undisciplined by classical culture.

In this sense, Mondrian is indeed a classicist. He sought in his pictures for a nucleus of truth that he identified with the totality of the real. Years before he arrived at neo-plasticism, he had already clarified his aim as representation that gathered together component visual elements according to an essentially moral attitude. True, this attitude tended to suppress the merely contingent in order to attain the rationality of the real, and it rejected everything that was not absolutely objective reality. It achieved, however, a rationally and therefore universally normative language, by adopting one point of view (or realization), which is universally shared because common to all (the relationship with reality as *existence,* not with an arbitrary episode).

Thus, *The Red Tree,* as early as 1910, was composed by Mondrian as the essence or Platonic idea of the tree. More profoundly, it was the essence of the real in one of its aspects, and not only the aspect of nature, for both man and nature are to be found in it. The presence of man creates form of the object. Invoking the formal precedents of Van Gogh, the sense of this work (which may be considered as typical of rational abstraction though preceeding the deliberately abstract approach) is totally new and autonomous, appearing humanistically as the search for an absolute that is a norm of life before being translated into a linguistic norm.[1]

What sense, then, is there in speaking of Pollock as a romantic? Using the word to describe a category of the spirit–the irrationality of the emotions

1 See A. Busignani, *Mondrian,* London, 1968.

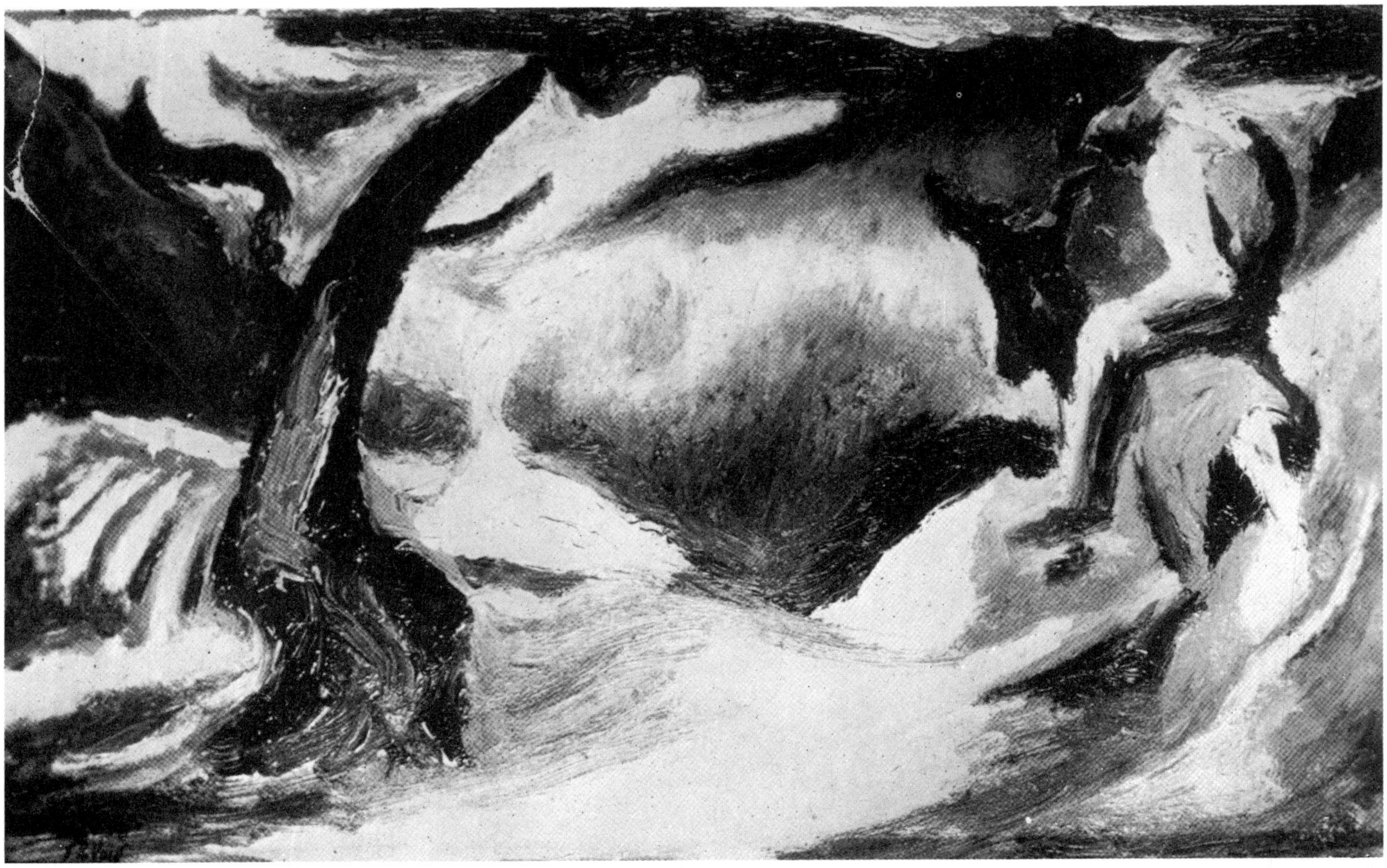

1 *Landscape with Rider*
1933, oil on tin
Whereabouts unknown

and senses–then Pollock is a romantic because he rejects the norm, and with it the rationality of form. He is a romantic because he is non-formal in comparison with the classicism and formalism of Mondrian. But this is hardly sufficient explanation. It is perhaps necessary to investigate the roots of American romanticism, of which Pollock's work represented a major and conclusive achievement.

The Romantic movement of the 19th century significantly marked the full bloom of nationalism in Europe. The universality of the 18th-century Age of Reason had seen in classicism its own ideal and the manifestation of the idea of supranational history; hence neoclassical art (though neoclassical art survived the imperial interlude and the Restoration, but only to become a denatured consumer object). The growing self-awareness of national states coincided with the search for autochthonous, anticlassical origins, which resulted in the cult of medievalism, neo-Gothic, and finally, romanticism in its revivalist aspect. The exaltation of the individual virtues of nations, in opposition to the universality of the Roman Empire in which Europe had till then recognized its image resulted too in the substitution of bards and druids for Plutarch's heroes; Wotan, Odin, elves, witches and goblins replaced the gods and heroes of the Greco-Roman heritage.

None of this happened in America. The origins of the United States had become identified with the principles of the Age of Reason, and the American tradition was predominantly neoclassic. It was this tradition that inspired the 19th-century revival, which was neoclassical (or perhaps, neo-neoclassical) rather than neo-romanesque, neo-Gothic, or even neo-medieval as it was in Europe.

A new tradition was forged in the United States in the 19th century. It was a *folk* tradition, a tradition of the frontier and the Far West; it was the sense of freedom conveyed by the opening prairies; it was the America that later gave birth to the myth of the Western.

From these roots, American art and literature elaborated that regional realism which, with its individual historical characteristics and causes is the true American romanticism. It was from this tradition, with certain European experiences grafted on, that Pollock created the first authentic American painting. Pollock's romanticism, as the eternal condition of existence, as the

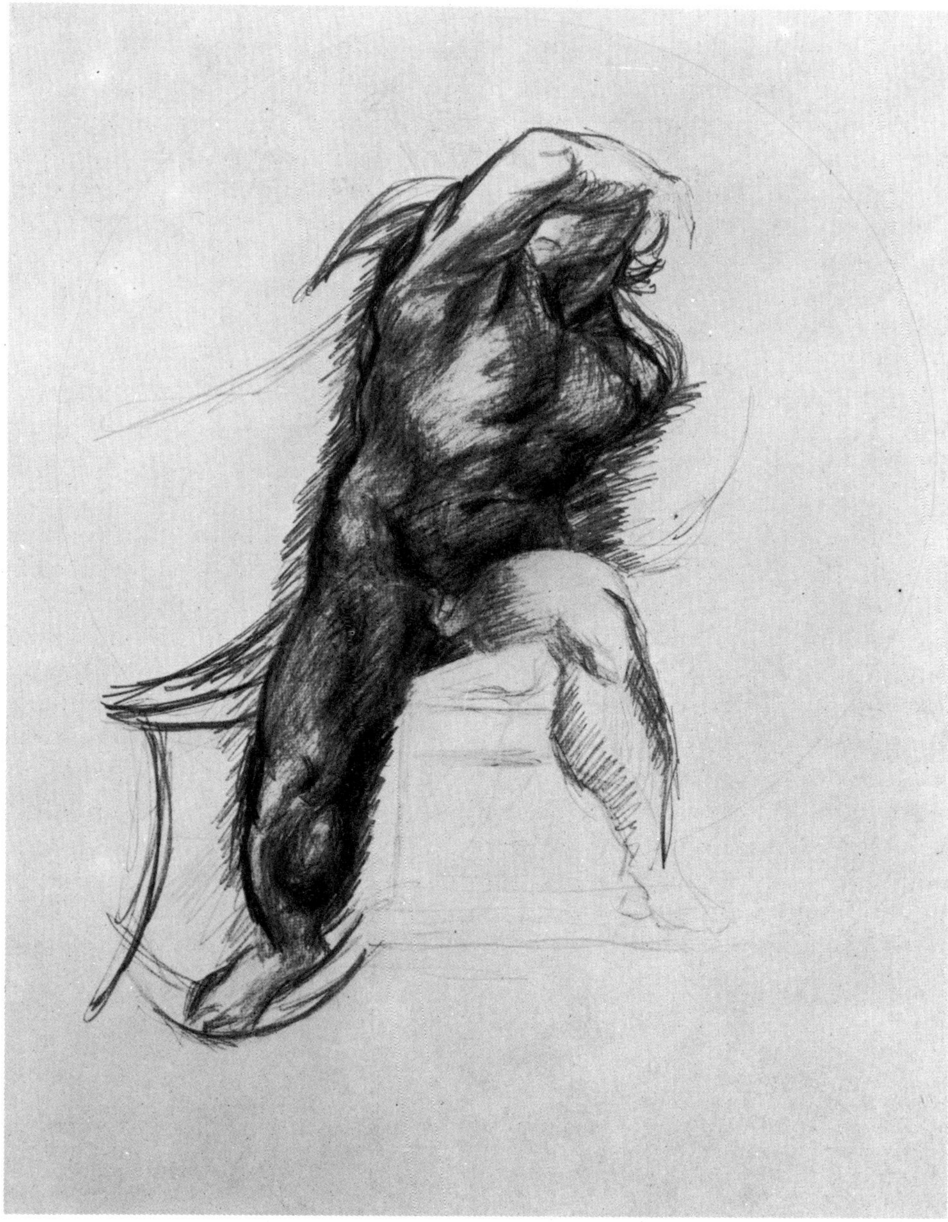

2 *Michelangelo Nude*
c. 1931–34, pencil and coloured chalk drawing on paper
18 × 12 in (46 × 30·5 cm)
Lee Krasner Pollock collection, New York

prevalence of feeling, was enriched by this tradition, and became defined as the conclusion of a process of cultural formation that had involved American society from the time of its constitution.

Man, history and nature

The manner in which Pollock's experience matured confirms his romanticism, even in the historical sense of the word. From his birth in 1912 until he moved to New York in 1929, Pollock lived in Wyoming, Arizona, and north and south California. When he was about fifteen he worked in land-surveying with his father and brother, Sandford. He was thus physically immersed in the vastness of the 'Big Country', and in contact with the plains and distant mountains that were the source of American romanticism and of the American autochthonous tradition.

It is difficult to reconstruct his environment or to analyze his particular experiences at this time.[2] But it is reasonable to postulate a relationship

2 From Bryan Robertson, *Jackson Pollock,* London, 1960: 'This early background to the age of sixteen can only be very sparsely charted and any inferences to be drawn from it can only be tentative. But it is clear that Pollock's taste was sophisticated from an early age, and that he was a rebel by nature and not attracted by tradition or by authority. It is clear also that he lived on the land and was close to it in a very real way and must have been conscious of the dramatic distances and spaces of the western landscape. He must have observed the land and its formations at close quarters and working on a geological survey, he would have seen surfaces and, textures and markings of minerals and ores and at least become conscious, always with an artist's gaze, of the colours and properties of rocks and stones and earth. His later work shows always an extreme consciousness of surface and texture.'

But in this passage Robertson has turned to an analysis of form, and the reason he has appealed to Pollock's prehistory is to justify the elaboration of these forms–a procedure whose legitimacy

between the expansion of open space offered to him as a physical and historical condition, and the attack on the subsequent destruction of European experiences in action painting and the romanticism of the non-formal.[3]

Here again, a comparison with Mondrian is revealing. The formulation of a rationalistic naturalism in the work of the Dutch painter was deeply affected by the strongly humanized and geometric-looking landscape of Winterswijk, Uden, Oele, Brabant and Zeeland. Equally, and inversely, it was the natural violence of the West that gave Pollock the presupposition for what was to become known as his personal baroque–the expansion of matter in the space that does not confine it but is created out of it. In the American landscape, space cannot be reduced to rational conventions, as in Europe. It is not a conditioning factor, but an outcome of matter. Because of its very immensity and non-humanity, it appears not so much as space (in the historical concept of space conferred by the classical tradition) but rather as a limit–as the subjectivity of the rule of perspective.

In New York from 1929, Pollock attended the lessons of Thomas Hart Benton at the Art Students League. Benton was one of the major exponents of American regional realism, that same tendency which was the cultural presupposition of Pollock's romanticism. Nevertheless, as Tomassoni (following Robertson) rightly says: 'traces of his influences in Pollock's paintings are virtually non-existent. Benton's heroic and highly dramatic compositions, designed to create a new American landscape tradition, and his frequent use of allegorical references, made little impression on his pupil, who was in search of something more authentic. Nevertheless, Pollock assimilated from Benton a rich, vigorous technique with a baroque kind of dynamism. More influential than Benton were the examples of Albert Pinkham Ryder and the Mexican painters, Siqueiros and Orozco. After 1935 Pollock's chief sources of inspiration were Picasso and the European surrealists'.[4]

we must doubt. On the other hand, what Robertson said about the 'Big Country' must also be quoted:

'If a man must continually prove his identity in America, he must also search for it. The search is conducted among a labyrinth of distractions designed to confuse most basic issues, but primarily to keep the land at a distance. For the space of America frightens its inhabitants. They are also proud of it. The space has been divided into territories, but few people in America live in the place where they were born. The search for an identity has to be made against the space, antagonistically. There are the travellers from the East on long-distance trains hurtling across California or Arizona for whom the continent exists only in terms of scattered relatives, or business appointments, or friends serving as refuge points. They do not look out of the windows of the club cars.

'Every individual is away from the place of his origin. A specific locality in space must be escaped from. The question: 'Where are you from?' plays an automatic part among civilities exchanged between Americans when they meet for the first time. The land is traversed, and warily encountered, and finally subdued.

'American books, plays, and films show a tendency towards inflation as a form of gesture that simultaneously embraces and dismisses the size of the continent. The form in each case is blown up and expanded beyond its usual limit. Popular novels like *Gone With the Wind*, *Anthony Adverse*, or *The Adventures of Augie March* not only revert to nineteenth-century literary dimensions but also overload the picaresque convention. An epic is woven around a nonentity, for in a country where the need for social conformity repeats itself in the severity of city planning, the waywardness of individual behaviour must sometimes be stressed and dwelt upon at length.

'The theatrical producer, Elia Kazan, shows in his production methods similar propensities for inflating, underlining, and spotlighting every nuance of thought and behaviour contained in a play–by an elaborate battery of theatrical devices which enlarge a simple situation into Wagnerian proportions. The Big Country demands a big art form. In some ways, this is a Germanic characteristic, but the tendency is not entirely explained by the German faction in America. Size impresses most Americans because they need it in order to find their bearings.

'The large scale of so many Americans art forms not only reflects the scale of the country but also shows an urge to fight back at its immensity and so diminish it. The scale of recent American painting shows in some degree a similar urge to attack the vastness of the land mass as well as to echo it.'

3 It may be noted, in parenthesis, how the importation into Europe of non-formal painting had had effects that were either completely useless or absolutely unrelated to their transatlantic origin–obviously because of the lack of any historical substratum to justify the non-formal.

4 With regard to Pollock's 'Bentonian' origins, let us quote Tomassoni again: 'Research into Pollock's apprentice years (1929–31) should properly be focused on the characteristic romanticism of Benton's world. In the atmosphere of chauvinism which prevailed after the financial crisis of 1929, Benton had consciously turned his back on European modernism in order to propagate, in the name of local values, a regional realism that would be unmistakably American. It was nurtured by a traditional mythology and tales from domestic and rural folklore, as used in the previous century by the American mannerist painter, John Shinn.

'Benton's paintings, and the paintings of artists such as Grant Wood who shared his ideals and his social conscience, transcend the limits of verisimilitude by a process of singling out an event from

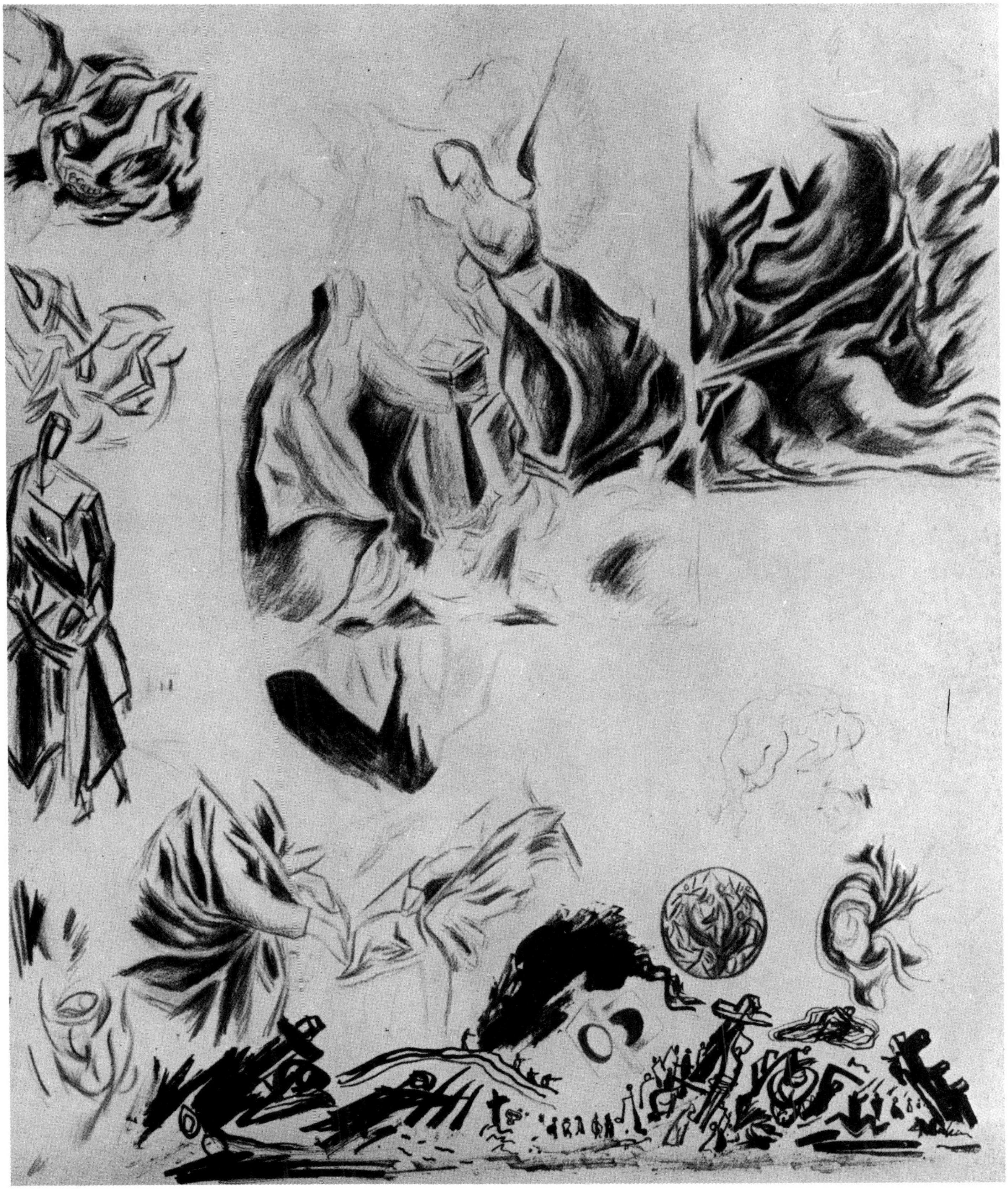

local everyday life and resiting the figures in a well-known illustrative myth: schematic and rhetorical, but nevertheless–even on the stylistic plane–rich in plastic synthesis and in well-defined, meaningful cultural content.

'Obviously Pollock dissented from his kind of undertaking: he declared that the "idea of an isolated American painting, so popular in this country during the thirties, seems absurd to me just as the idea of creating a purely American mathematics of physics would seem absurd". About his teacher, Benton, he said that his work "was important as something against which to react very strongly, later on".

'Having assimilated Benton's synthetic and vaguely baroque-expressionistic methods, not of course in their ideological and figurative aspects, but purely from a technical and stylistic point of view, Pollock reverses his teacher's whole outlook; he is pre-occupied with recording an episode from his own creative life, not with singling out someone else's story to narrate. At the same time he amplifies the energy put into composition (Benton is obviously strictly confined within the boundaries of his figurative narration) and this, iconography and content having been devalued, lends even greater power to the actual means of expression which now comes to be considered as something valuable

3 *Studies of figures and draperies*
c. 1931–34, coloured crayon and encre de chine on paper
$13\frac{3}{4} \times 17$ in (35×43 cm)
Lee Krasner Pollock collection, New York

This is undoubtedly true of the formal relationships and the concrete aspects of the works, but Pollock had to go beyond Benton's culture to make the transition from the Mexicans to Picasso and the Surrealists (Ernst, Miró, Matta). He had to find the non-formal in order to create alone, the American landscape for which Benton did not have sufficient perseverance.

Pollock's beginnings, from 1930 to 1940, may seem rather disconcerting. To some extent, they even resemble a series of scholastic exercises in the manner of such classic artists as Michelangelo, Tintoretto, El Greco, or Rubens. Nor does it seem that attempts to discern signs of baroque interest in this period characterize the painter's personality in any significant way. The drawings, briefly, are rather dull, despite the interesting traces of contemporary artists, Picasso above all, that occasionally shine through them.[5]

Figs. 2 to 4

Figs. 5 to 9

In my opinion, baroque themes are to be found not so easily in these studies of movement as in the urgent colouring of the few paintings that belong to these years, *Landscape with Rider* (1933), *Seascape* (1934), *Untitled* and *Flame* (both 1937). Pollock's baroque rejects historical qualification. It is no Rubensian revival, and the term, because it is linked to a certain type of pictorial achievement, should be used only to indicate developments–a taste for brilliant matter, chromatic intensity, negation of space in matter–which were anyway justified by romanticism.

Fig. 1, Pl. 2

Pls. 6, 7

Thus, Pollock is baroque just as Delacroix is baroque, and he came to reconsider the pictorial experiences of the past mainly from the viewpoint of technique, for their chromatic values and for what they suggested about material that might be abandoned. It is clear, too, that the initial negation of human measure imposed on space, innate in American landscape and history, and linked to the impossibility of transferring the European cultural tradition to so different an environment, gave Pollock a glimpse of pictorial truth in those artists who rejected the post-Renaissance classical and rationalistic attitude in the 17th century.[6]

in itself (and it should not be forgotten that Pollock took a great interest in baroque painting). To the intellectual romanticism of Benton and his followers Pollock added cultural and figurative romanticism culled from the work of Albert Pinkham Ryder, a nineteenth-century American painter and visionary who painted ghostly, deserted landscapes (see Pollock's *Seascape,* 1934).

'Pollock abstracted from Ryder as he had from Benton, assimilating rules of composition which made possible the careful rhythms and synthetic forms of his work. He also adhered to a conception of painting as the exaltation of the imagination and the vehicle of passion, totally and tangibly expressed outside of all mimetic considerations.'

5 Let us quote the opposite view of Robertson: 'The drawings and studies relating to the period *c.* 1930–34 are most revealing: all the seeds are contained in them for Pollock's future development. They embody in the simplest terms his essential characteristics as an artist. The first impression is of an almost incessant preoccupation with movement. Even in the few isolated nude studies there is no concern for repose or stillness. The figures are static but they share in common a declamatory note, almost of rhetoric. A dynamic attitude emerges, imposed over the basic subjects, which is of more interest than the mere posed presences of the figures themselves. Some of the nude studies appear to be after Michelangelo, but the general graphic conception behind all of them is essentially Northern: dry, sharp, and unsensuously compressed. The treatment of the figures or the means taken to realize them detach themselves from the figures they are intended to summarize, and establish themselves too positively and autonomously to allow for any further penetration into the original form. There is less concern for the human body than for the marks made on the paper and the way in which the casing of contour lines and structural accents combine together to make new abstract shapes that are independent of the complete figure.

'This tendency is more fully realized in the studies of Baroque drapery and the pencil notations which refer to compositions by Rubens, Tintoretto, and El Greco. Here we find, expressed in the most obvious way, Pollock's concern to detach movement and energy itself from the object containing that movement and energy, for as Kenneth Clark observes in his book *The Nude,* in discussing the portrayal of energy in Greek sculpture:

"... the chief aid to the representation of movement which art has to offer: the rhythmic line of drapery. Clinging drapery, following a plane or contour, emphasizes the stretch or twist of the body; floating drapery makes visible the line of movement through which it has just passed. Thus the aesthetic limitation of the nude body in action, that it is enclosed within an immediate present, is overcome. Drapery, by suggesting lines of force indicates for each action a past and a possible future".

'Even in these early studies, Pollock is trying to get through and beyond the restrictions of physical reality and to capture and transmit a distillation of energy, drawn out of the flux of human experience and thrown back again into the flux of time. And he sought, as many great artists have done, to represent energy in terms of depth and volume, as well as movement.'

6 Let us quote a long passage from Robertson which is, to a certain extent, an attempt to make Pollock part of a continuous and constantly self-renewing tradition: 'For art achieved the all-over intensity of Pollock's late canvases, in different pictorial conventions, at a time when the spiritual exaltations of man reached one of their highest levels: the medieval period. No part of the surface in a medieval painting is more important than another. Consider the work of Van Eyck or Van der Weyden. Their panels are suffused with an all-over intensity–or anonymity–of paint and an equal

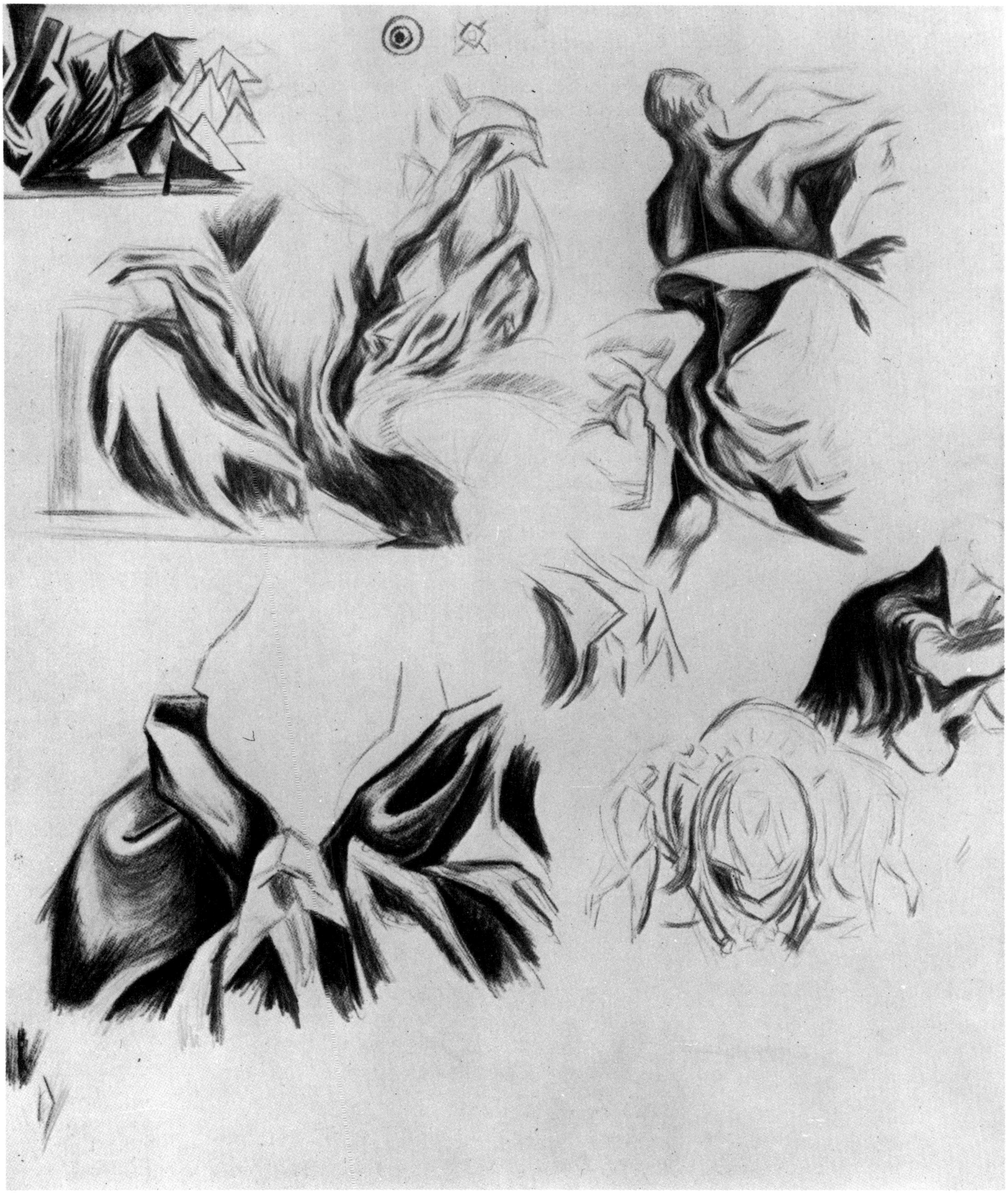

sharpness in the even registration of detail which springs from a unified faith, a concentration on spiritual values at the expense of materialism, and a complete integration between belief and practice. This spiritual unification was often destroyed by war, bigotry, physical catastrophe on a horrifying scale, and independent spiritual dissension. But the spirit was there and it is faithfully mirrored in the all-over painting of the time.

'Art began to lose this radiant unity during the Renaissance, a period when the spirit had to come more radically to terms, in a changed world, with materialism and artists began to concentrate on individuals and individually dramatized incidents. The estrangement from unity was complete by the seventeenth century, a period of mannerism in most countries. But in Dutch paintings of this period, light is a transmission of spirit as an enveloping and unifying agency. In the flickering landscapes of Ruisdael or Hobbema, no less than in the motionless interiors of Vermeer, light is the dominating factor. It fills these paintings as religious fervour and piety once charged and unified the paintings of an earlier time. But light only unifies Dutch painting indirectly as a by-product of natural phenomena; it illuminates, more precisely, separate parts of each canvas. The play of light on the pearls round a woman's throat, the light on the ringed hand snatching at a fold of drapery,

4 *Studies of figures and draperies*
c. 1931–34, coloured crayon and encre de chine on paper
$13\frac{3}{4} \times 17$ in (35×43 cm)
Lee Krasner Pollock collection, New York

5 *Study*
c. 1934–38, coloured pencil on paper
14 × 9¾ in (36 × 25 cm)
Lee Krasner Pollock collection,
New York

The airlessness noted by Robertson in the pictures of these years can be explained by Pollock's perhaps unconscious opposition to the European humanistic tradition, the rational spatiality that Mondrian had taken to its supreme conclusion. Pollock's is in fact the first affirmation of the American landscape and of the new American romanticism. It is the emotional and physical impetus that actually creates and fills the environment, denying the very basis of the Old European cultural tradition together with its latest and greatest exponents–Cézanne, the Cubists and neo-plasticism. Later, Pollock had to reckon with this tradition, and with Picasso in particular, but only to deny it again in a more conscious way.

The *Landscape with Rider* mingles figure and environment, man and nature, together in a single representative cluster of paint, and reduces the two realities which have been constantly distinct in European painting to a single order. Mondrian in his pre-Paris period (1912), when his work was still to some extent naturalistic, resolved the duality by the rationalization of the landscape taken as an instrument of the search for a universally valid nucleus of total reality. In this equally prophetic painting by Pollock every distinction was denied. The horseman (a Western cowboy) is an episode in the landscape and is incorporated in it both materially and chromatically.[7]

Fig. 1

The same may be said for the hint of a white sail caught in the vortex of an intensely elementary nature in the 1934 *Seascape*.

Pl. 2

But this is not all. In the two above-mentioned pictures we have mentioned the submersion of the human element represented in the picture itself, which detaches the object from the author, the work from its painter. In fact, the real relationship between man and nature in Pollock's work (the 'submersion') is shown in the relationship between the painter and the work: it is Pollock, Jackson Pollock born of Le Roy McCoy and Stella McClure at

the flash of light in a stormy sky: in each instance, light is used as a dramatic device rather than a totally unifying source. In some ways, possibly, light was also equated by the Dutch with virtue. Physical light became, above all, a substitute for the light of God, and so was used to fragment and to isolate separate parts of pictures which sang the praises of a new materialism. And landscape, as a receptacle for light, was seen, gradually, as a vehicle for ethics and for morality.

'With Impressionism in the nineteenth century, light emerged as an entity in its own right and was no longer equated either with virtue or with spirit. An entirely materialist society saw light, as it saw nature, only in physical or optical terms. Turner alone, before the Impressionists, again transformed the concept of light and carried its spiritual-substitute meaning over and above Impressionism into a new visionary field which only Monet, unconsciously, was to inhabit later.

'For Monet's interest in light as a physical entity causing particular optical effects became obsessional, and so turned his late work into a kind of all-over visionary painting. His abstract use of paint and his concern for an almost hallucinatory all-over close-up view of a subject caught the imagination of a later generation in Europe and America–the abstract Impressionists: but many of these artists, lacking his genius as well as his astigmatism, have only seized upon the superficial attributes of Monet's style and inflated it without its motivating vision–as some kinds of cool jazz popularize the style of Satie, Ravel, Bartok, or Stravinsky, and so make a new analgesic: middle-class chamber music. But the nature of Pollock's inner vision removes his work entirely from abstract Impressionism or abstract Expressionism. Both terms described a legitimate extension of language in the early fifties but are now journalistic clichés and refer to mannerism. Pollock's work, in all its stages, has its own momentum and inevitability, built by his obsessive progress through and against an entirely personal range of imagery.

'Throughout his life, he fought a sustained battle to unify the picture plane and to achieve an intensity of feeling and emphasis in each picture. He broke through by absorbing life and the outward signs and portents of living and by seeing all things in the universe as part of a vast general order, as in medieval art. He was in many ways a metaphysical artist, for a dormant religious sense sometimes externalized itself in early work through a preoccupation with the anthropological aspects of religion and their appropriate fetishes. He allowed his apprehension to life to re-emerge at a new altitude in his eventual handling of paint and by striving to be "in" the picture.'

It cannot be denied that this type of wide synthesis leaves one completely perplexed: medieval spiritualism and the materialism of the Renaissance are concepts that modern historians have largely rendered obsolete, while the mention of Van Eyck or Van der Weyden as 'medieval' defies all historical probability. Moreover, it is typical of a large number of non-Italian art critics (despite Berenson's teachings) to make the beginnings of the Renaissance coincide with the period of Lorenzo de' Medici and the Florence of 'Il Magnifico' so that the term medieval becomes even less significant (although this immensely long period embraces neo-Byzantine art and Giotto, Provençal Romanesque and courtly culture, Chrétien de Troyes, Dante and even Brunelleschi perhaps). As for Renaissance individualism, this is a problem already present in Van Eyck and Van der Weyden in Flanders, not to mention their Florentine contemporaries and precursors. Nor does it seem to me that one can easily speak of light in painting as an abstract value without historical modifications ('a transmission of the spirit, a component capable of developing and unifying the work'). To conclude, the placing of Pollock at the end of a process seen in such a summary and arbitrary way seems to me no less arbitrary and just as useless.

7 Which should be equivalent to a 'cowboy of the West' though it is clear that such American terms have undergone and suffered from a process of mythification which has totally distorted their original meaning.

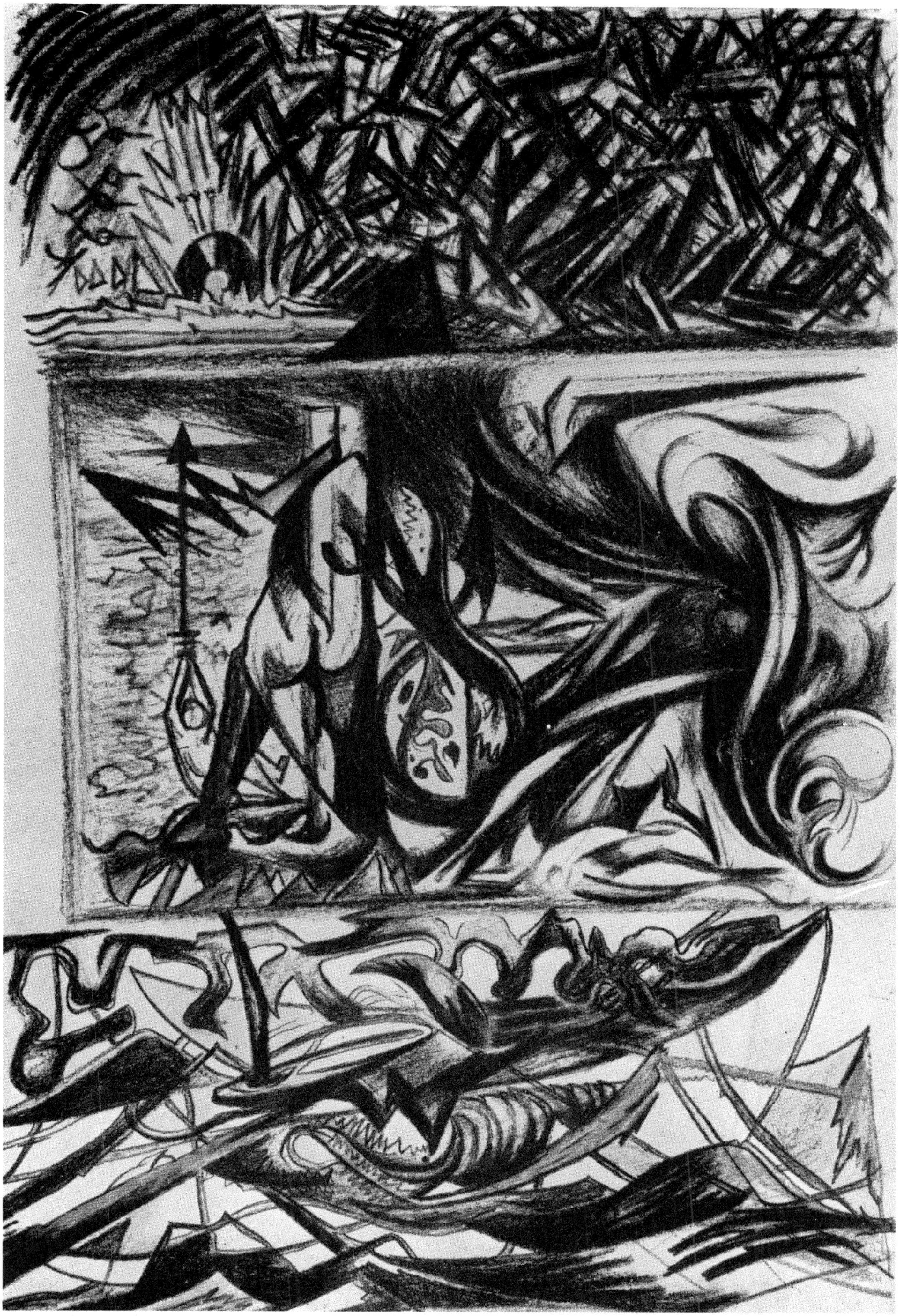

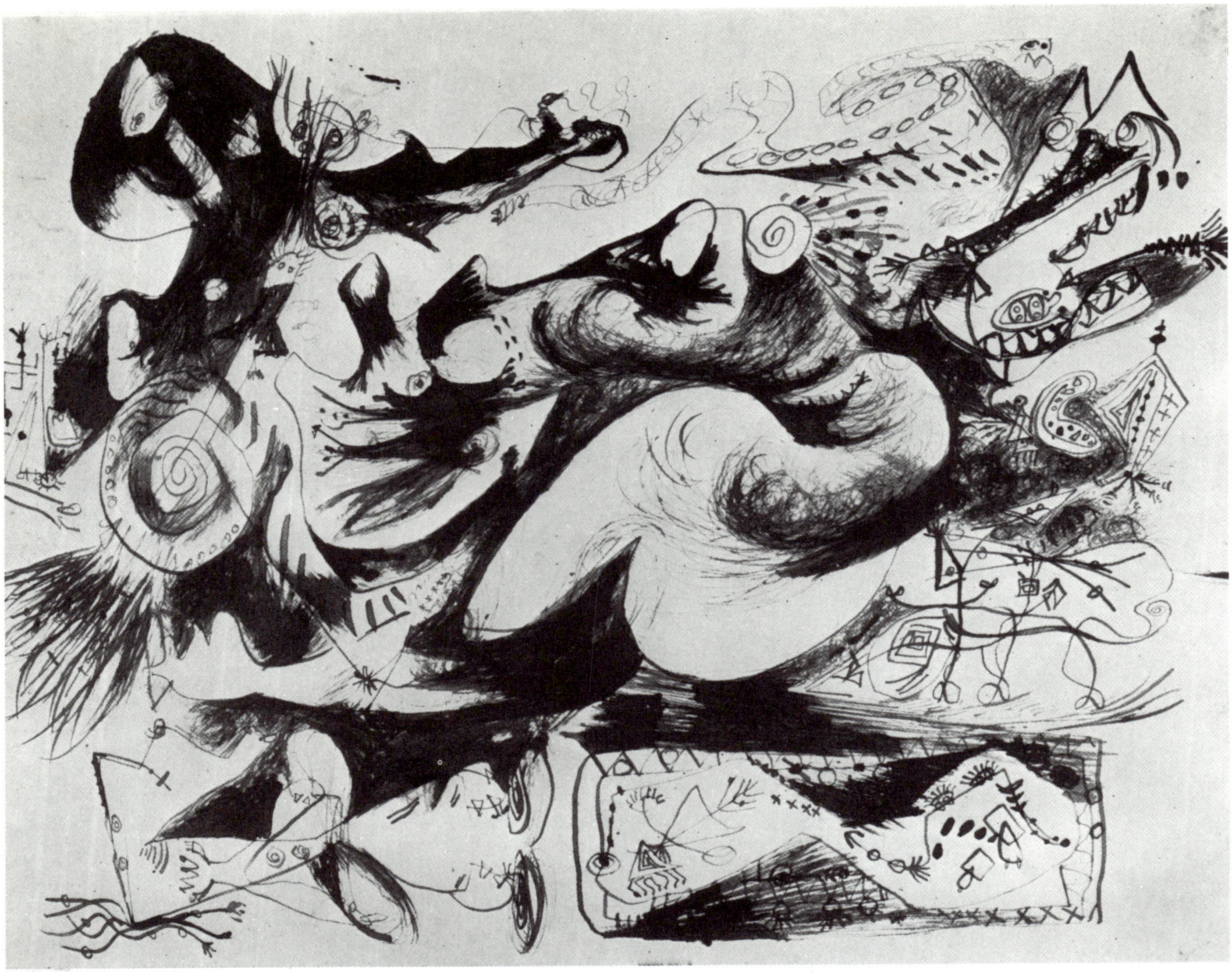

6 *Untitled*
c. 1934–38, encre de chine on paper
$8\frac{3}{4} \times 11\frac{3}{4}$ in ($22 \cdot 5 \times 30$ cm)
Lee Krasner Pollock collection,
New York

Cody on January 12th, 1912, who is cancelling himself out as an anagraphically identifiable person in this already effervescent magma which landscape is for him. It is Jackson Pollock who 'is' and who is a part of life, inasmuch as he unleashes on to the canvas the violence of existence which he resumes in himself from nature and which he verifies not at the moment of representation but by recreating it in an autonomous manner in the painting. In short, this is already action painting, or at least, a sort of pre-awareness of action painting, the creative gesture which derives its value from negating representation by replacing it with direct participation, with the immersion of the man in the painting, which thus becomes his own history.

For Pollock then, history became identified with nature and this was his romanticism.

Negation of American society

In the meantime there matured in him an awareness of European experiences which were immediately exploited in the prevailing interest in matter, not only in the sense of pictorial technique, but matter because of Pollock's identification of man (the protagonist of the pictures of Picasso and the Surrealists) with matter. The three untitled paintings of 1936–37, here reproduced, adopted Picasso's infallibility of the sign but employed it (in an uncontrolled, sentimental tumult) in a way that is as inexorably anti-classical as Picasso is fundamentally classical.

Pls. 4 to 6

Further examples may be found in the series of drawings made between 1934 and 1938 (apart from those that are academic or, as some would describe them, baroque). Here, the relationships with the Surrealists, and most importantly Miró, which may appear easily recognizable, are in fact vitiated by a fundamental negation. Along his phosphorescent snails' tracks, Miró unwinds the limpid subconscious, denying, with irony if not snobbery,

Figs. 5 to 9

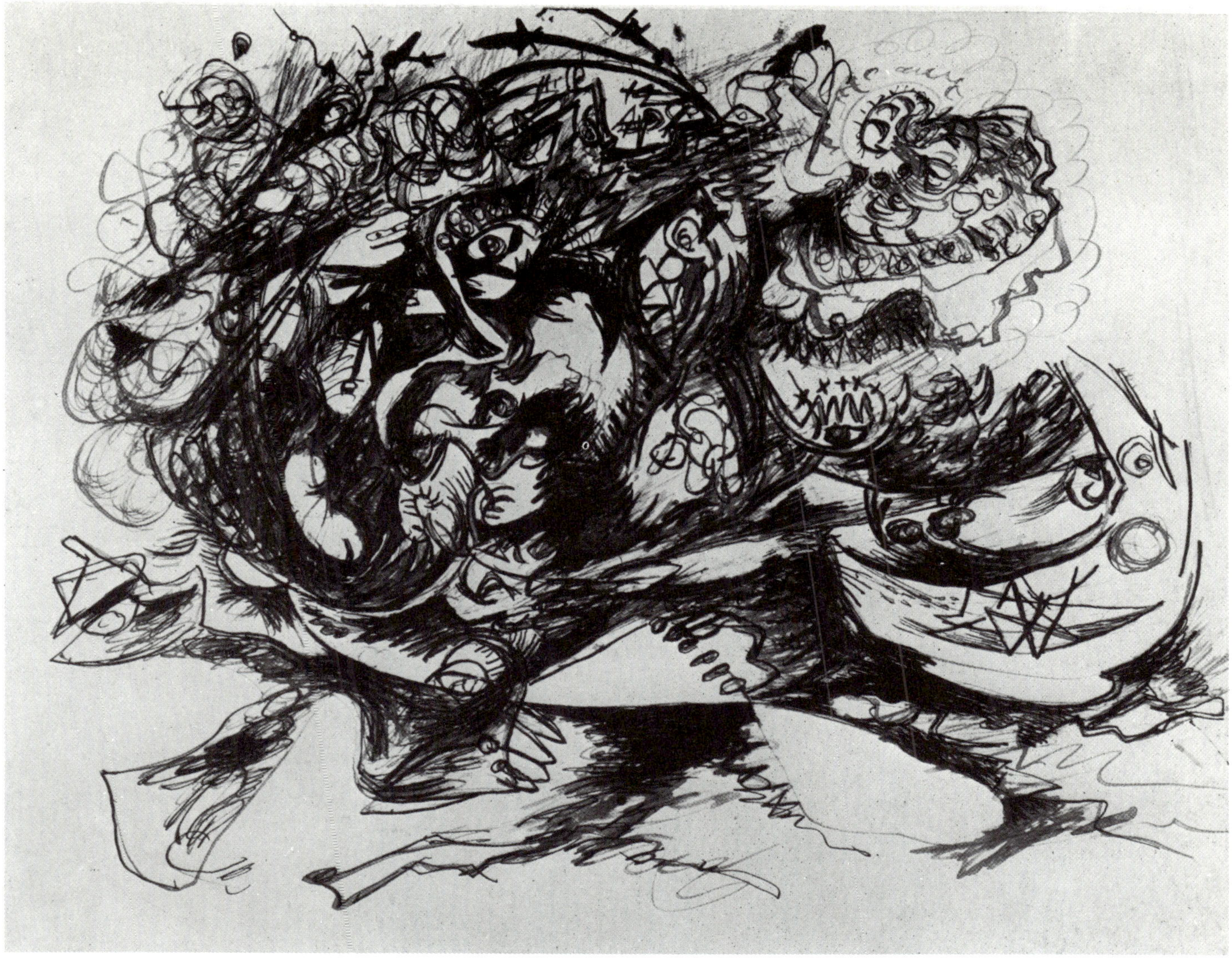

7 *Untitled*
c. 1934–38, encre de chine on paper
$8\frac{3}{4} \times 11\frac{3}{4}$ in ($22{\cdot}4 \times 30$ cm)
Lee Krasner Pollock collection, New York

three thousand years of humanist culture. He identifies, while aware of the lie, the subconscious with his fabulous inventions. But in the repetition and the shattering of the sign he borrows, he really unleashes matter that is not of the subconscious, but merely subrational.

Another fundamental component in Pollock's work may be discerned, side by side with nature. It is the theme of the unrestricted profundity of the soul. In nature felt as an almost primordial agglomerate of matter, man is an equally primordial agglomerate of thoughts and sensations, with thought becoming absolutely identified with feeling, the *res cogitans* with the *res extensa.*

We should probably see in this attitude Pollock's revolt, not against technological society in itself (exalted by Mondrian to the supreme morality of reason), but against the exploitation of man in a consumer society. The consumer system reduces man and the natural environment to episodes of the productive machine and, in an economically advanced society, the freedom to 'drop out' must be sacrificed. Not to pursue wealth and social status, not to become part of the machine whose value is money (which, according to Protestant ethics assumes a moral significance) – this fundamental freedom is lost.

Moreover if Pollock's revolt against this type of respectability is expressed in his painting, it is equally clearly expressed in the everyday occurrence of alcoholism in life, the usual libertarian and liberating 'gesture' of the American genius even after the Roaring Twenties, when Pollock contracted the vice (if vice it may be called). Robertson notes: 'It is possible that his spasmodic and finally compulsive life-long addiction to alcohol began at this time (1928–29), for he was working on the land, in tough conditions, with groups of men mostly older than himself'.

8 *Drawing*
c. 1938, ink on paper
$13 \times 10\frac{1}{4}$ in (33×26 cm)
Lee Krasner Pollock collection, New York

With regard to the relationship with American society, it is interesting to note how a rejection of man's role as a producer-consumer-unit in the vicious circle of consumption, which was basically analagous to Pollock's, affected another American genius, Frank Lloyd Wright. His conclusions were partly similar to Pollock's and partly opposed to them, but they took him to the summit of that society which Pollock had totally contested.

And indeed, from the time of the Prairie houses, Wright's theme and his

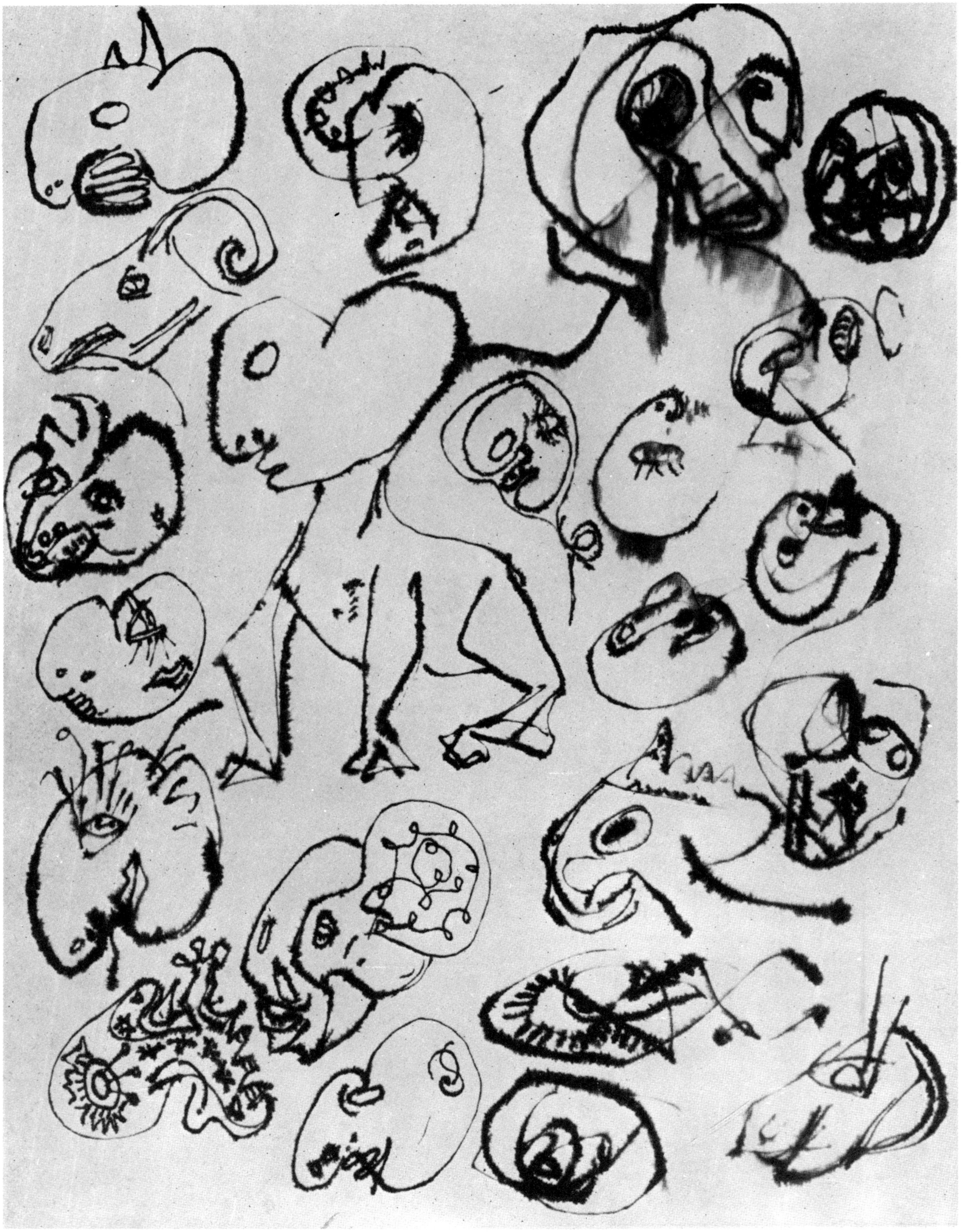

principal interest was the adoption of nature as the basic module for dwelling and, consequently, for living. Man must repudiate the metropolis and the artificial structure of consumer civilization (besides the debris of a history that has nothing to offer contemporary society) to create and to live in Broadacre, the Utopian city which, with the multiplication of dwellings integrated in natural surroundings, will end by populating the whole immense space of America, creating a city-continent, or a non-urban city.

9 *Drawing*
c. 1938, encre de chine on paper
18 × 13¾ in (45·5 × 35 cm)
Lee Krasner Pollock collection, New York

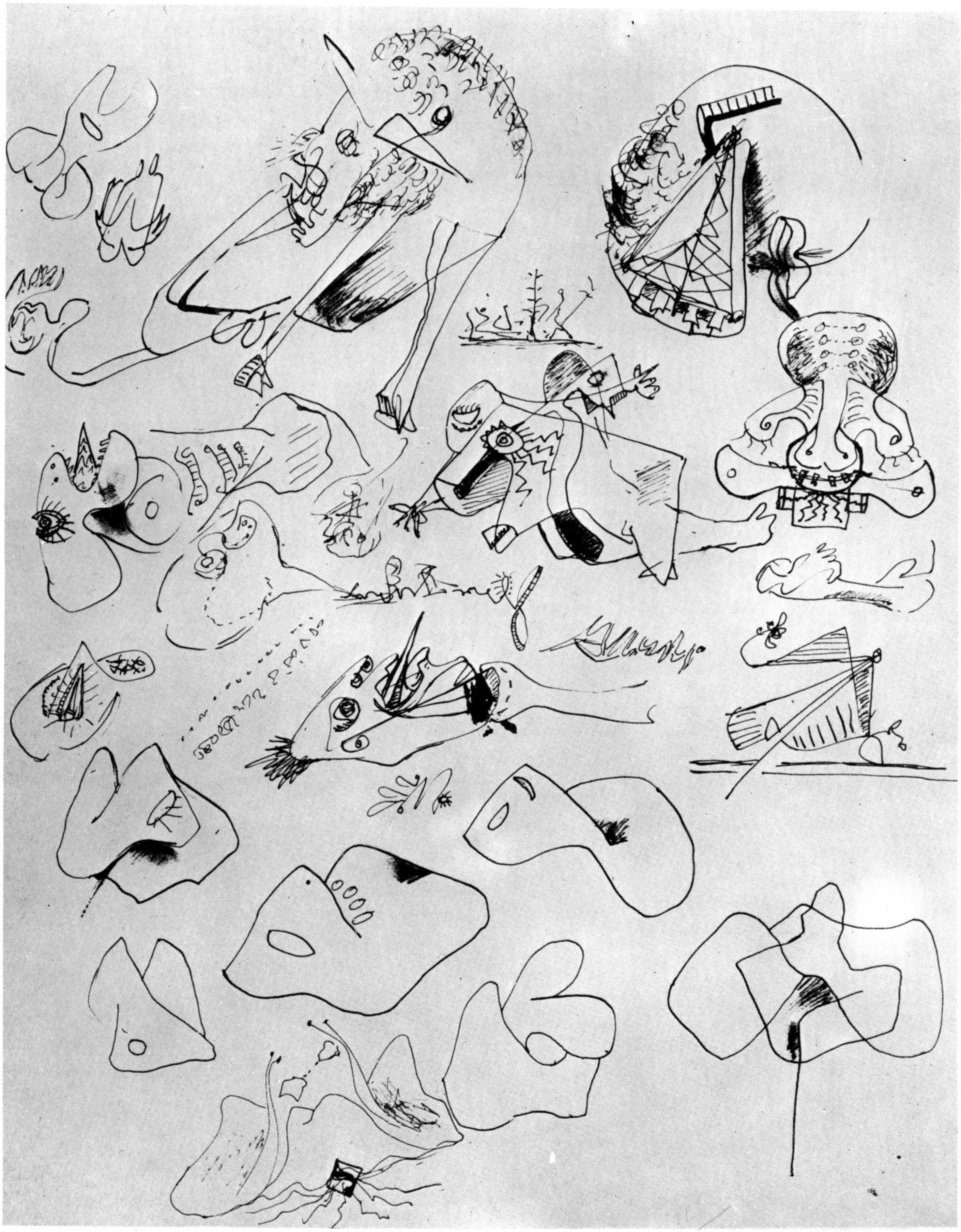

(Wright yearned for this utopia with an almost naive faith in technological progress, in rapidity of means of transport and in the instantaneity of means of communication which would make it possible.) From this legitimate beginning, Wright only managed to achieve what was possible i.e. dwellings for the rich. Unlike Pollock he accepted the spirit while rejecting the 'manner' of the consumer society.

It is worthwhile here underlining the morality of the operation conducted by Le Corbusier who, starting from European rationalism rather than from American romanticism, attempted to integrate nature in dwellings for all – really for all – adapting it to human modules in his *villes radieuses*. All in all, a comparison between Le Corbusier and Wright might be made as a parallel to that between Mondrian and Pollock. But such a comparison can be made in an exemplary sense only, and as an illustration of the relationship

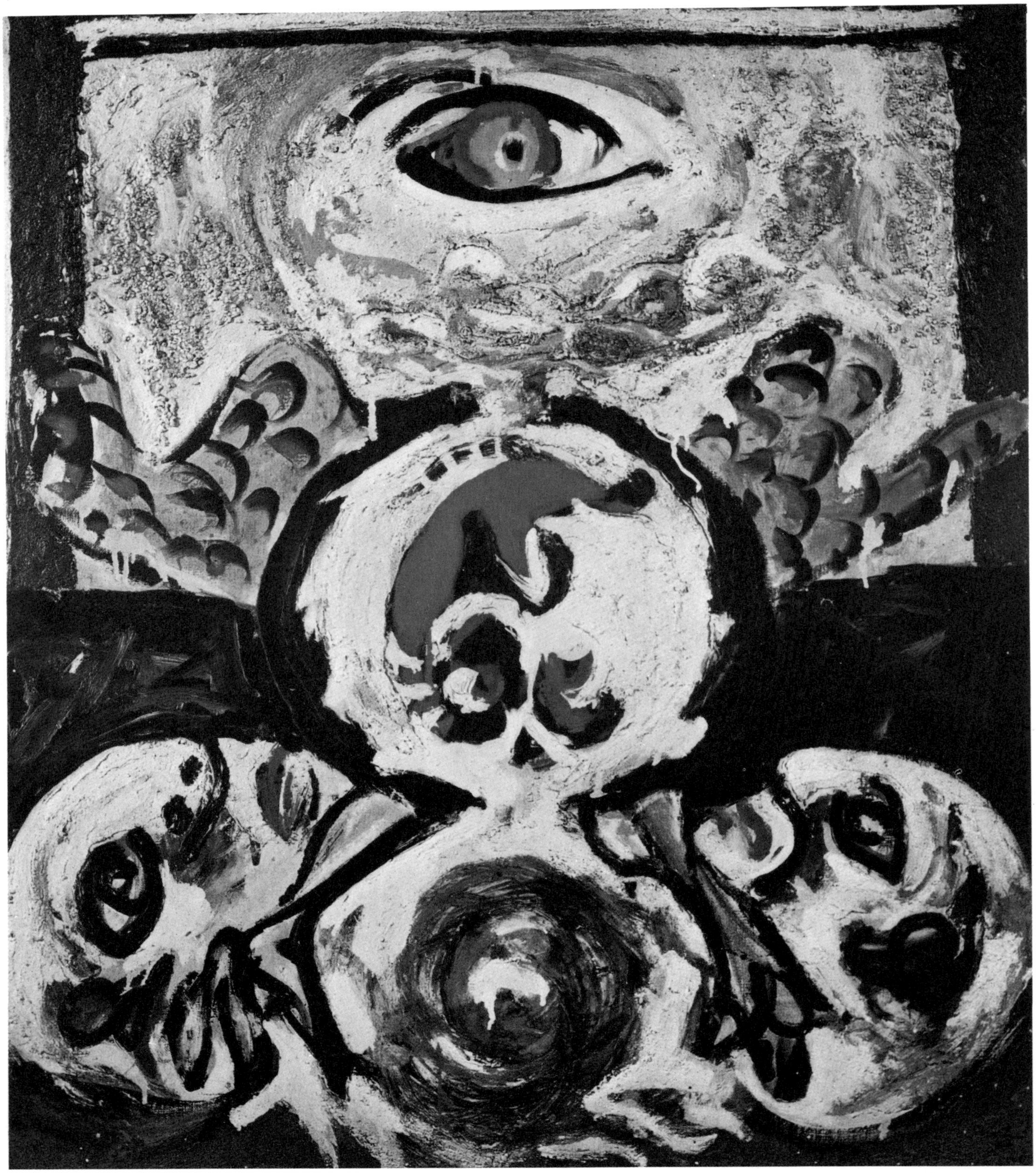

10 *Bird*
c. 1941, oil and sand on canvas
$28 \times 24\frac{3}{4}$ in (71×63 cm)
Lee Krasner Pollock collection, New York

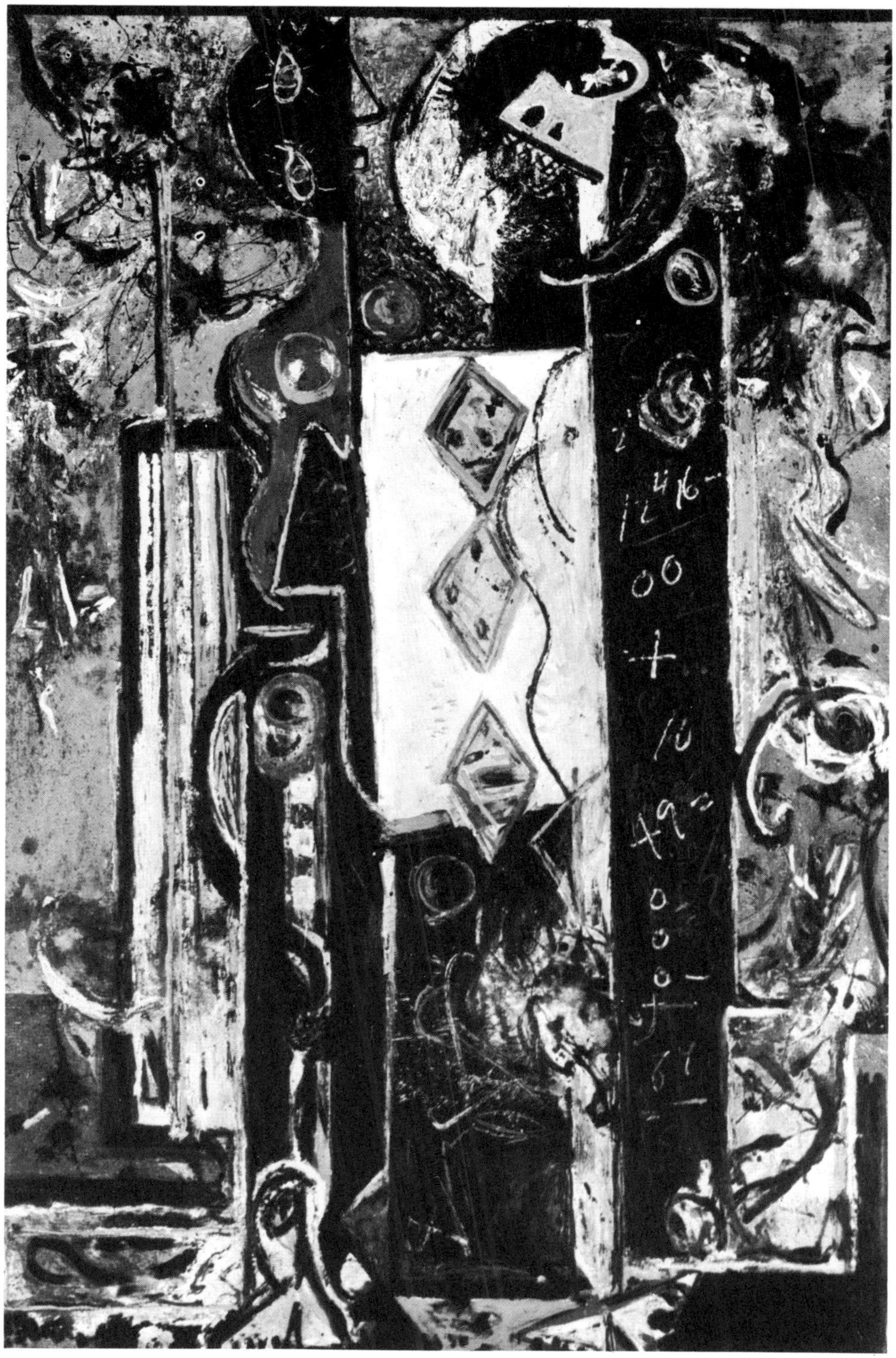

11 *Male and female*
1942, oil on canvas
$73 \times 88\frac{1}{4}$ in ($186 \times 124{\cdot}4$ cm)
H. Gates Lloyd collection,
Haverford, Pennsylvania

between European and American civilization. (And it must be noted that Wright represented the optimistic and Pollock the pessimistic aspect of American romanticism.)

Sand painting and totem art

We have seen how the nucleus of Pollock's painting was emotional urgency, and that it was matter that determined technique. The rejection of a history that Pollock did not feel to be his own (and the rejection of European experiences by a negation of classic form) was accompanied by his acceptance of another kind of history, intimately linked to nature, magic, symbols etc., irrational and primitive. Pollock found it recorded in the practices of the American Indians, especially in the sand paintings of the Navaho.[8]

8 From Robertson: 'The liquidation of the image effected by Pollock between 1947 and 1953 came also from a most loving understanding of an extraordinary kind of traditional pictorial art made by the Navaho Indians in New Mexico in the American South West. Pollock was born in Wyoming, and travelled in the South West in his youth. He made spasmodic trips to that area after he came to live in New York as a young man and his consciousness was conditioned, always, by early memories of the West.

'As fertility symbols, as invocations to the natural sources of rain, wind, and sun which they see

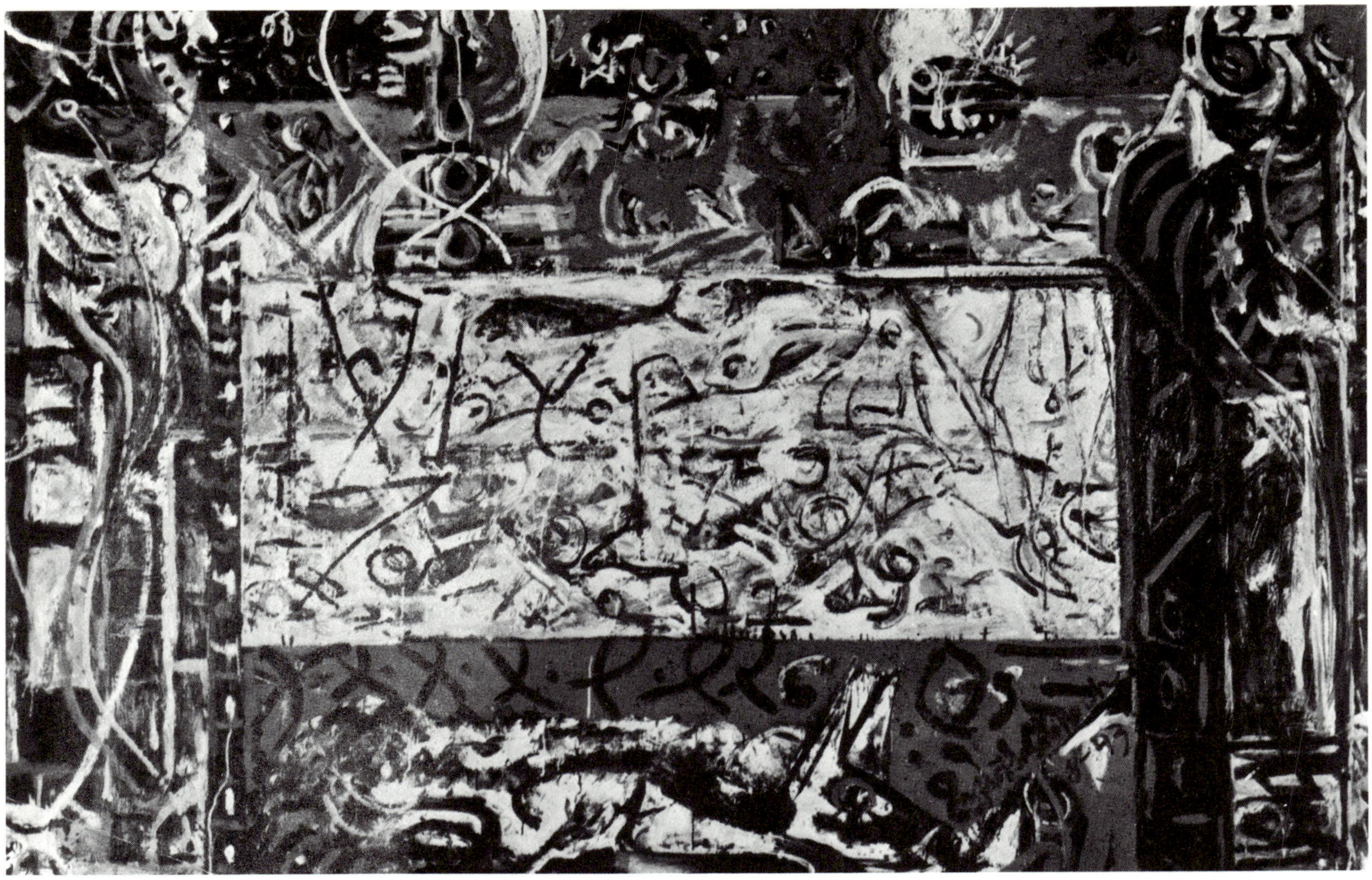

12 *Guardians of the Secret*
1943, oil on canvas
$48\frac{1}{4} \times 75\frac{1}{4}$ in (122·8 × 191·3 cm)
Museum of Art, San Francisco

13 *Gothic*
1944, oil on canvas
$84\frac{1}{2} \times 56$ in (214·5 × 142·3 cm)
Lee Krasner Pollock collection, New York

Such works were ephemeral (sand paintings disappear by sunset), they were significant as action rather than representation. The gesture of execution was more important than the result, and the gesture linked the spiritual matter of man to the great forces of nature, the wind, the sun and the rain (primitive art always expresses the magical relationship between the being and the environment, whose forces are identified with the divinity). All these were cultural precedents for Pollock's definitive achievement in action-painting: the recognition of the self in the act of painting.

Pollock's relationship with Indian art goes even further. From *Birth* (1938), the totemic image connected with Indian culture is a frequently

as gods, and as two-dimensional flat totems on the earth, the Navaho Indians make pictograms flat on the ground by spilling sand and coloured earth through their hands on to the earth surface. Records in the form of accurately coloured charts kept in Santa Fé show a predominantly linear treatment of natural forms and archetypal shapes which represent the Indian deities and their mythology. These sand-paintings, as they are called, are ephemeral. They are made at sunrise, and the magic they are intended to invoke cannot materialize unless all traces of them are dispersed by sunset.

'Certain elements of design, patterns, and emblems from Indian sand-painting can also be found in the Spanish Colonial art of New Mexico. The Spanish element in the church decorations and the popular art of this region is occasionally stimulated by purely Indian influences no less than the more obvious Mexican derivations. The Spanish Colonial iconography is further complicated by Central European influences; the Pennsylvania Dutch *factura* in the Philadelphia Library, for example, show a form of Bohemian and Southern German folk art used to decorate the borders of birth or marriage certificates which appears unmistakably in the wall decorations of churches in New Mexico. Traders and early settlers in the South West from the East, but of European origin, had carried their papers with them and gradually all three art forms were merged together. Pollock was conscious of this iconography and it can be seen in his paintings of the early forties; notably in *The She Wolf* and *Guardians of the Secret,* but he was most directly affected by the practice of Indian sand-painting.

'The form of art is part of a ritual. Its conception is opposed to the modern European idea of art as a separate activity for its own sake, with no magical properties and with no part to play in a ritual. European art is permanent: we conserve it and restore it, we guard it in museums, and we buy and sell it as a commodity. The idea of a temporary art made only to serve a ritual mythology and placed at the mercy of the elements is strange to us. The idea was not strange to Pollock, and his sympathy for it provides us with the crux of his personality as an artist and the most radical clue towards an understanding of his pictorial inclinations.'

Pollock himself noted: 'My painting does not come from the easel. I hardly ever stretch my canvas before painting. I prefer to tack the unstretched canvas to the hard wall or floor. I need the resistance of a hard surface. On the floor I am more at ease. I feel nearer, more a part of the painting, since this way I can walk around it, work from the four sides and literally be "in" the painting. This is akin to the method of the Indian sand painters of the West.'

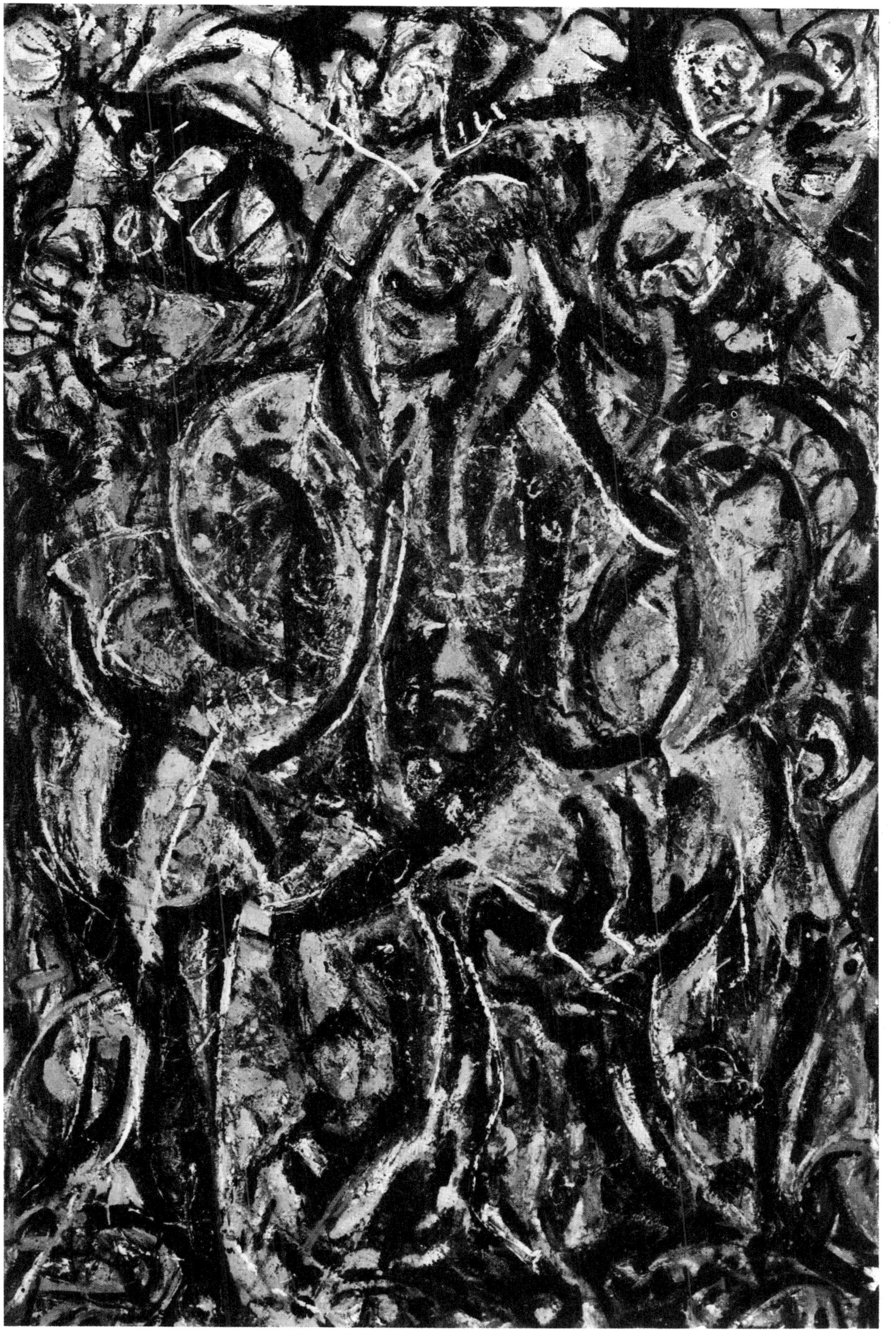

14 *Totem I*
1944, oil on canvas
$69\frac{1}{2} \times 43\frac{3}{4}$ in ($177 \times 111{\cdot}5$ cm)
E. Walker collection,
Ridgefield, Connecticut

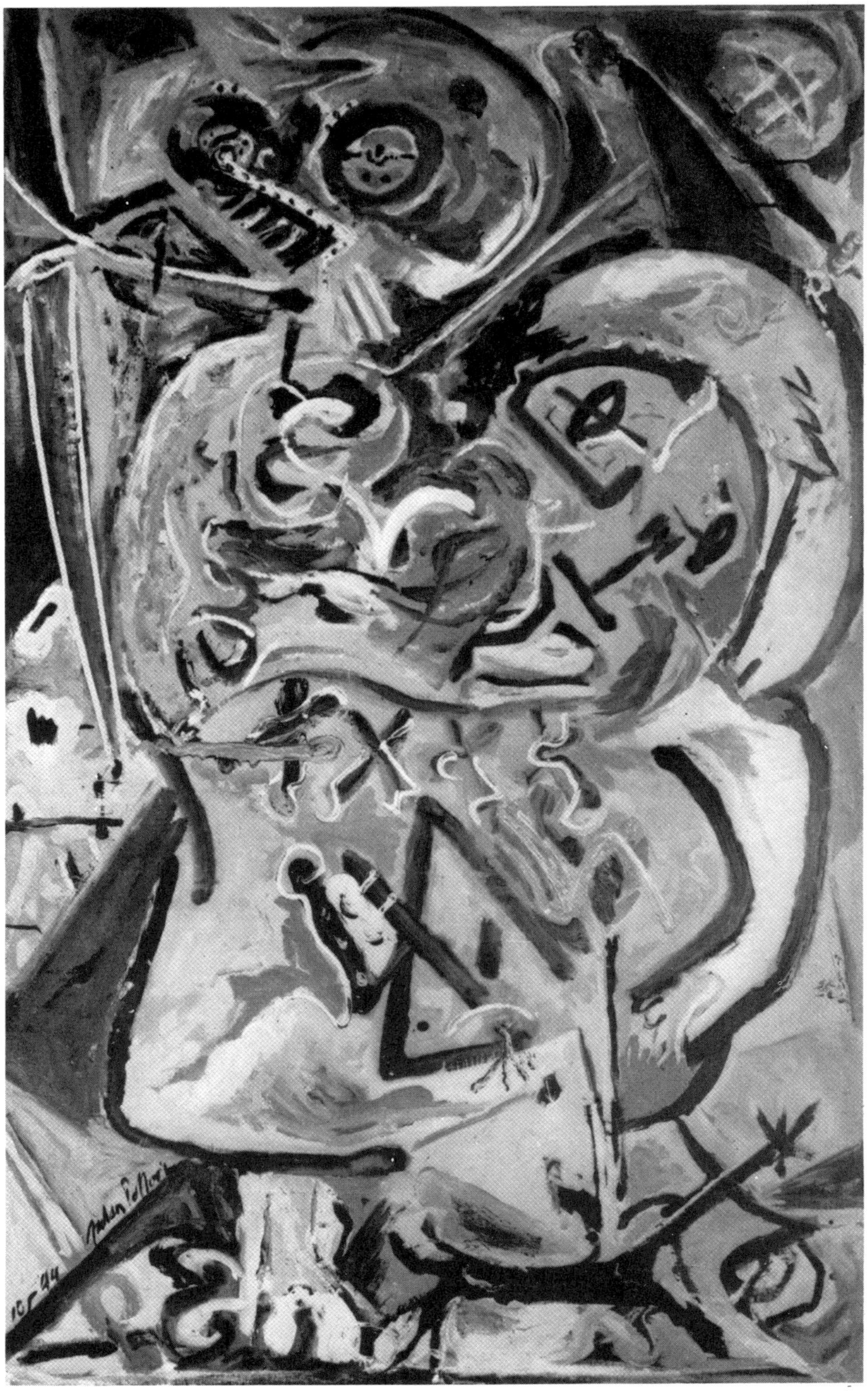

recurring theme in Pollock's art (it emerges again in the famous *Blue Poles* of 1953). It is clear that this kind of imagery had a significance for Pollock quite different from that which the discovery of African masks had for Picasso. African art, for Picasso, presented above all a formal value–by singling out the object and stripping it of all superstructure. In essence it offered the experimenter of Cubism a repertory of elementary forms. Pollock's totemic image, while it certainly encouraged some strange formal solutions, was in the first place loaded with obscure existential allusions (remembering the constant sexual implications). It was therefore a 'sign' of that 'natural' history that Pollock adopted, which joins man and nature in a relationship that is not rational, but religious or magic.

Pl. 8 *Birth* is a particularly good example, because the components that are enunciated in it can be analyzed.

In it, according to Robertson's interpretation, 'sexual imagery, derived from Mexican art and made less definite by the more plastically emancipated

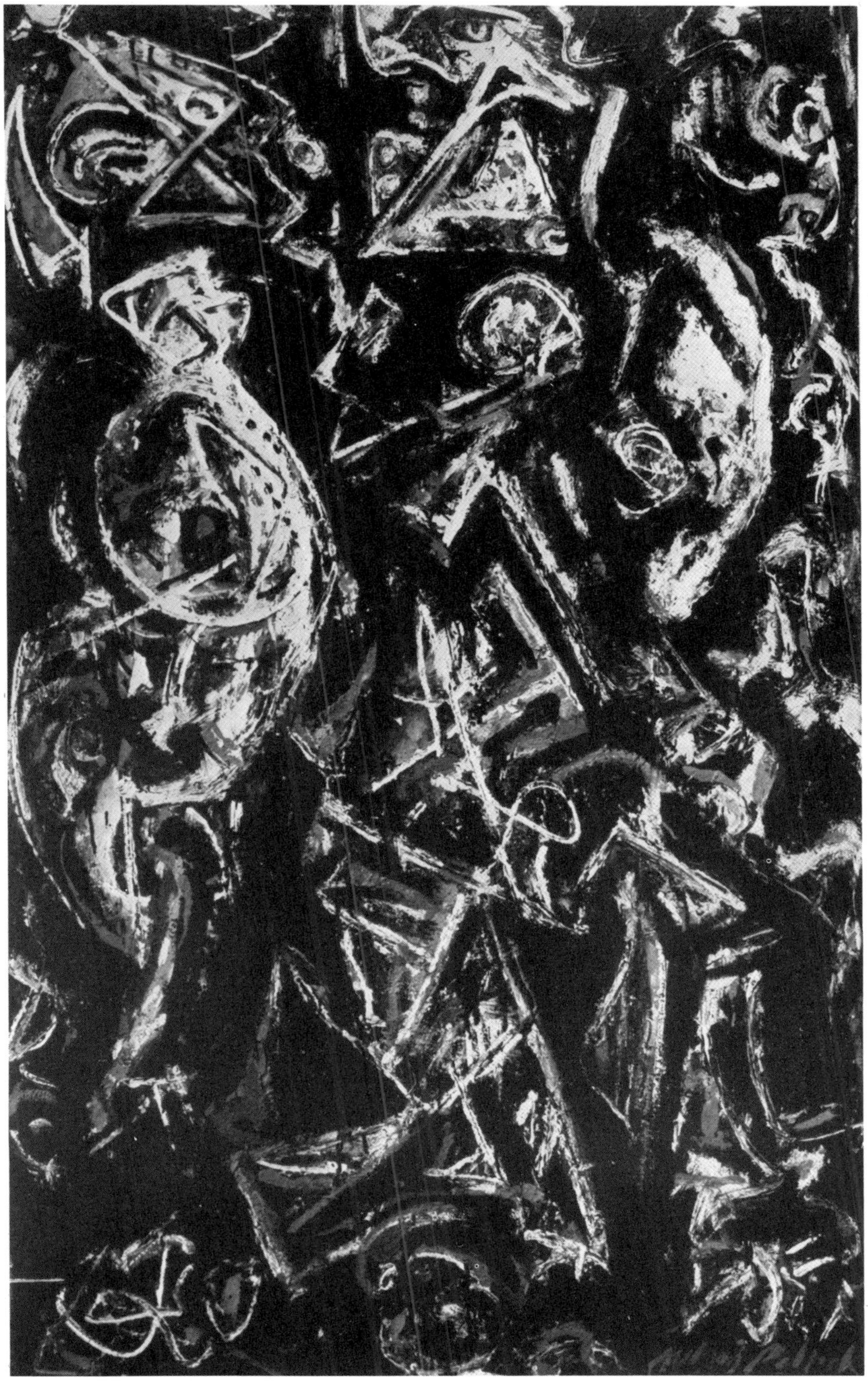

15 *Night Ceremony*
1944, oil on canvas
$71\frac{1}{2} \times 42\frac{1}{4}$ in (182×109 cm)
B. J. Reis collection, New York

and painterly influence of Picasso, is bound together in a rearing vertical totem shape, not dissimilar formally from the totems of the North-West American Indians'.

In my view, the Picassian sign has already disintegrated in the whirl of the recurrent object, which excludes all possibility of space and creates a vortex of motion, intended as a sort of natural effervescence. These allusions to women and masks suggested the magical ferocity of man which was to appear in the theme of *Pasiphaë* (1943), and lead man back to a natural event, to an episode of that infinite, totally present, rich, absolute, primary and absorbing nature.

Meanwhile, in the same year, 1937, Pollock painted two pictures which seemed to make a break with all these experiments, with European and with what may be called totemic culture, and to move towards total abstraction. Whereas we can still distinguish a recognizable image in *Flame* (but it is symptomatic that the subject is fire, a tumultuous and unleashed force Pls. 6, 7

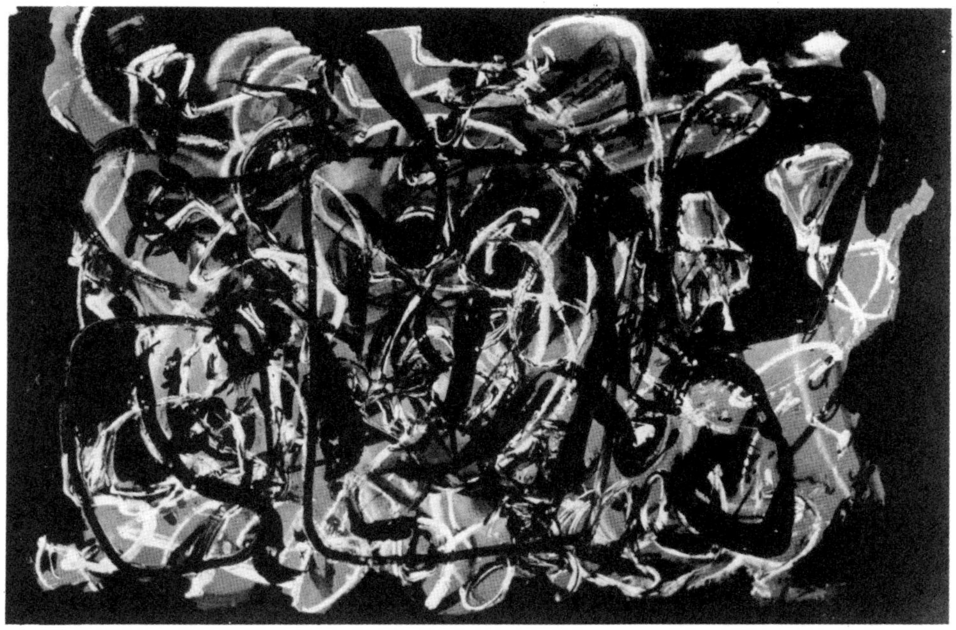

16 *Painting*
c. 1944, gouache on paper
$11\frac{1}{2} \times 17\frac{1}{2}$ in (29×44 cm)
Lee Krasner Pollock collection, New York

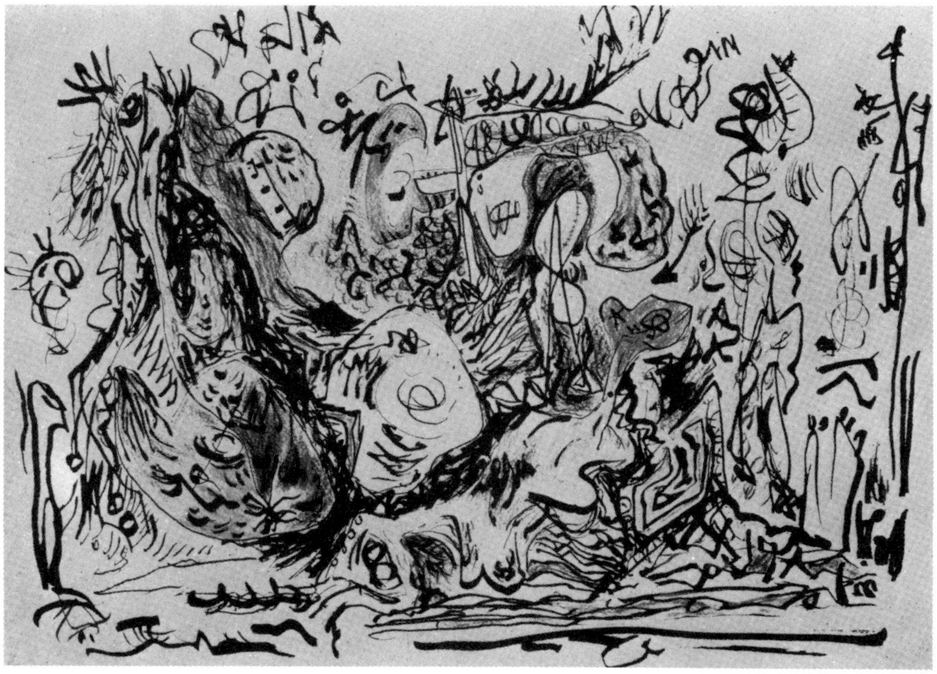

17 *Drawing*
1944, ink and coloured pencil on paper
$13\frac{1}{4} \times 16$ in (34×41 cm)
Lee Krasner Pollock collection, New York

which is resolved pictorially in the ascent of vertiginous matter), in the *Untitled* in the Lee Krasner Pollock collection, the renunciation of the still-identifiable object is complete and the result is a primary naturalism.

The painting instinct

So far we have dealt with the problem of Pollock's artistic formation (almost a spontaneous generation) and the initial components of his problem. Otherwise the acquisition of various cultural data which concurred in forming his poetic vision does not follow a simple chronological order that would allow us to define the growth or evolution of his language. We should speak rather in terms of horizontal enrichment than of vertical development. We should recognize a perceptive capacity which operated in different directions from a basis of fundamental and constant experience – the recognition of self in the organic natural magma – without the successive acquisitions of the reality with which the painter came in contact necessarily formalistically and linguistically in a consequent evolution of style.

Pl. 6 Pictures like the above-mentioned *Untitled* of 1937 suggest the conclusive liberation of the painter in informed poetic vision. But we must also consider works that, in a sense, are conceptually anterior – Europeanized, totemic, even figurative – all variously conditioned by the lively potential of the painter. Pollock was reacting to cultural pressures in terms that repeated his attitude to the existential condition; he therefore renounced both the rationalism of the critic and the exercise of choice on the level of a precise awareness of values. He immersed himself in experience, trusting to instinct and to the possibility of realizing himself and his own vital violence, which he substantially reassembled in undifferentiated nature-matter.

It was not mere chance that impelled him, apart from local and totemic inclinations, towards Picasso and the Surrealists. The elementary force of Picasso is, as expressive possibilities go, probably the most overwhelming factor of our century, while the Surrealists, of course, provoked the explosion of the uncontrolled violence of the subconscious.

18 *Shimmering Substance*
1946, oil on canvas
$30\frac{1}{4} \times 24\frac{3}{4}$ in (77×63 cm)
E. Walker collection,
Ridgefield, Connecticut

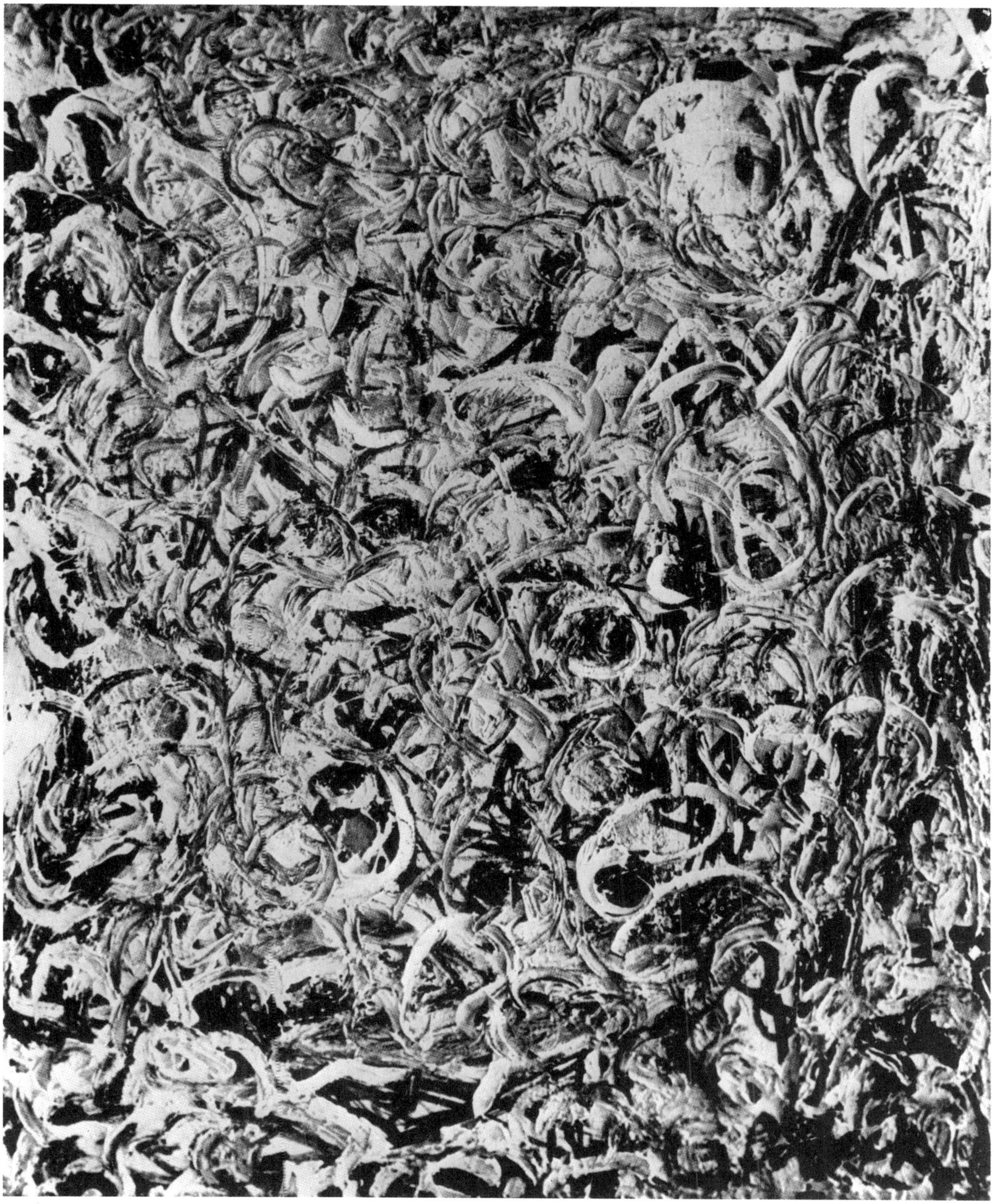

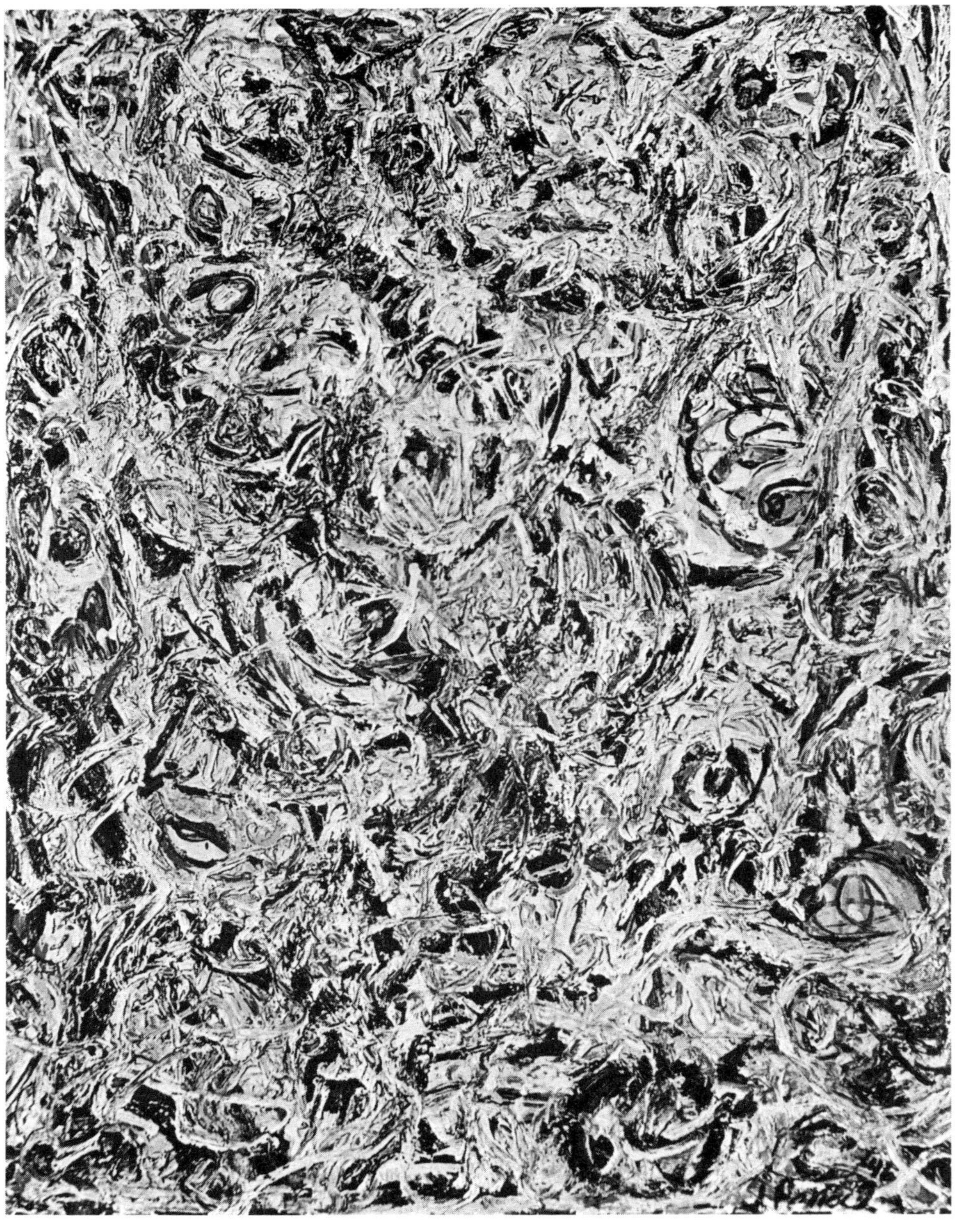

19 *Eyes in the Heat I*
1946, oil on canvas
54 × 44 in (137 × 112 cm)
Peggy Guggenheim collection, Venice

From 1938 to 1942 Pollock worked for the Federal Arts Project, a Rooseveltian answer to the needs of artists in the New Deal society of the United States. The relationship with a public organization, which demanded a public type of painting (or, at least, a type of painting appropriate to public buildings), raised the question, a fundamental one in contemporary art, of function. It is evident that the aim of the F.A.P. was to give back to painting and sculpture, if not architecture, the status it had lost since the 19th century – to recreate the role of the artist as part of society, commissioned to produce work the function of which, practically if not necessarily in principle, determines his work.[9]

Such conditions for artists, which prevailed until the 19th century, demanded that the work of art should be a means of communication, a vehicle for information or an instrument of education, a language capable of communicating at determined levels. During the Middle Ages, painting

9 Robertson: 'Economic depression and the weight of materialism against art in American life in the twenties and thirties are two further reasons for the modesty of American art until the forties. Before then, large paintings had occasionally been produced: Shinn's genre scenes of New York in the Oak Room Bar at the Plaza, painted at the turn of the century, were among the first; Benton's own murals in the Art Students' League in New York, painted in the early thirties, are another step forward. In the late thirties, under Roosevelt, the Government-sponsored Federal Arts Project began, designed to give work to artists during the economic slump. Public patronage using public money demanded public art. For the first time, American artists were encouraged to produce murals for public buildings, and a considerable number of painters now working on a large scale had their first taste of this new freedom within the terms of the F.P.A., under the enlightened directive of Holger Cahill.

'Including Pollock, whose work for the F.P.A. was unsuccessful, presumably through its lack of any obvious or literal public meaning. At this time, *c.* 1938, Pollock's painting was semi-figurative and incapable of adaptation to the needs of decorative mural paintings.'

and sculpture had literally performed the task of divulging the sacred and profane themes that interested both the society of commoners and that of nobility. In the Florentine Renaissance, the figurative arts were transformed in the atmosphere of a new, free and democratic republic. Taste in art became progressively more private and personal with a corresponding flight in art from the representation of great public and religious themes, and the replacement of a public by a private buyers' market. With the Counter-Reformation, art was asked to perform a promotional or propagandizing task: hence the celestial glories painted on the ceilings of churches or the family glories on the walls of palaces. The resort to Greek and Roman art by neoclassicism between the 18th and 19th centuries corresponded to the

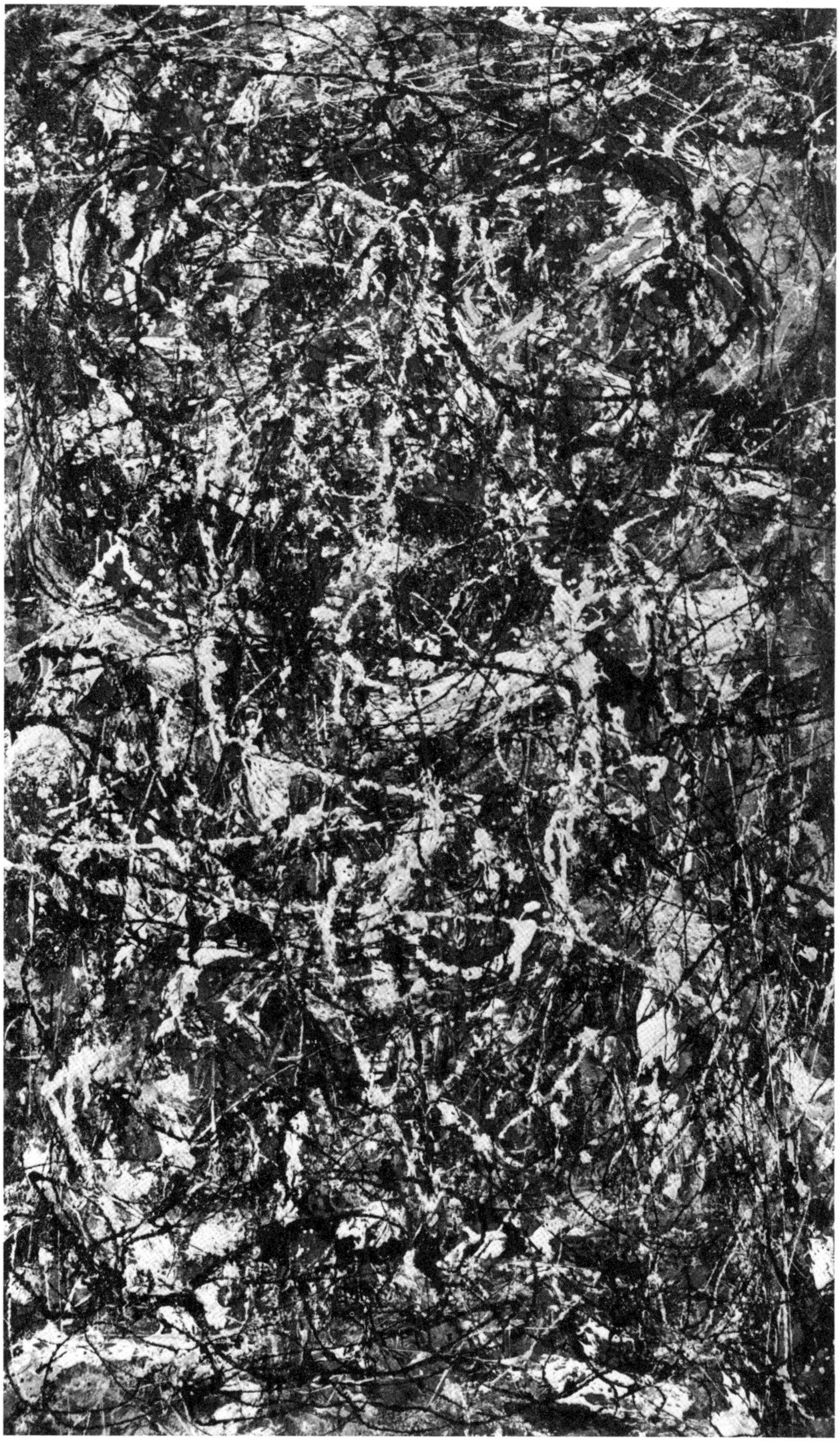

20 *Full Fathom Five*
1947, oil on canvas
$50\frac{3}{4}$ × 30 in (129·2 × 76·5 cm)
Museum of Modern Art,
New York

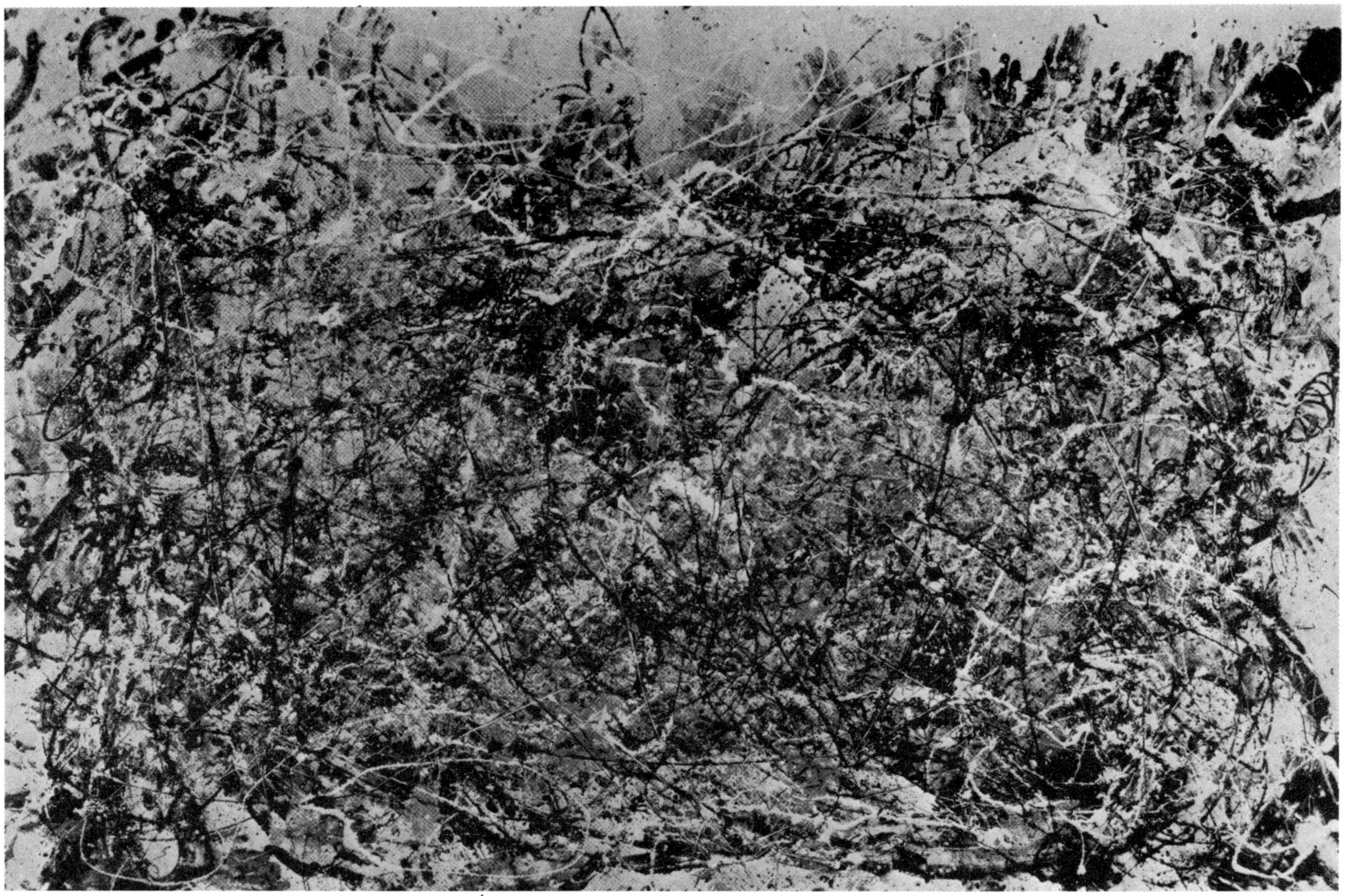

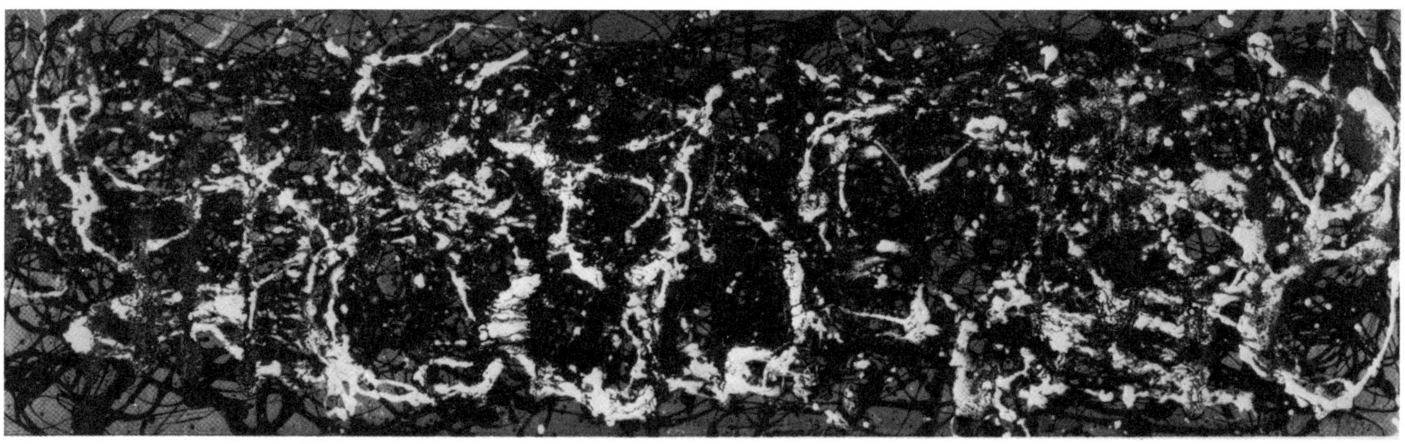

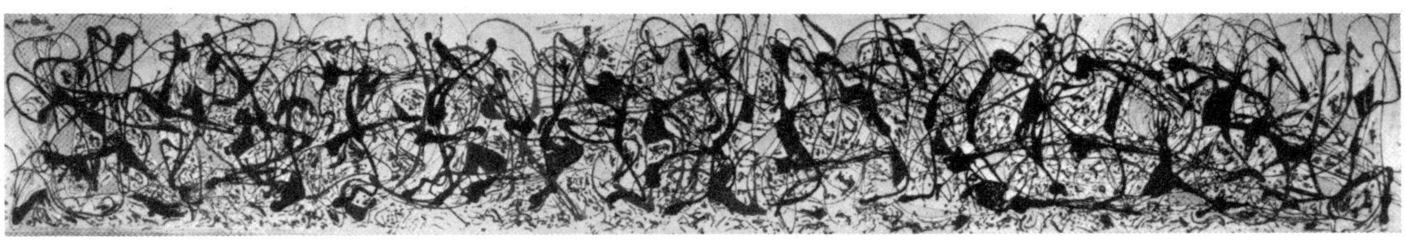

habitual republican identification with antiquity and with meanings traditionally linked with it, such as liberty, firmness, and austerity in costume, and still had a social significance. It was with the advent of a bourgeois society that figurative art tended to lose its function as a message-bearer and to acquire a purely decorative function as a drawing-room ornament. It was at this time that the artist became freed from patronage and ceased painting the pictures that he had been ordered to paint in order to sell the pictures he had painted. This reduced the possibilities of art as a means of communication, while the level of appreciation was raised. New means of communication, beginning with photography and ending with present-day mass media, definitively deprived figurative art of its function as a

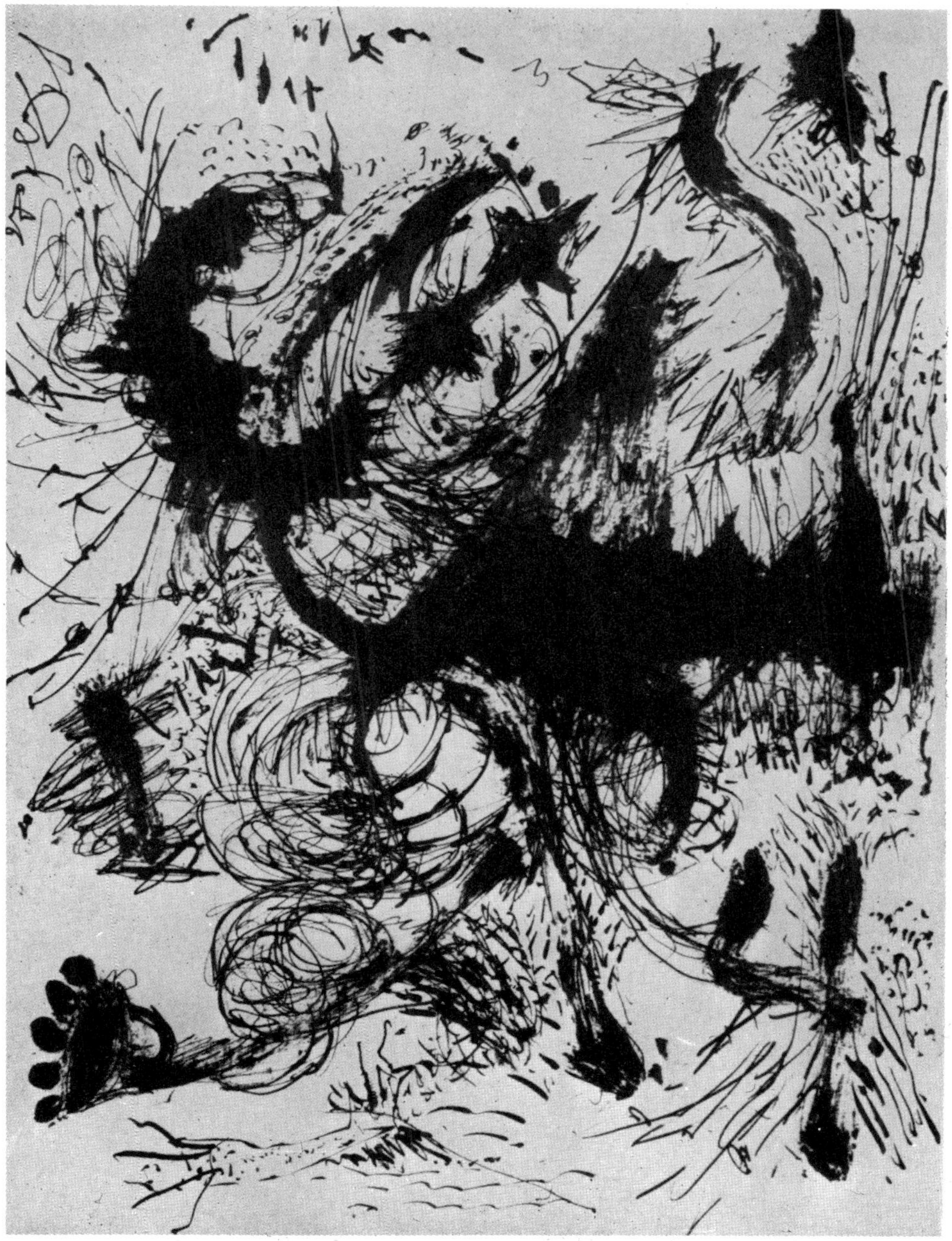

21 *Number One*
1948, oil on canvas
$67\frac{3}{4} \times 104$ in ($172{\cdot}5 \times 264{\cdot}5$ cm)
Museum of Modern Art, New York

22 *Number Twenty-Four*
1948, oil on canvas
$34\frac{1}{4} \times 11\frac{3}{4}$ in (87×284 cm)
Lee Krasner Pollock collection, New York

23 *Summer Time*
1948, oil and Duco on canvas
$33\frac{1}{4} \times 216\frac{1}{2}$ in ($84{\cdot}5 \times 550$ cm)
Lee Krasner Pollock collection, New York

24 *Drawing*
c. 1948, encre de chine on paper
$11 \times 8\frac{1}{4}$ in (28×21 cm)
Lee Krasner Pollock collection, New York

mass medium, which it had always held until the 19th century. We have already had occasion to note how all this led the artist to lose interest in representation and to neglect the episodes of reality in order to approach the totality of the real, and to reject figurative art in favour of non-figurative art.[10]

10 See A. Busignani, *Mondrian:* '. . . a greater consideration of the content . . . of the work of art in accordance with the oft-stated hypothesis of its identity with the form, especially in the visual arts, tends to favour a purely formal interpretation and consequently implies that the "function" of a work of art is a decisive constituent element. This may appear rather strange in connection with a painter whose fundamental non-figurative approach makes him avoid if not content at least the hypothesis of a subject, were it not that episodic qualification of the subject itself having been exhausted in a long figurative process, contemporary art has not identified this subject with the totality of the real, clarifying its various inclinations according to artists and tendencies, thus: rationalistic concreteness in abstract painting, subconscious use of colour in surrealism, or violent sentimentalism in expressionism. This cannot be blamed on the devaluation of the episode in reality (universalized in the past in the historicity of the work of art) nor on the decline (often cited by certain critics) of the figurative or linguistic medium. Instead, the thought springs spontaneously to mind, concerning the matter of the "function" of representation, that the role of episodic description has passed on the other means of expression, leading perhaps to a justification of the old assertion that the photograph has a greater capacity for meaning in the reproduction of a contingent reality (and consumer demand is, or was, relative to the reproduction of a contingent reality) than painting. The fact remains, however, that no matter how materialistic such a thesis may be, how directly it may spring from an ingenuous belief in technical progress, the great figurative medium, which in the past satisfied all artists aiming at immediate and generally accessible representation, has now disintegrated into other media, mass communications etc., and the visual arts in the traditional sense are now in turn attempting to approach the new media in the hope of acquiring a new universality, a new immediacy, new modes of appreciation.

'Without striving after paradox, it may not be wholly fanciful to suggest that had the means been available, the patrons of the thirteenth, fourteenth and fifteenth centuries would have replaced the

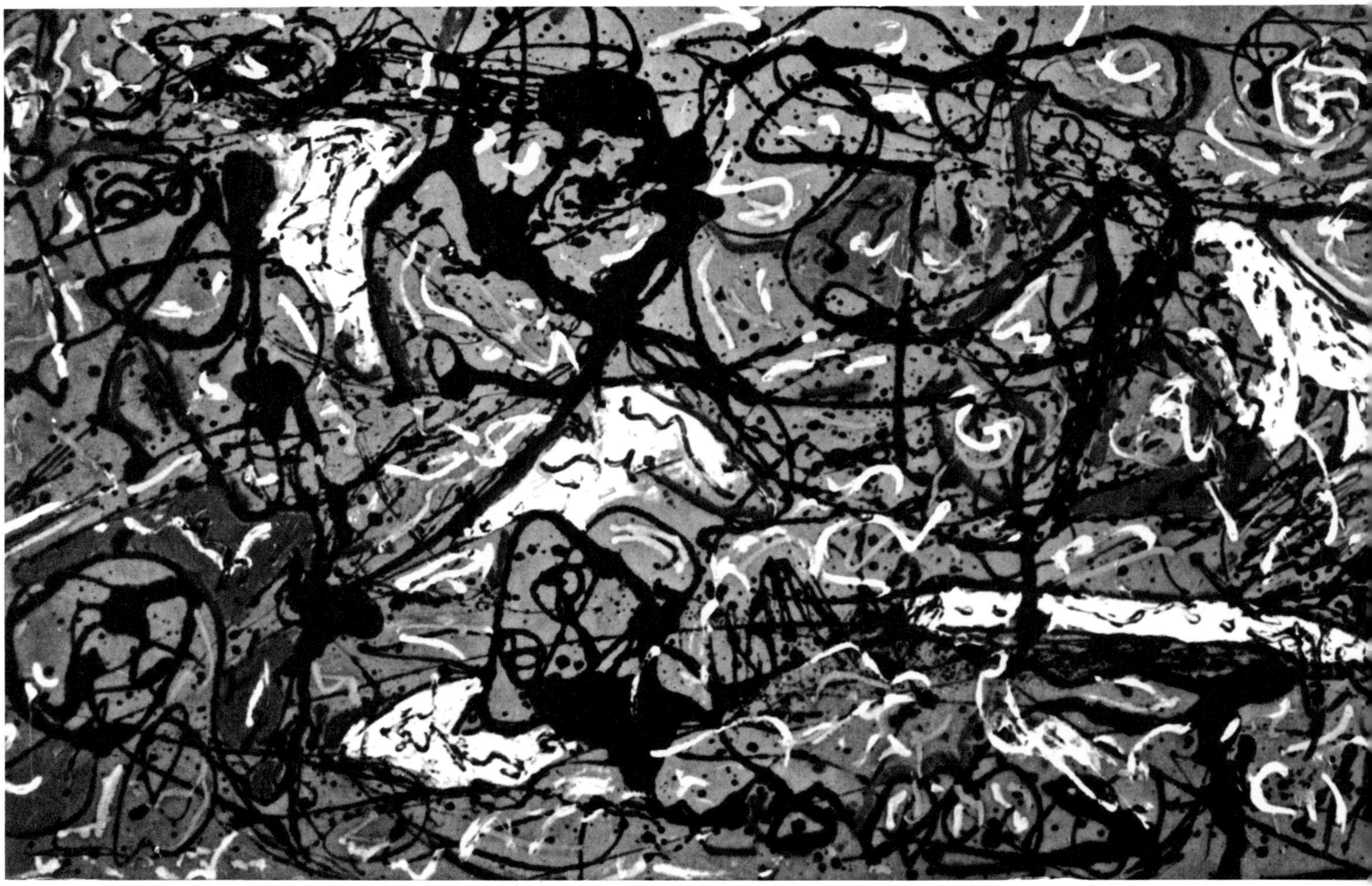

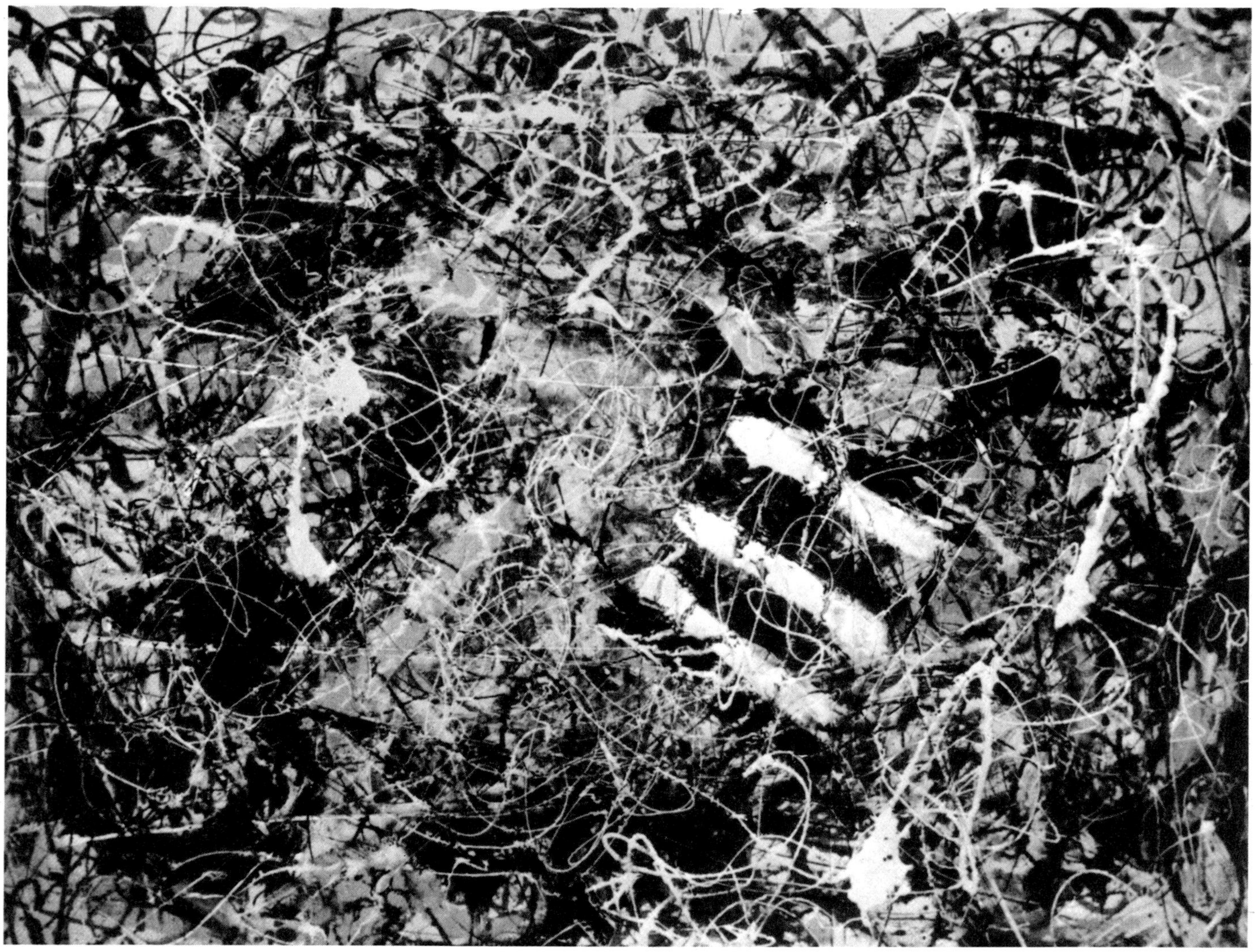

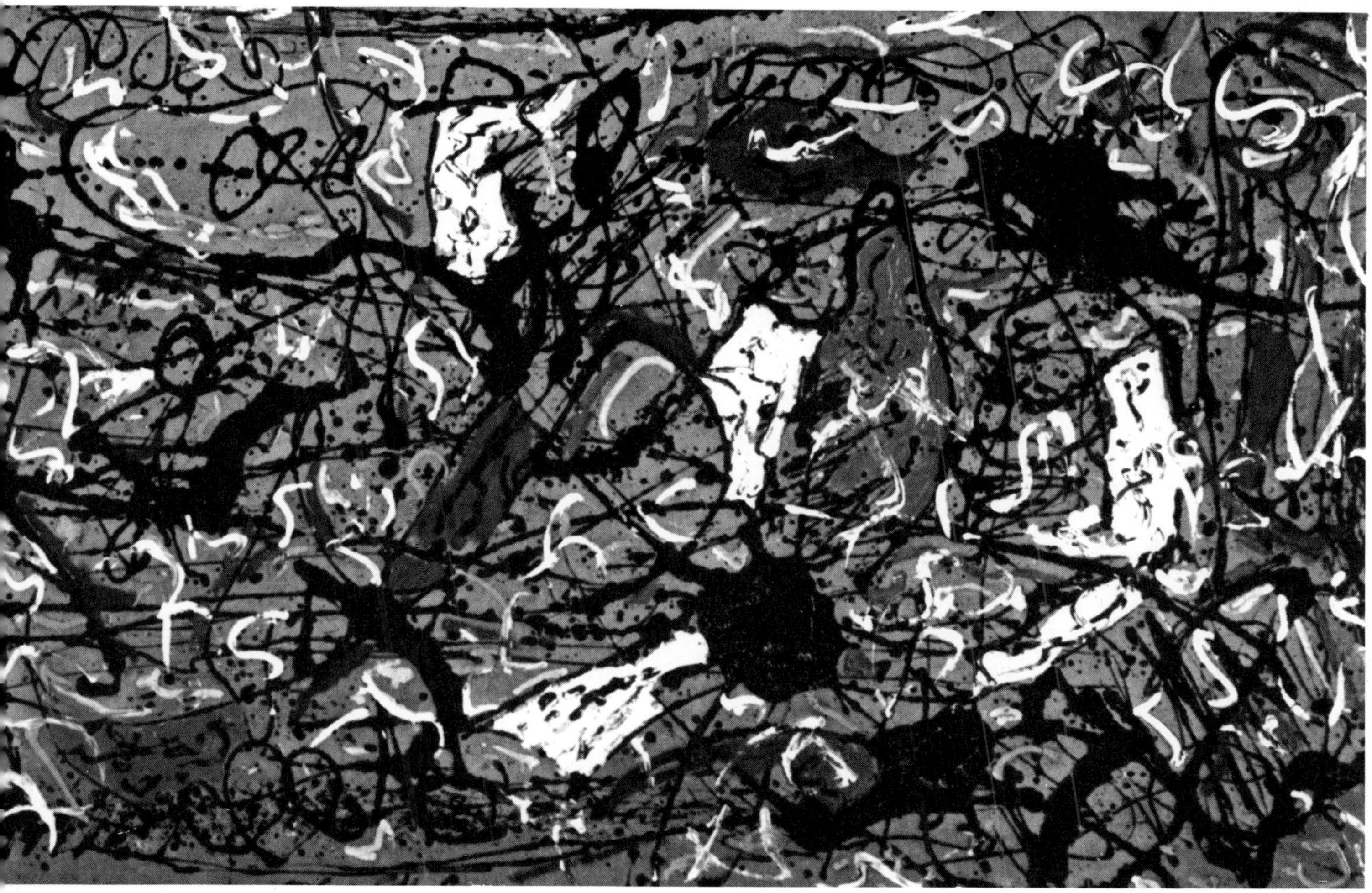

What the F.A.P. was essentially doing was to ask Pollock to reassume the role of a public painter while offering him nothing 'public' to say. Nor could American society give rise to the phenomena of a revolutionary painting imbued with political meaning as, for example, in Siqueiros' Mexican paintings.

This led to the failure of the F.A.P. or at least of Pollock's work for it. It is enough to examine the evolution of Pollock's art to become aware of the effective detachment of the painter from any consumer demand, be it that of the state as represented by the F.A.P. or private collectors.

25 *White Cockatoo*
1948, oil and Duco on canvas
$35\frac{1}{2} \times 114\frac{1}{4}$ in (90×290 cm)
Lee Krasner Pollock collection, New York

26 *Number Seventeen*
1949, oil on canvas
30×40 in (76×102 cm)
Private collection, Paris

The symbology of sex

From 1938 to 1943 (after his years with the F.A.P.) Pollock's painting appeared increasingly conditioned by the interests which we have called totemic, and the symbology of sex already announced in *Birth* became more pronounced. Indeed, the paintings which are probably the most important of the period, the *Male and Female* of 1942, *Pasiphaë*, the *She-Wolf*, the *Guardians of the Secret*, all of 1943, are all orientated in this direction. According to Robertson's formal interpretation, the *Guardians of the Secret* betrays Pollock's struggle to 'unify the picture plane and to avoid fragmentation for its own sake or as decoration'.[11] This opinion is based on the concept of the formation of Pollock's spatiality that Robertson himself has outlined ('Pollock was making a new kind of space, indivisible from the imagery and

Fig. 11, Pls. 12, 13
Fig. 12

biblia pauperum of the painted wall frescoes with filmed representations, leaving the artists free to experiment with a different, if not necessarily deeper kind of reality which was not the result of necessary narrative conventions.'

11 Robertson: 'In *Guardians of the Secret*, painted in 1943, Pollock has devised a fragmentary border surrounding an inner rectangular space of complete abstraction and all-over unification. If this rectangular space is studied independently of the border, a later painting by Pollock is unearthed, in embryo. In many of Pollock's drawings and paintings in different periods we find variations on the idea of an enclosed plane, usually in the form of an inner rectangle repeating the exterior pictorial boundary, in which the calligraphy is either contained or spills over into the surrounding border. In the same way, there is also a recurrent alternating divergency between the activity in a painting or drawing being contained within the frame, and the movement or activity by implication extending beyond and outside the picture's edge. One method of composition provides us with a section of an unconstricted flow of life and energy; the other gives us a set-piece, a composed tableau inside this flow of energy and movement. The idea is similar to a public square surrounded by buildings, an

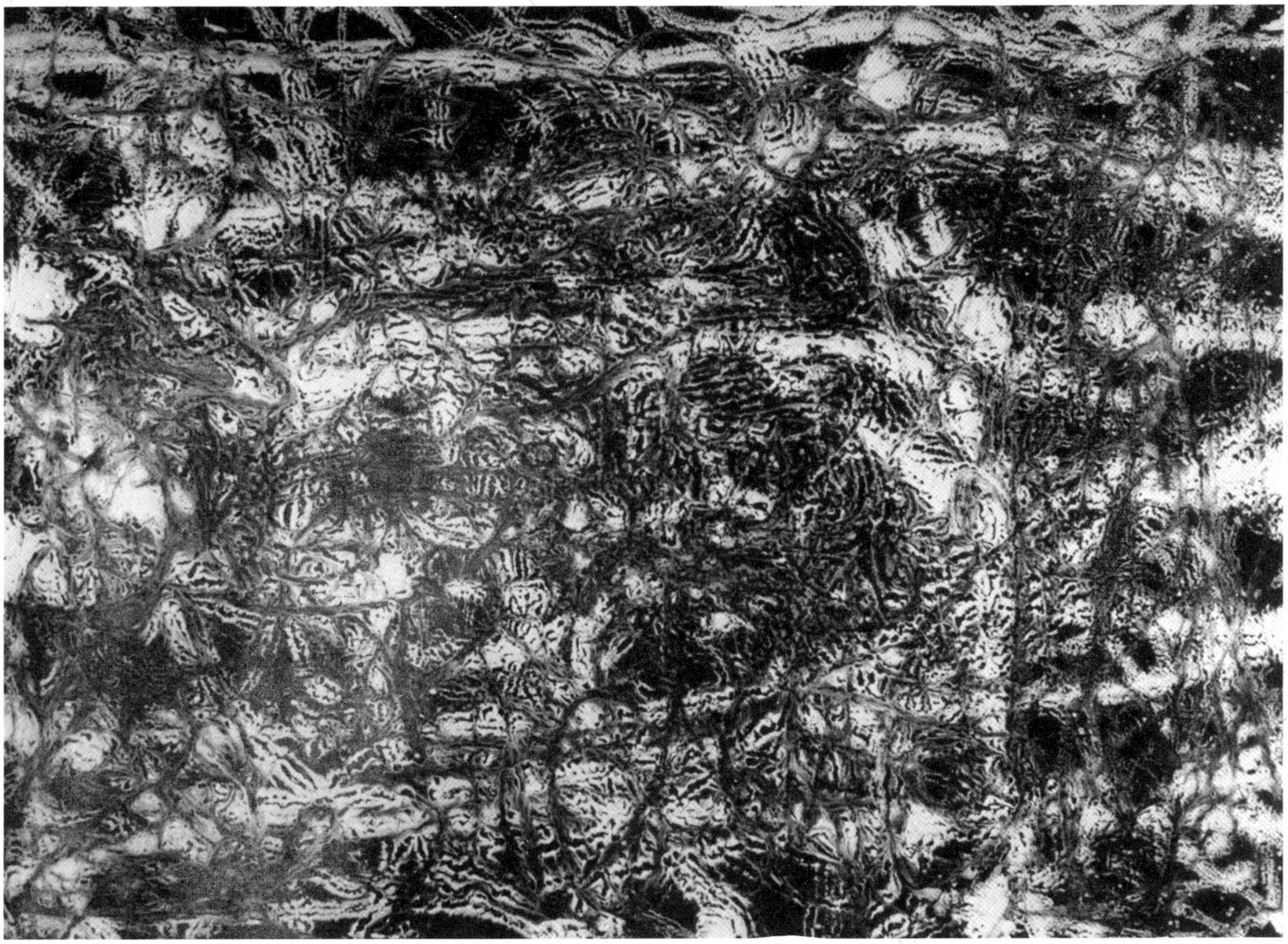

27 *White on Black II*
1949, oil on canvas
13 × 18 in (33 × 46 cm)
H. Ralston collection, Chicago

the technique. The separate strands of image, colour, texture and brushwork were all coming together').

Now even if we agree with such a concept (though I prefer to speak not so much of a new space as of a negation of space in the non-space of matter), it also seems to me that Pollock achieved this space or non-space from the very beginning. This was therefore the germinal condition of his pictorial experimentation, and not the result of a stylistic progression of which the *Guardians of the Secret* constitutes a more or less important stage.[12] On the other hand, in the work we have started with, *Landscape with Rider,* the space which Robertson has alluded to is already present, no matter how minor the quality and how awkward the achievement. All this seems to bear out what has been said above with regard to the horizontal development of Pollock's language and his ability to project himself in different cultural experiences from the constant basis of his romanticism in pictorial matter.

But Robertson's other proposition seems more concrete to me:

'. . . The evolution of this date, *c.* 1946–47, shows a spasmodic but steadily

enclosed garden, the old notion of Paradise, a document containing the marks of a finite truth surrounded by a generalized decorative border, an arena, or a specific picture plane placed in a generalized space.

'*Guardians of the Secret* is heavily symbolic of Pollock's pictorial problems at that time, as well as his inner, human problems, for the rectangle of free space and all-over calligraphy is beset round its perimeter by a bestiary that represents the tangibilities of life, translated into archetypal forms, which Pollock had to pierce and subdue in order to gain complete freedom as a painter. The guardians still retain the secret, but the problem is stated here in the most pointed metaphysical and plastic terms.'

12 With regard to the theme of space, I think it useful to quote Tomassoni's complex introduction to Pollock: 'Action is a performance and also the result of that performance. For Pollock, action meant physical exertion, movement in all directions, pauses for thought, struggles. One can only guess what the equivalent of this action would be in spatial terms; space can exist without action but action can never dispense with space. "Space" in this context, even when expressed in painting, is not, of course, the abstraction of neoplastic geometry, structured and reducible to a theorem; nor is it psychological space, the visualization of an interior dimension; not yet, as we shall see, is it a perceived entity against which experience can be oriented. Pollock's space is without doubt closely tied up with the phenomenology of perception, but it is above all an existential space in as much as it is inherent in action, in the painter's gestures and in the material consistency of his painting. It is something that can be perceived in the natural world, a non-critical concept that arises directly from sensation, from

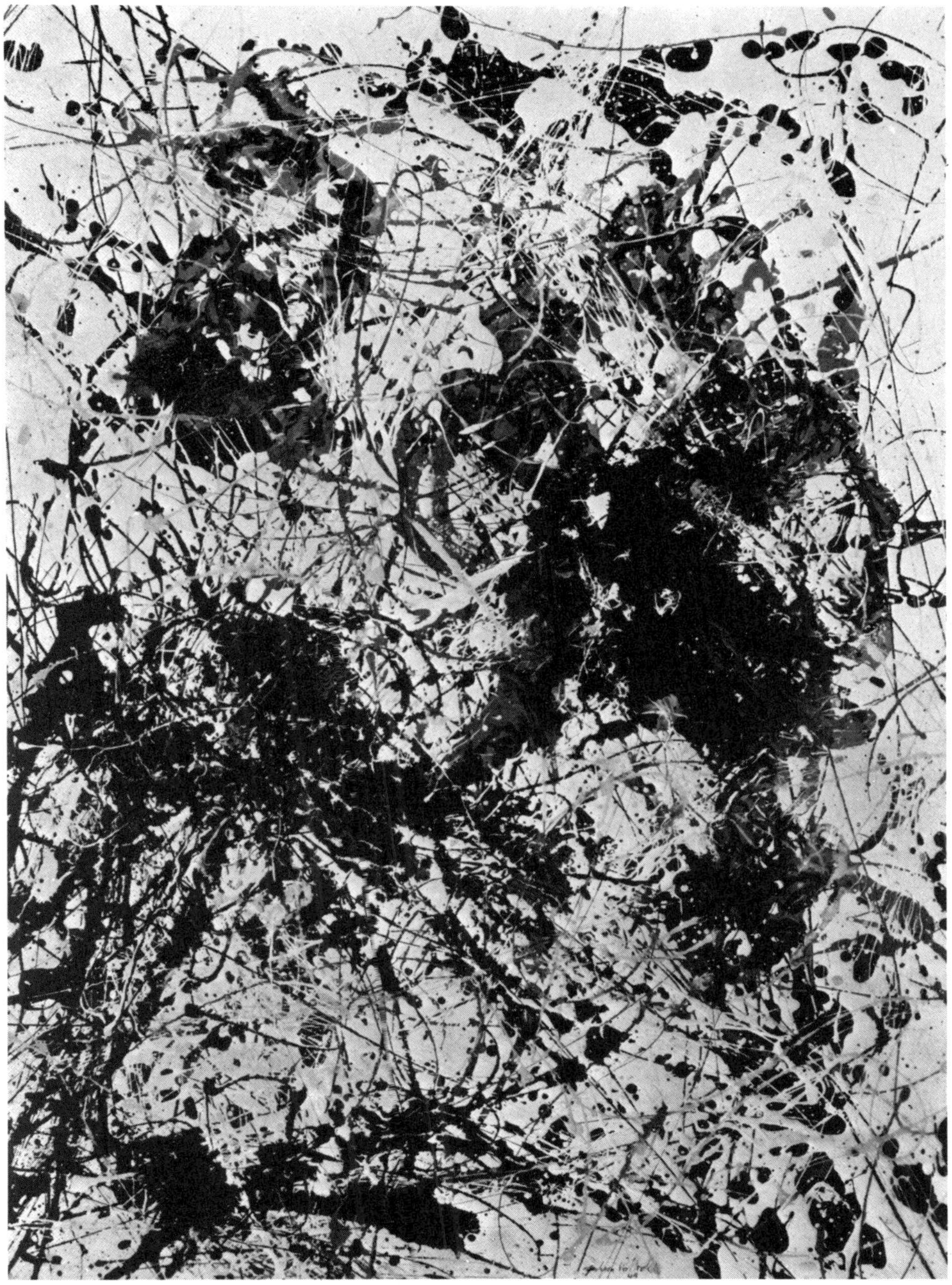

28 *Number Twelve*
1949, oil on paper
31 × 22 in (79 × 57 cm)
Museum of Modern Art, New York

accelerating progress towards abstraction by means of successive phases of imagery selected for formal characteristics that might lend themselves to abstract treatment. Pollock was greatly influenced by the writings and teachings of Jung, and there is no doubt that his search for images of the widest possible reference and implication exactly coincides with his parallel search for an abstract statement of the utmost potency and tension: an abstraction that would be informed and regulated by the banished imagery so that it achieved the weight and suggestiveness of a graph or cipher, derived

immediate intuition. For Pollock it assumed a vital dimension because his painting is like a physical extension. Unfolding his own convulsive action in a real spatial dimension, which he always attacks frontally, he longs for space as a suffocating man seeks for air.

'But to say that Pollock's painting has its origins in space is not to say that it formulates a hypothesis of space or determines a concept of space–just as living does not mean interpreting life or formulating a theory of life. Pollock regards space as presupposition of existence, a physical element which permits him to have physical experiences. Pollock "is" in space simply by being in contact with objects "other" than himself: first and foremost the canvas, the locus on which he realizes an event by flinging himself upon it, occupying it physically and conferring on it the specific character of an area of space during a certain period of time. However, since objects are situated in events, and Pollock's use of space reflects the physical side of the human condition, his paintings do not present space as a thesis (as it was for Mondrian) nor as a hypothesis (as it was for Klee); space is a physical expression of the artist himself and is entirely within his control.

'If Pollock's spatial horizon is that of physical existence (meaning the consciousness of being alive and of continuing to live) then this immediately introduces a very close relationship between space and time: together they create the concrete condition of experience. Pure time, a regular progression of instants without duration which can only be apprehended in the sum and relationship of these instants, does not exist, Pollock seems to imply, following in Whitehead's wake: time to the individual is an abstraction made from the flow of empirical events, from a succession of related events.

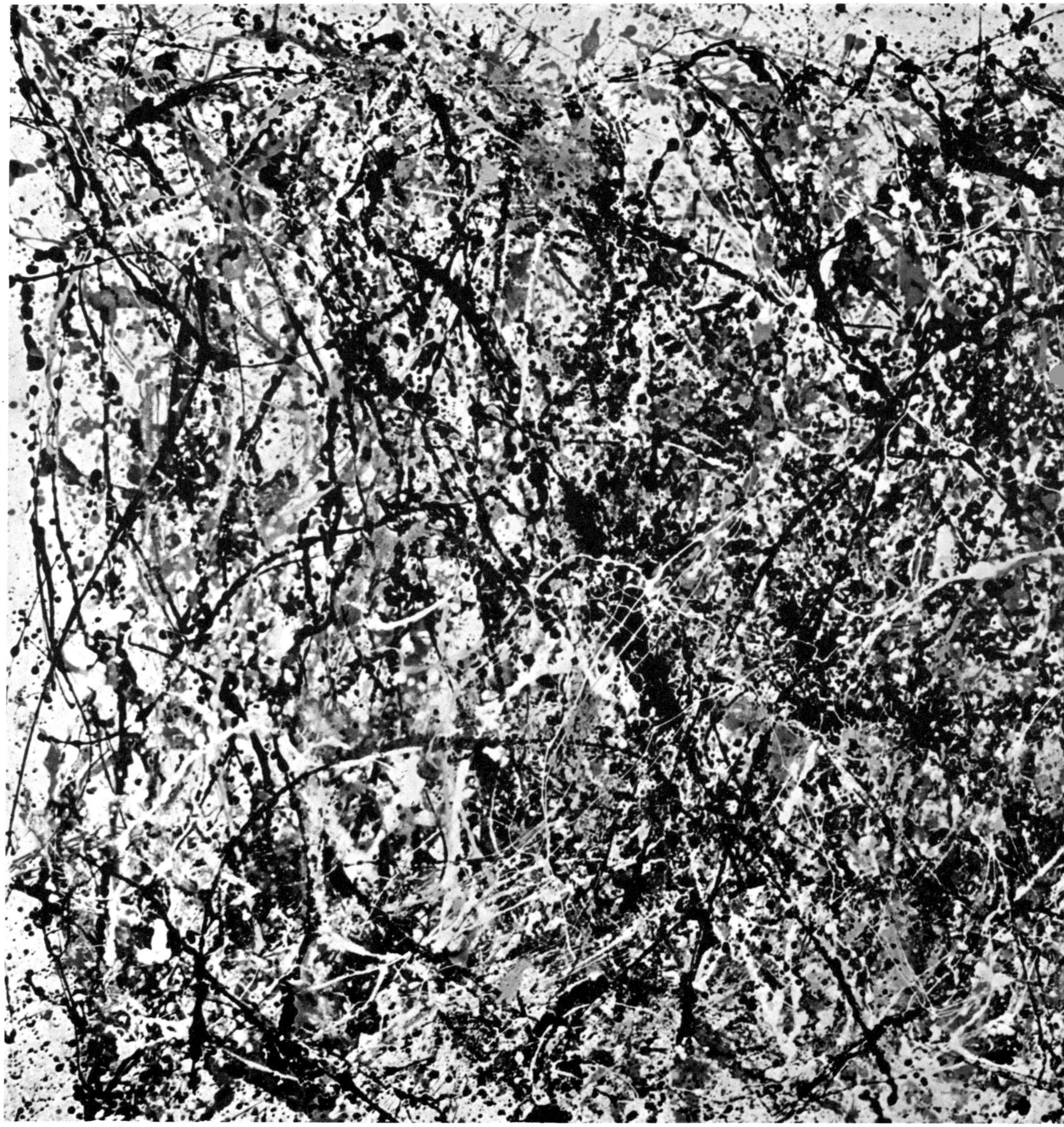

29 *One*
1950, Dev-o-lac,
Duco and aluminium on canvas
$106\frac{1}{4} \times 210\frac{1}{2}$ in (270 × 525 cm)
B. Heller collection, New York

from the earlier presence of the imagery and its movement in space.'

In my opinion, however, Pollock's fundamental pictorial theme in the pictures mentioned and in others that were more or less contemporaneous was the symbolic emergence of the image (totemic experience) and its envelopment in undifferentiated matter (which Robertson defines as 'movement in space').

In 1942, Pollock met Peggy Guggenheim, who was probably the only type of client with whom Pollock could agree. She gave him a five-year

The flow and the relations of events can be seen as a continuous process, one time unit tending to over-lap with another one. Pollock's painting is the sum of these two moments, the coinciding of two different time scales: he paints with one unrestrainable movement, which culminates in the alienation of the body, the more dramatic and tragic because two time scales tend to become confused towards the limits of their duration. This is painting in process which will remain in process.

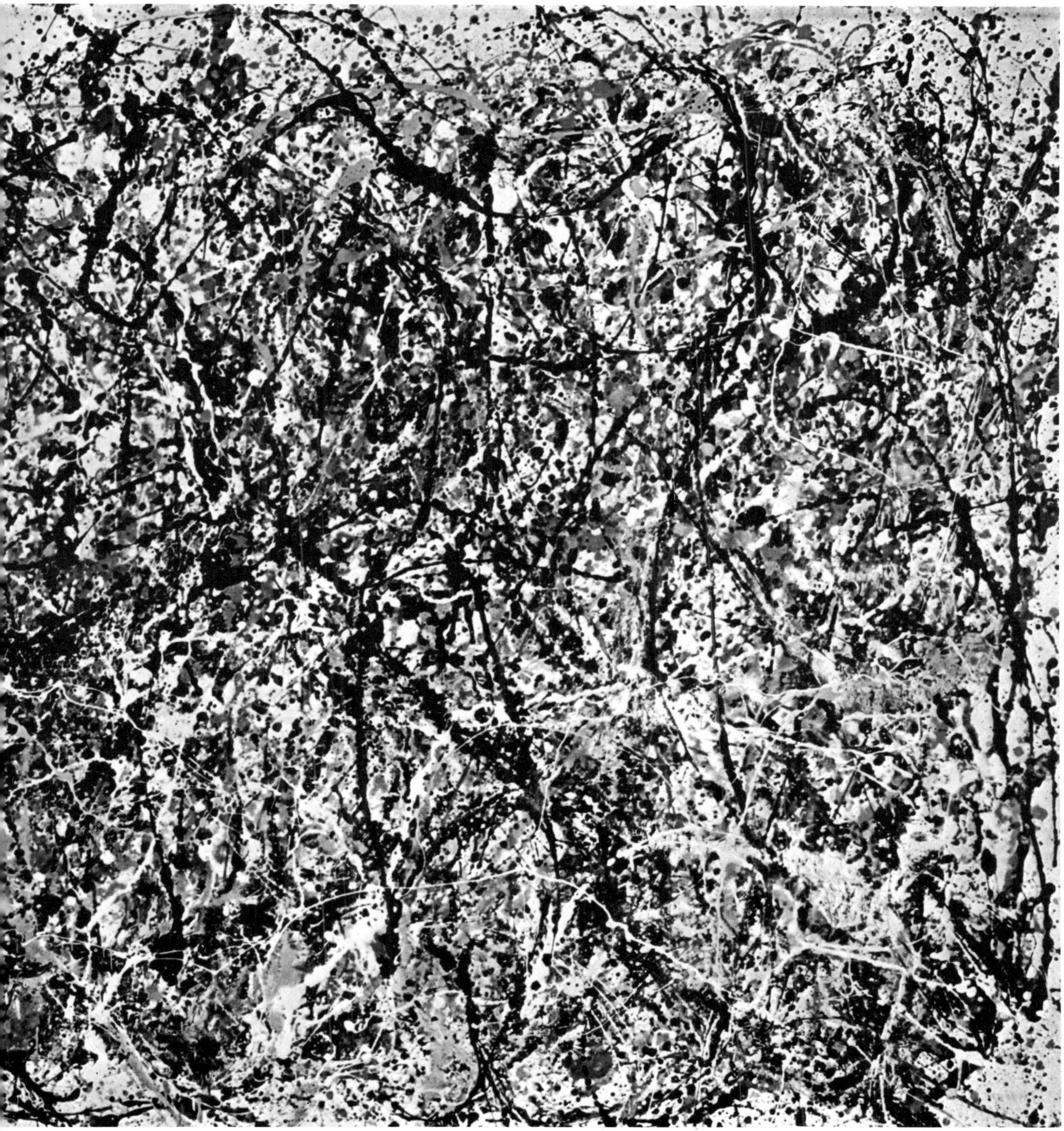

contract and organized his first one-man show in 1943. This was a decisive event for Pollock's future, as was the appreciative article by the critic Clement Greenberg (in *The Nation*) which began to outline and clarify the terms of Pollock's pictorial poetry.

The non-formal approach

Pollock spent the last ten years of his life at East Hampton in Long Island, where he moved in 1946 with his wife Lee Krasner (whom he had married four years previously). It is probably right to take this period, at least for the

'If the traces that the artist leaves in time constitute his deeds, the traces that he leaves in space should correctly be called his signs. If Pollock had confined himself to deeds he would have been a dancer or an actor; his action painting represents the deed of a moment in time made tangible in the form of a sign. By becoming visible it ruptures the bonds of time as a dimension, breaking off its passage by taking on the opaque and finite substance of paint. But space exists only where the sign

sake of explanation, as marking the total resolution of Pollock's language in non-formal terms, in paintings like *Eyes in the Heat* or *Shimmering Substance*. A year later the goal had been reached. This was the time of *Cathedral* and *Full Fathom Five,* works which completely justified what Harold Rosenberg, the theoretician of action painting, was to write later: 'At a certain moment, American painters one after the other began to consider the canvas as an arena in which to act rather than a space in which to reproduce, redesign, analyze or "express" an actual or imagined object. Thus the canvas was no longer the medium for a picture so much as an event'.[13]

Figs. 18, 19
Pl. 27, Fig. 20

How clearly Pollock recognized his own attitude may be seen from his own emphasis on the Navaho painting mentioned in note 8. It is probable that at this point the term romanticism, which has been used so widely here, came to assume a greater significance. The coincidence between representation and action, or even the annihilation of representation in action, constituted the ultimate act, the final truth of a conception of existence which brought together history and nature, past, present and future in the act of creation. The 19th-century image of the romantic poet who himself assumes an ethical as well as an aesthetic responsibility is defined in this henceforth absolute identification of being with doing and of doing with creating. The only morality, and therefore the only truth, lies in becoming totally intermingled with one's creation, making painting and the act of painting a constant intervention into reality.

Blue Poles

After completely breaking free from figuration, Pollock made a partial return to it in the period of black and white paintings, between 1950 and 1951 (*Number Five* of 1951 for example). But, naturally, he used it with a new liberty which in some successive works like *Sleeping Force, Four Contraries, Easter and the Totem,* and *Ocean Greyness,* all of 1953, achieved an extraordinary image-nature symbiosis.

Fig. 36
Pls. 36, 38

Pl. 37

In the same year, 1953, Pollock painted *Blue Poles,* which was perhaps his masterpiece (though I do not altogether accept Robertson's interpretation of the work, which attempts an exegesis in the formalistic key, precisely in the picture in which the artist most completely expresses his non-formal conclusions).

Figs. 34, 37

Apart from *Blue Poles,* the great milestones leading to his last work are essentially two: *Frieze* of 1953–55, and *Scent* of 1955. It is difficult to say whether they represent the effective epilogue to Pollock's painting apart from his life; what is certain is that one year later, as Robertson says, 'the search was ended, the great gesture made, and the exorcism was complete. The effort killed him'.

Conclusion

After examining Pollock's development by trying mainly to collate it, or even to justify it, in a historical situation, it is obvious that a conclusion on his work cannot be reduced to an aesthetic judgement based on traditional criteria constructed for formal art, which no longer suffice. Nor today, fifteen years after his death, does Pollock's art any more appear as a decisive subversion of traditional modes of expression.

gives its substance, and this is not enough—it tries to free itself of the sign, to get rid of its material encumbrance, and to move towards a beckoning future away from the torment of eternal non-fulfilment, and to feel free again to be translated into a deed. But the deed then collapses and becomes anguish and torment. Pollock's world is seen as a space-time continuum, and the account he gives of it in paint, using his dripping technique, is an expression of his *Weltanschauung*. The interval of time between one painting and the next is what in phenomenological terms would be called the "pause": a transient moment unrecognized or unidentified by his consciousness. This infinite repetition of selection and the state in which the concrete physical act is conducted, outside all ideological premises, are the conditions in which Pollock's art is realized. It is the result of the interpenetration of time and space. But if motion by antithesis presupposes quiet, Pollock's activity, by opposing everything that remains static, should show some dynamic kind of development. In fact the equation of space and time means also that the past is brought to terms with the present: the sign, disposed rhythmically over the canvas, is a constant recollection of the present moment yet left for a moment it slides back into the past. It would be wrong to suggest that Pollock's paintings make full use of horizontal and vertical space, but lack depth. He borrows a practice frequent in a different medium—free verse: the present moment, in which he is submerged, turns back on itself and becomes a labyrinthine web, an all-enveloping tangle, and since this moment derives from a perpetual motion

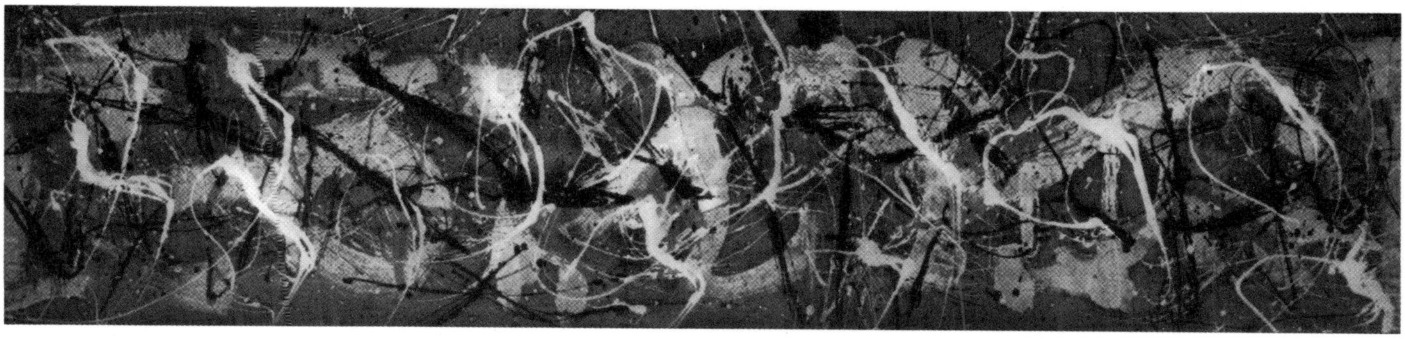

30 *Number Seven*
1950, oil on canvas
24 × 106 in (61 × 269 cm)
M.L. Mark collection, New York

What has happened since 1956 gives a new dimension to the anticlassical Pollock, the Pollock who burnt himself out in a pictorial gesture, in an artistic space which yet remains always that of the image, with its evocative, narrative, descriptive, all-in-all figurative possibilities intact. By dwelling on the romantic theme, the relationship with nature (and leaving it to writers quoted in the text to clarify other aspects of Pollock), this account has stressed his traditionalism–despite the enormous break with the past that action painting represented. For though action painting suggested a different existential relationship between the artist and his work, it maintained not only the work's communicative function (criticism has been able to receive its message even as an image, not only as a gesture) but even its habitual quality as an object of a certain type, endowed with historically acquired characteristics. The fact that Pollock had made use of non-traditional paints –Duco or Dev-o-lac–and used them with a technique borrowed from the Navaho, extending the canvas on the ground and walking upon it to be the better 'within' the work, does not alter the substantial 'being a picture' of the paintings, nor their capacity to retain their meaning when fixed to the walls of a house or mixed with other paintings in a museum collection.

The effective destruction of the visual arts in their traditional aspect happened after Pollock's time, with movements ranging from Pop art to *art pauvre,* which all aim at a gesture that does not occur within the work, as it did for Pollock, but outside it. Also, the gesture acquires meaning in the corrosive relationship between the object proposed and the fact that proposes it. The gesture, therefore, is totally consumed in the moment in which it is accomplished.

Just as extraneous to Pollock's experience as this new Dada which gathered fragments of our civilization to throw them at us was that other contemporary movement–probably the most deliberate–of seriality in the work of art, and consequent negation of the *unicum* (typical of non-mass culture) in the possibility of a production multiplied by the number of the consumers (a trend linked to Mondrian's rationalism and to its fruits in, for example, the field of industrial design). It was precisely because of its gesture-like quality that Pollock's work was always a *unicum* and continually repeated the endeavour of a masterpiece.

Moreover, it is probable that we can find not only existential anguish at the root of Pollock's experience but the anguish of a true artist. We can

it manifests itself in a series of events which were contained within itself. The present moment which derives from a state of stasis does away with any semblance of duration–as in the case of Tapiès. Pollock, like Tapiès, uses time as a perpetual motion dominated by the need to repeat itself endlessly without pause: to interrupt the movement would mean breaking the space-time continuum. Only the ultimate liberation,death, can break the circle of repetition to which we are condemned for life. Along with European artists such as Van Gogh, Gorky and Wols, the American Pollock represents Heidegger's theory of "living for death", according to which liberty is attained only in the act of dying, because "in possessing oneself one loses oneself". Pollock, dying as he did in a motor car accident, went even further, demonstrating that involuntary death may be an act of choice, therefore a gesture of freedom.

'One key to Pollock's personality and work is the philosophy of Husserl: his longing to be in the public eye, his inescapable desire for physical experience, the physical presence of man in the world are what Husserl called *Lebenswelt,* the world of life, or *Erfahrungswelt,* the world of experience. Besides Husserl's theories, to which should be added the problem of alienation in the development of existentialist thought, as discussed in the works of Jaspers and Heidegger, and also the psychology of the *transfert,* we must take into account a representative group of Anglo-American thinkers, who have concentrated on the problems of experience and personality and have helped to create a typically

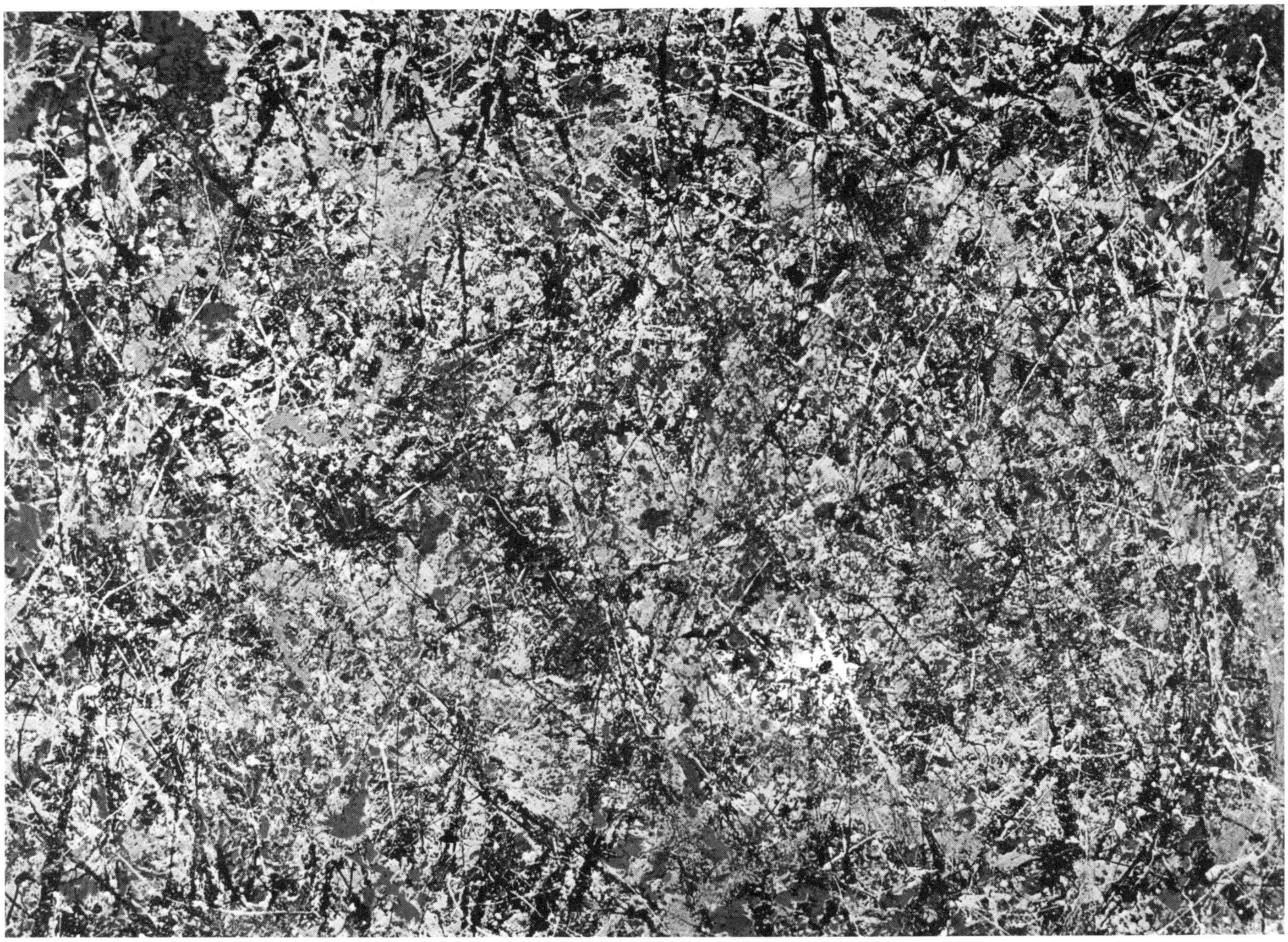

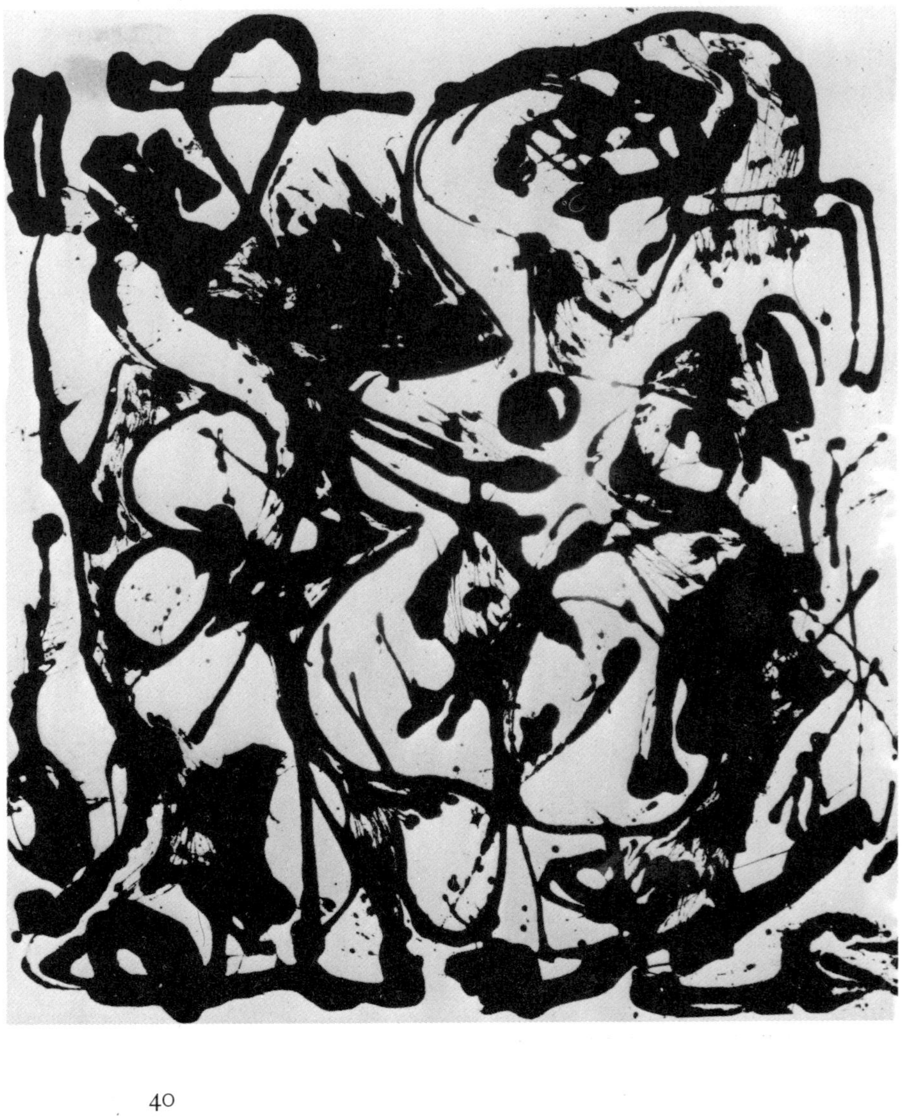

31 *Lavender Mist*
1950, oil, enamel and aluminium paint on canvas
$86\frac{1}{2} \times 119$ in ($220 \times 297{\cdot}5$ cm)
A. Ossorio and E. F. Dragon collection, East Hampton, New York

32 *Black and White Painting*
1951, Duco on canvas
35×31 in (89×79 cm)
Private collection, New York

33 *Number Seven*
1952, Duco on canvas
$52\frac{1}{4} \times 40$ in (133×102 cm)
Lee Krasner Pollock collection, New York

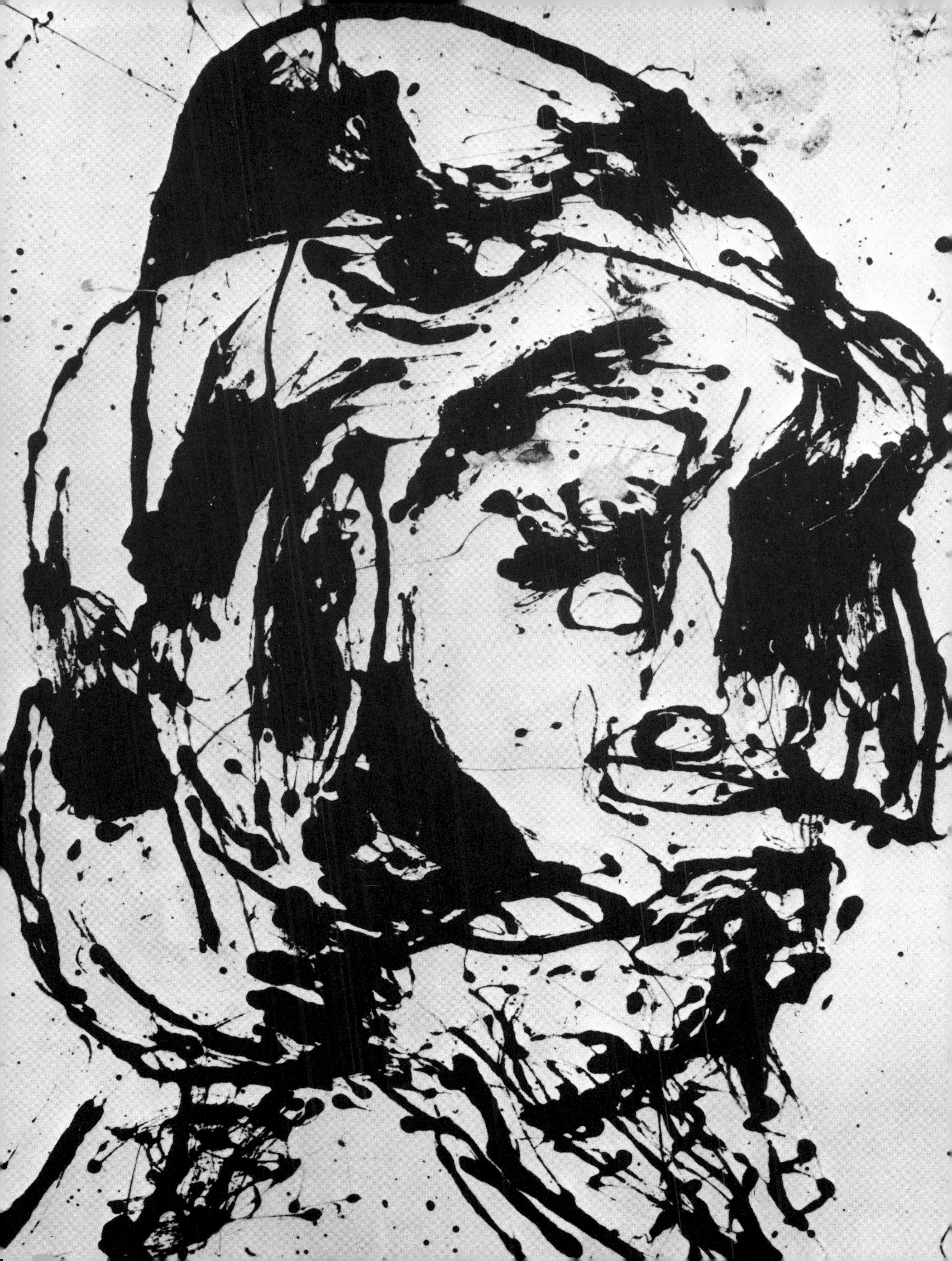

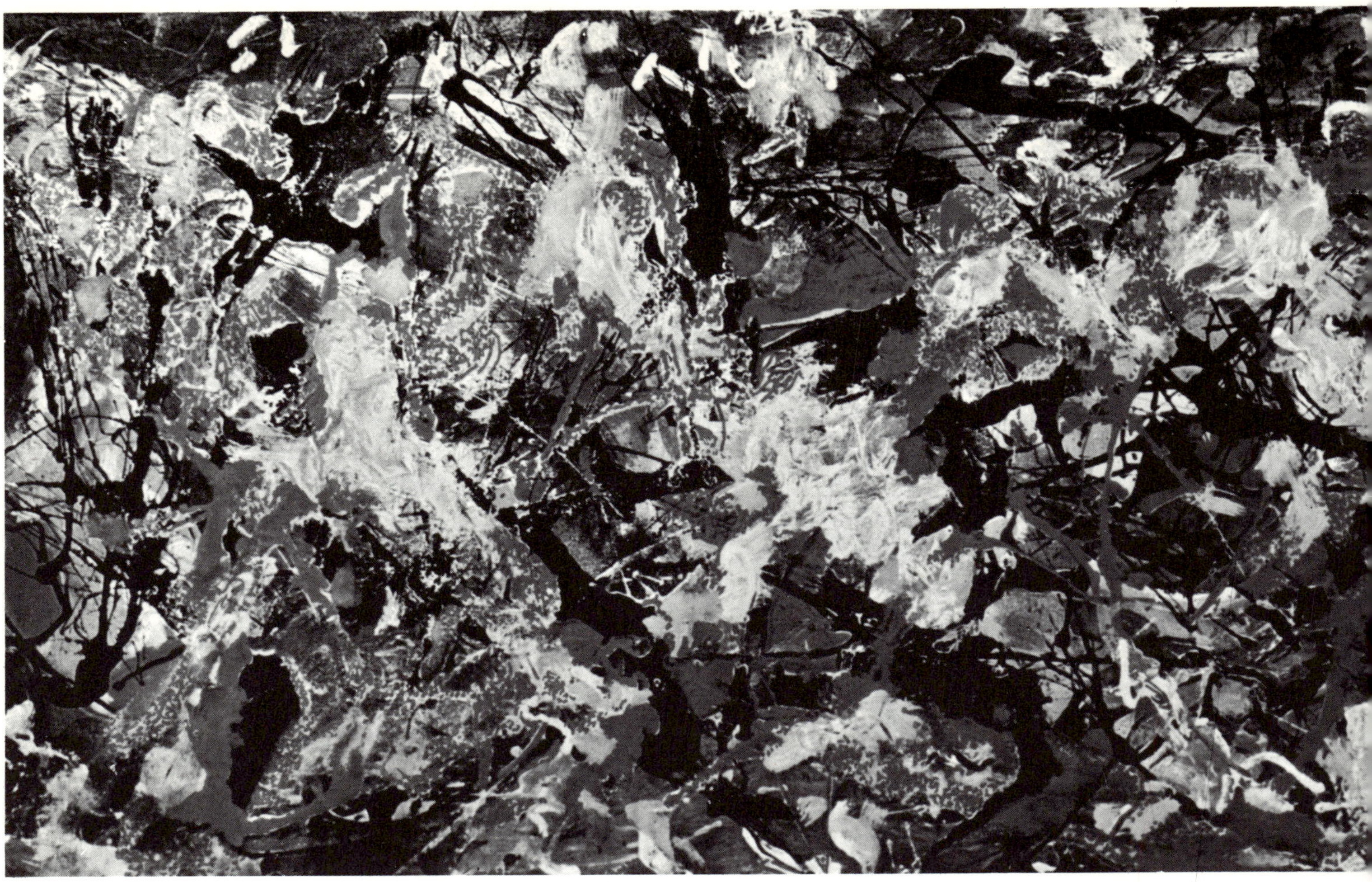

34 *Frieze*
1953–55, oil and aluminium on canvas
$26 \times 85\frac{3}{4}$ in (66×218 cm)
B. Tremaine Senior collection, Merion, Connecticut

single out his awareness of the inactuality of the work of art and of the impossibility of total communication, in which the function justifies itself. If the work cannot acquit itself of the almost messianic task of revelation, if the artistic language can no longer be simply explicative and descriptive through the effective solitude of the individual, then the relationship between the artist and the work can only resolve itself in the definition of the actuality of the work and in the artist's presence in the work (this is substantially its gesture-like quality), which offers itself to others as a message for what it is worth. This means that the three traditional links of the chain of poetic communication–artist, work, spectator–in which the first and the third maintain their individual personality and the work assumes the function of a medium, are reduced to two by the absorption of the artist in the work and the work in the artist. The relationship with the third link becomes one of shock, the impact of an action-expression monad against a fundamentally hostile terrain.

A judgement of Pollock's work (a judgement not of value but rather of mode of comprehension) must then spread itself between these two themes:

American type of consciousness: Charles S. Peirce, John Dewey and A. N. Whitehead. To Whitehead in particular, with his "apprehension" and "experience", his identification of perception with existence, were due the cogent critique of absolutist theories of time and space and the elaboration of the relativist and organicist vision which was to lead to a new "concept of nature", in which nature was understood fundamentally as a real process. If this area of perception is taken to be an emblematic vision of the world, then a direct and complete relationship between space, time and material is established; and if this relationship is restricted to an area of events which is constantly narrowing and becoming more circumscribed, then the artist materializes simply by being himself. To this condition of hyper-individualism ("these painters are experimenting with a unique kind of solitude", wrote Rosenberg) are attached the concepts of adventure, risk and failure, key ideas in non-formal painting. If we can see Pollock's work in purely phenomenological terms as an act of total self-revelation in the present moment, we perceive that it is governed in fact by a moving time scale which involves dashing forward in time and sliding back again into the present. The emotional equivalent of this condition is a state of worry or anguish. Since all actions are dangerous, each one is an adventure; adventure is risk, and death is always ahead as a final possibility; one's energy is used up in escaping from a sinking ship. Action painting is a paean of praise for absolute commitment, and therefore absolute risk. It is the acceptance of imminent catastrophe, of "living for death" through an aesthetic action which could be negatively described as a moment of failure:

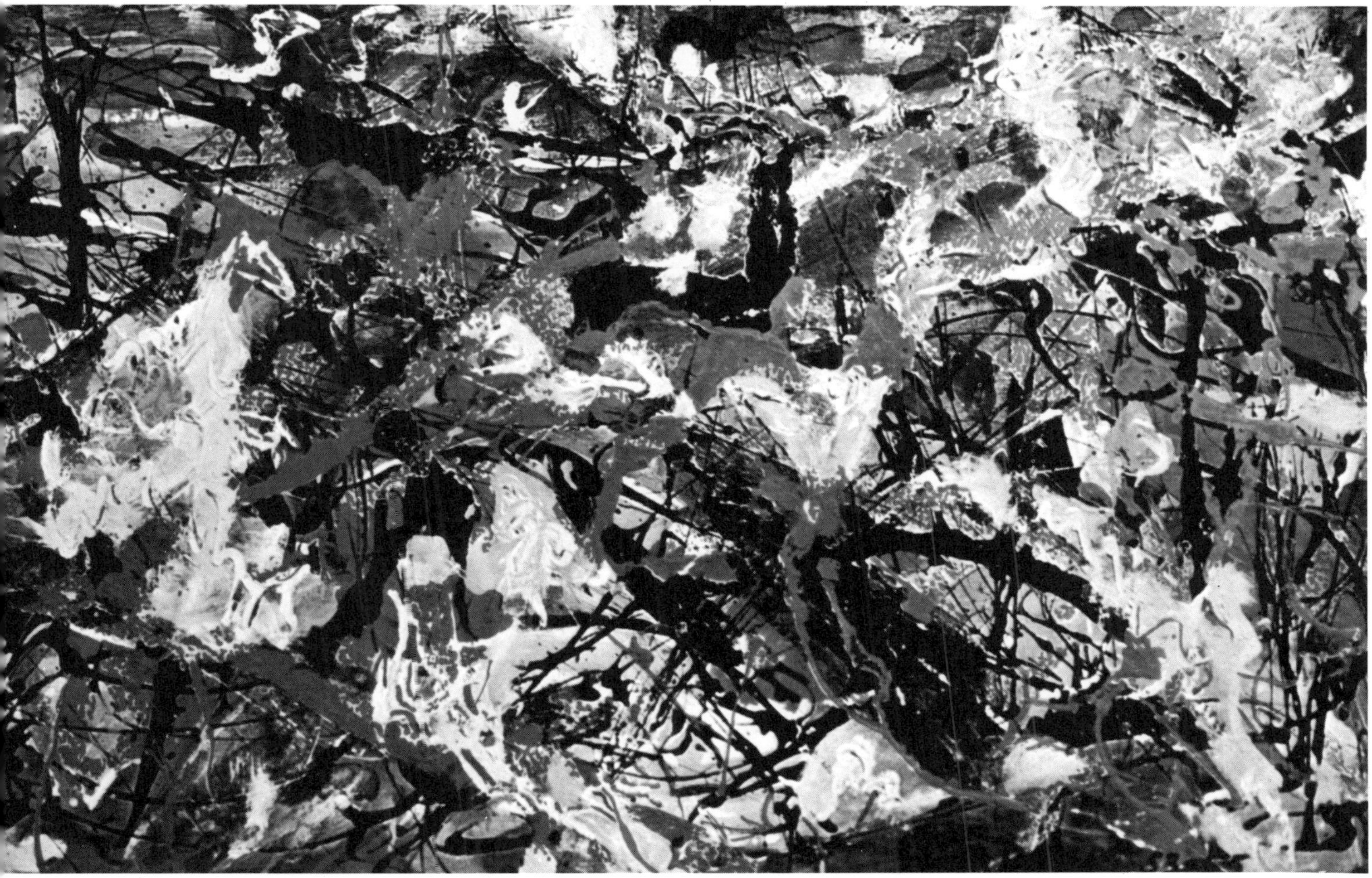

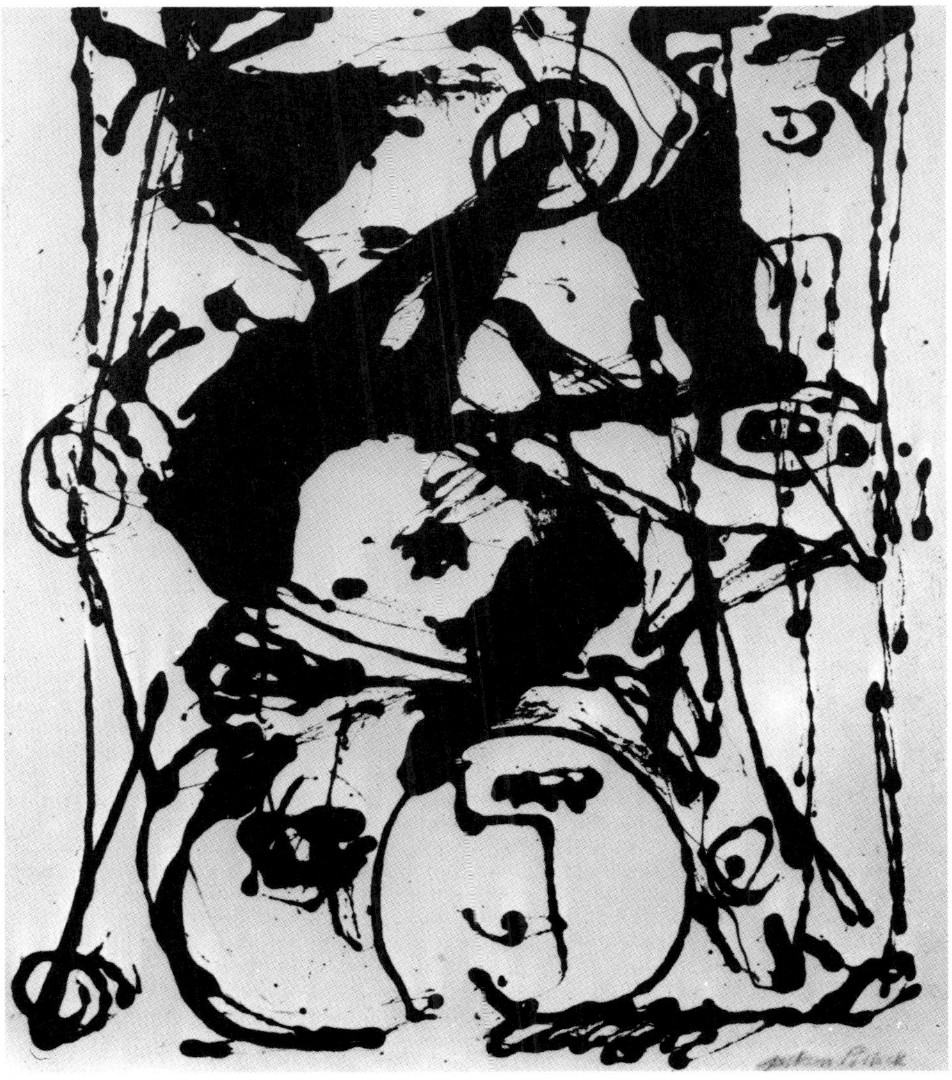

35 *Black and White Painting*
1951–52, oil on canvas
35 × 31 in (89 × 79 cm)
R. H. Patterson collection,
New York

36 *Four Opposites*
1953, oil, Duco and aluminium on canvas
$72\frac{1}{4} \times 51\frac{1}{4}$ in ($183 \cdot 5 \times 130 \cdot 2$ cm)
Leavitt collection, Hannover, Pennsylvania

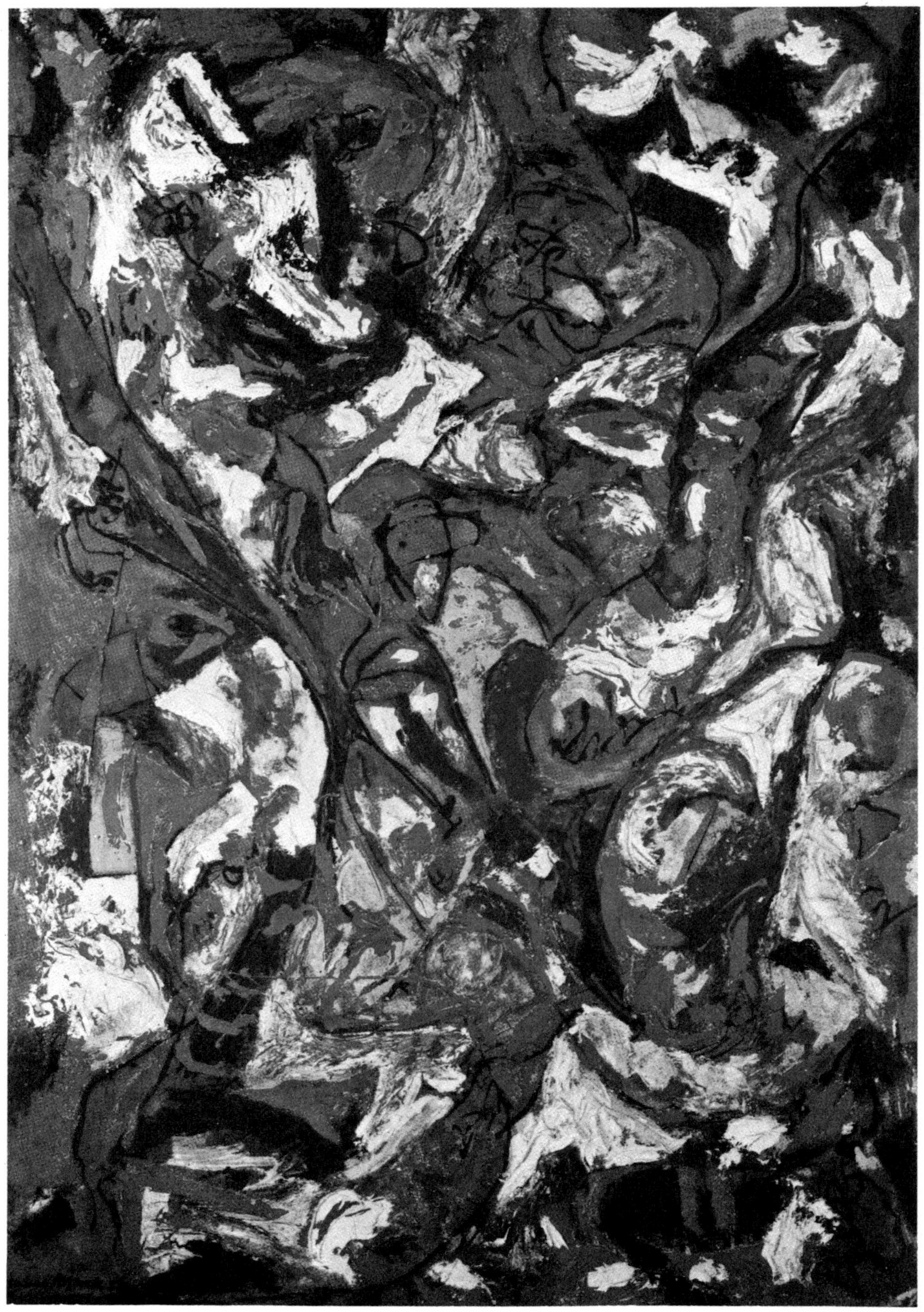

on the one hand, its historicity i.e. its location at the summit of a cultural process (which we have defined as American romanticism), that is profoundly different from that of Europe even if it is tied to it by an undeniable series of relationships; on the other, the conflict inherent in and peculiar to American society, between its history and the cultural process in which it tends to recognize its origins and its development, and the alienation deriving from productivism, technology and industrialization.

There remains the fact that beyond all this, and without any wish to

"the sudden, terrifying stoppage of the flow of existence, and in its place something which is not quite life and yet neither is it quite death" (Argan). It is a convenient moment to add here that, in spite of his familiarity with the theories of Jung, Pollock's state of mind was one of brilliant lucidity: his work is not only experimental; and he was not fundamentally motivated (as Sam Hunter and Sir Herbert Read would have it) by surrealist automatism. He was determined rather than hypnotized, overwhelmed by conflicting anxieties rather than passive and unconscious. "When I am painting I have a general notion as to what I am about. I can control the flow of paint: there is no accident, just as there is no beginning and no end." These words were part of Pollock's commentary to a short film made about him by Hans Namuth and Paul Falkenberg in 1951. Perhaps more than any other painter of our time he makes us feel that beyond the painting, outside the confines of the canvas, the void lies outstretched. This explains how, alongside the image of impending death, his canvases burst with an uncontrollable feeling of life: life materializes on the canvas, the struggle to paint is the struggle to commit a concrete version of life to the canvas. Pollock's action is the struggle of a prisoner, of a man condemned to death, of a wild beast, avid for freedom, pacing furiously up and down its tiny cage. His action is compulsive yet never automatic.'

13 H. Rosenberg, *The Tradition of the New*, New York, 1959.

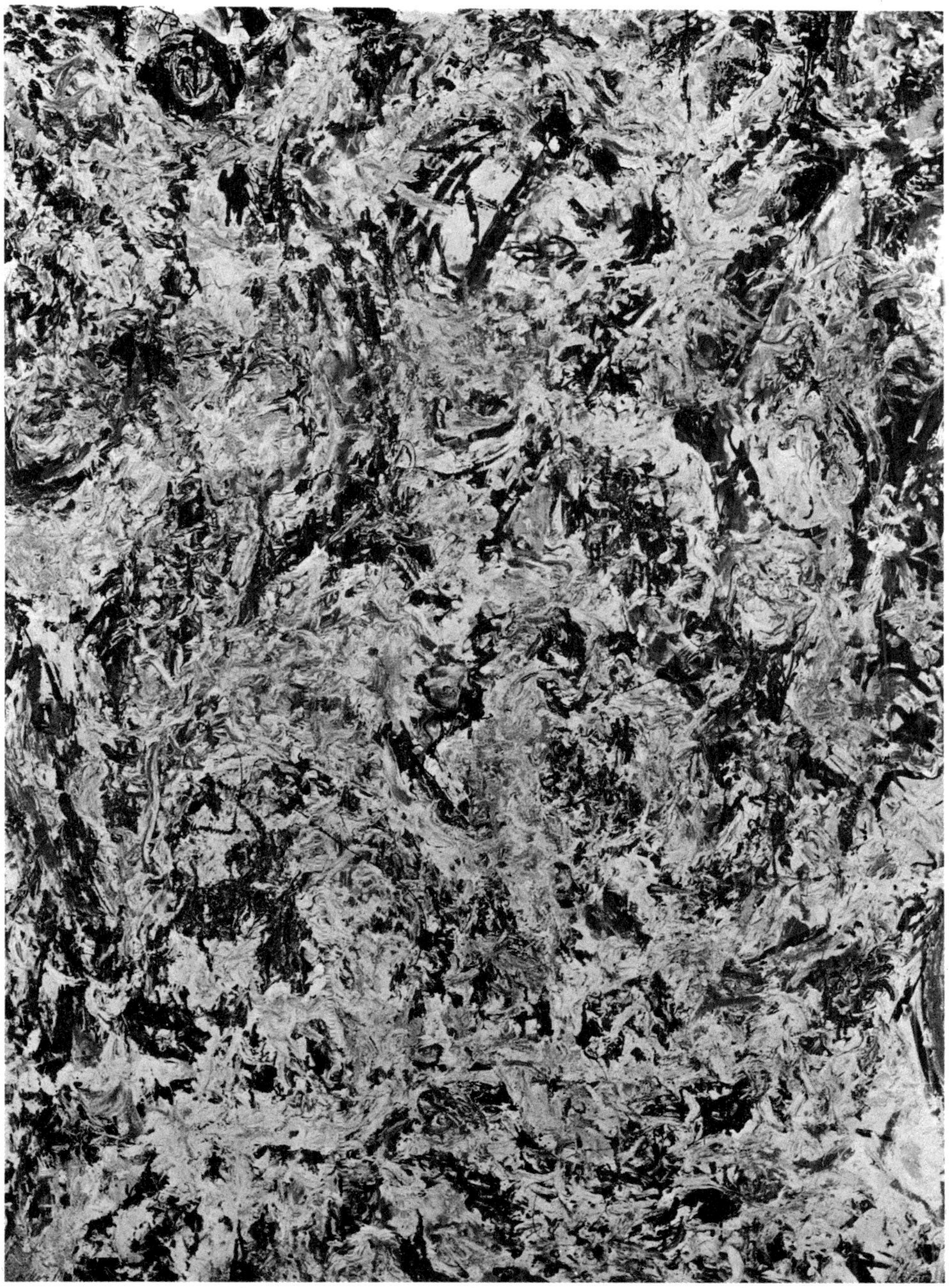

37 *Scent*
1955, oil on canvas
$78 \times 57\frac{1}{2}$ in (198×146 cm)
Leo Castelli collection, New York

formulate the judgement of aesthetic value that the works themselves have denied, Pollock's art falls almost magically into the category of poetry. Once the impact has occurred, once Pollock's gesture has entered into our awareness, these paintings succeed in completely arousing our feelings and in provoking our participation. This means that Pollock has made an intervention into our reality and into our history (not only in our imagination), has revealed to ourselves an aspect of our being and of our existential condition.

That we should subsequently try to express this enrichment, this new rediscovered truth, analogically by means of 'lyrical' transpositions (compare Robertson's remarks on *Scent* of 1955: 'The brushwork and the elaborate layers of paint have taken on a new complexion in describing something only just removed from nature, rather as travel to a far-distant country can make the native land more meaningful when the traveller returns'), is our personal way of justifying the quality of an emotion which we habitually relate to the traditional, consecrated sphere of the 'beautiful'.

Colour plates

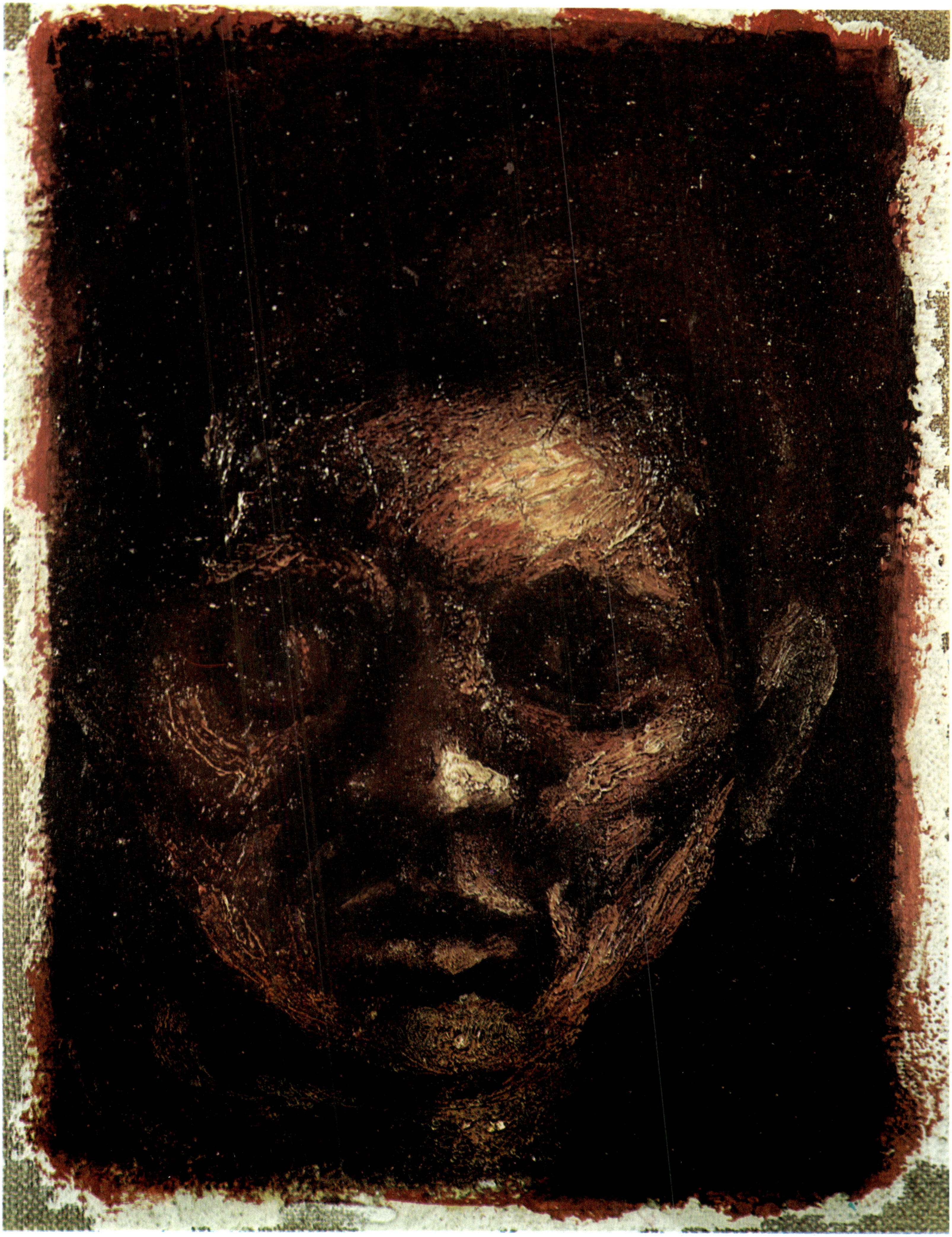

1

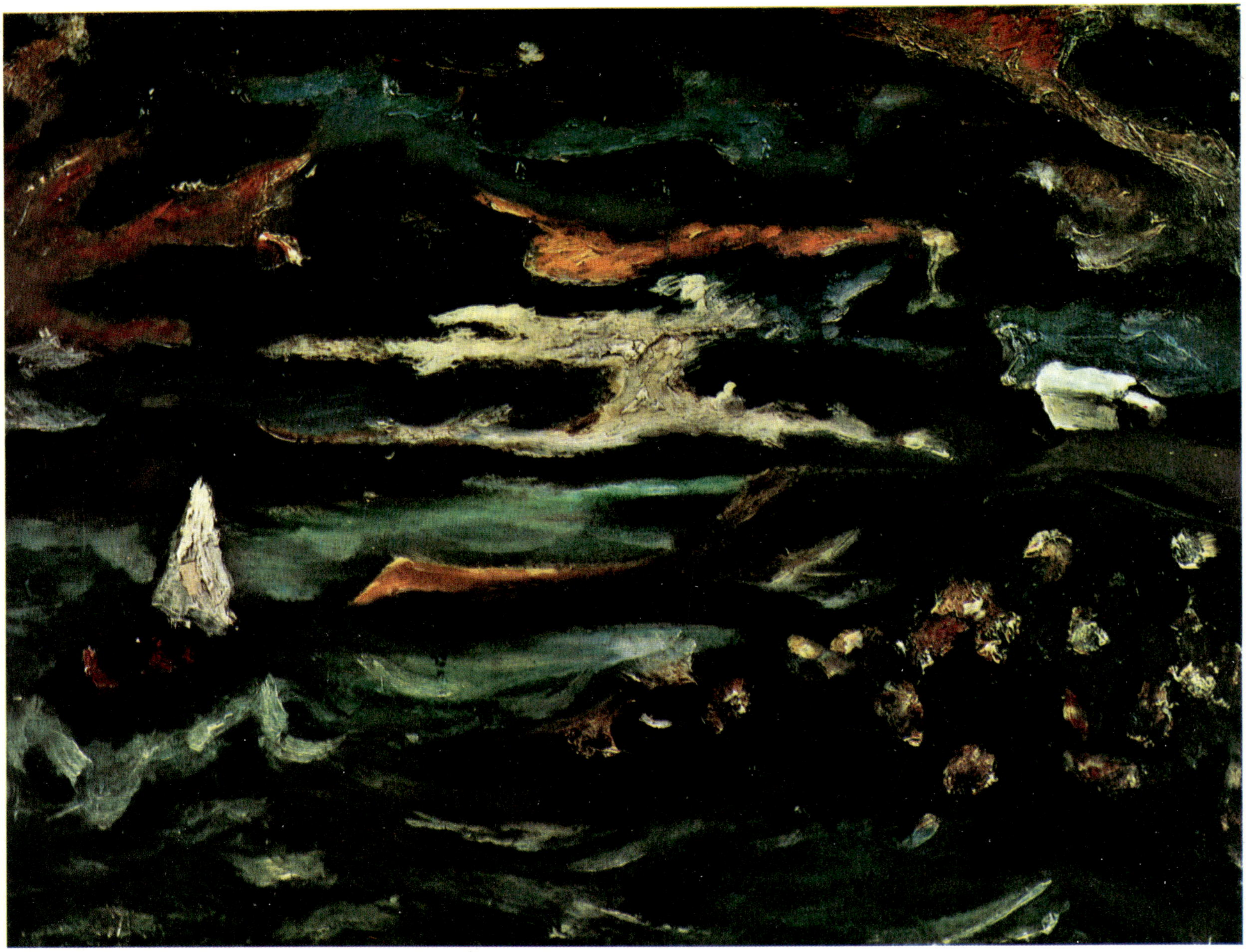

2

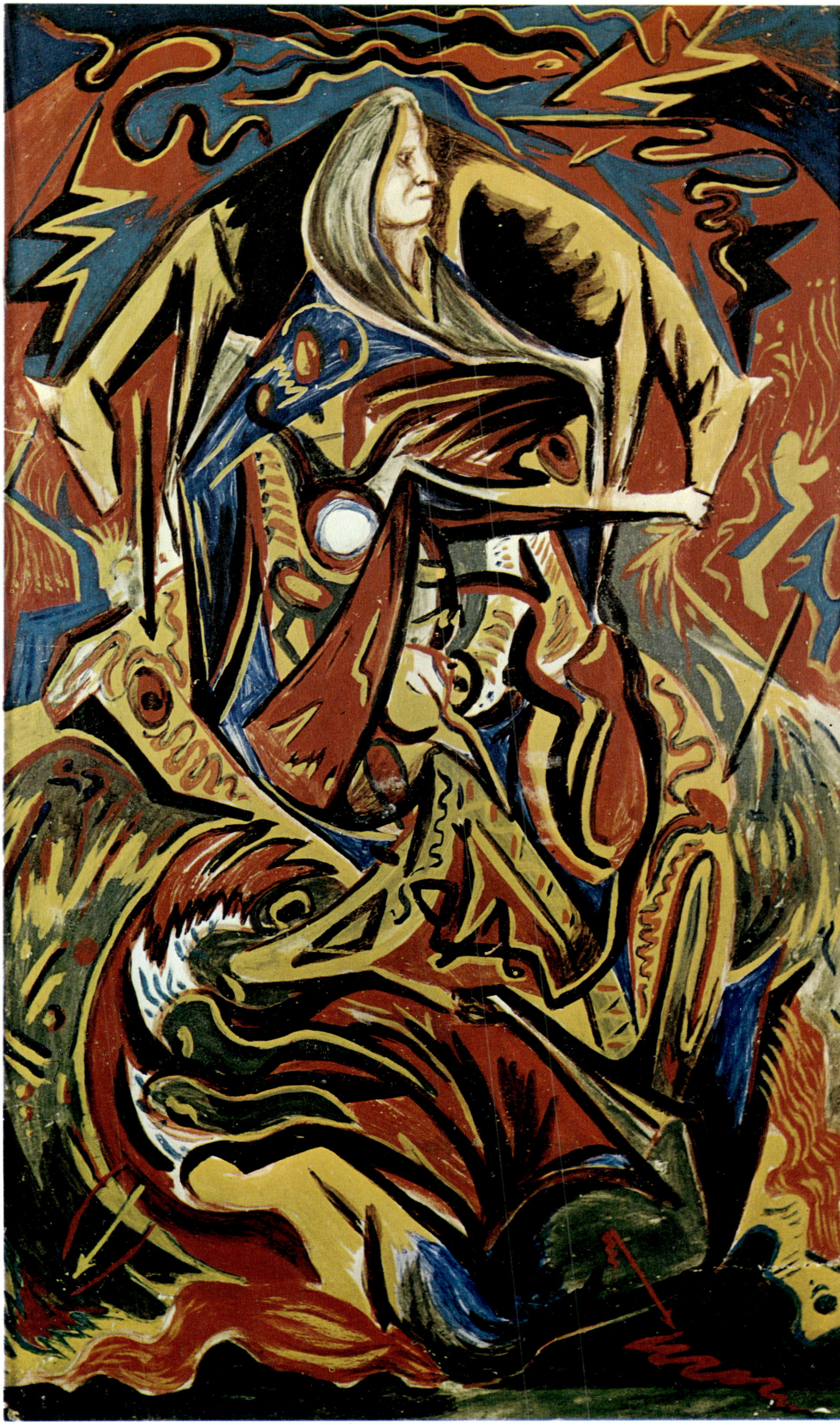

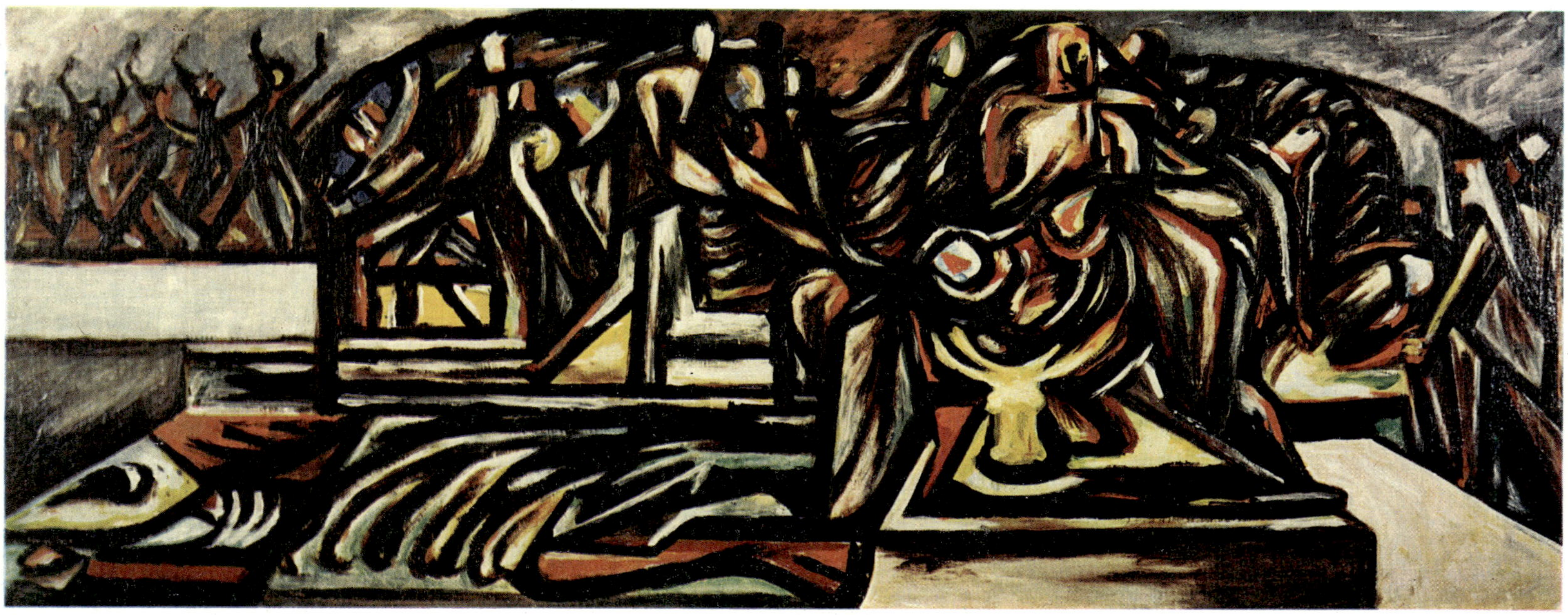
4

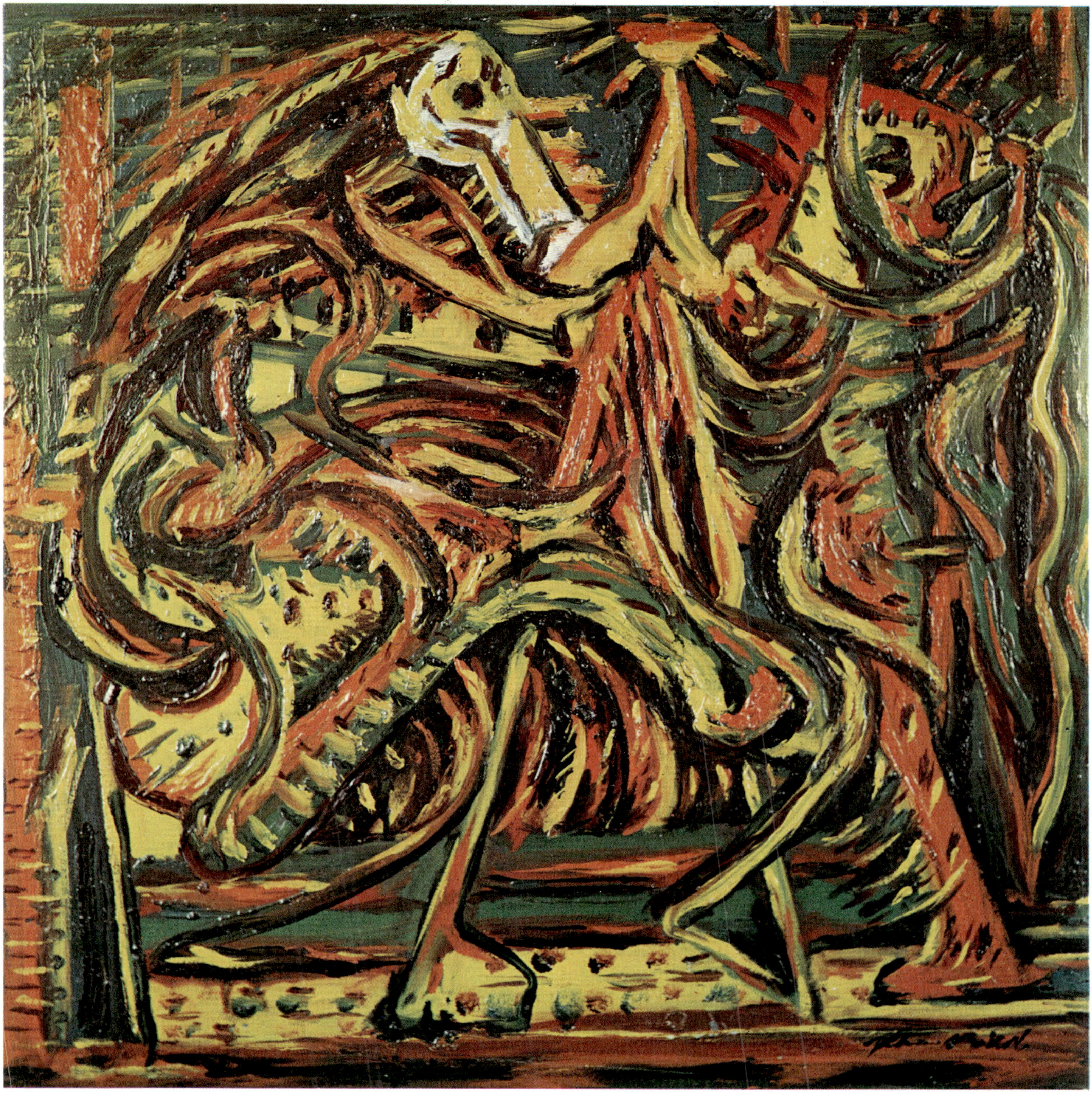

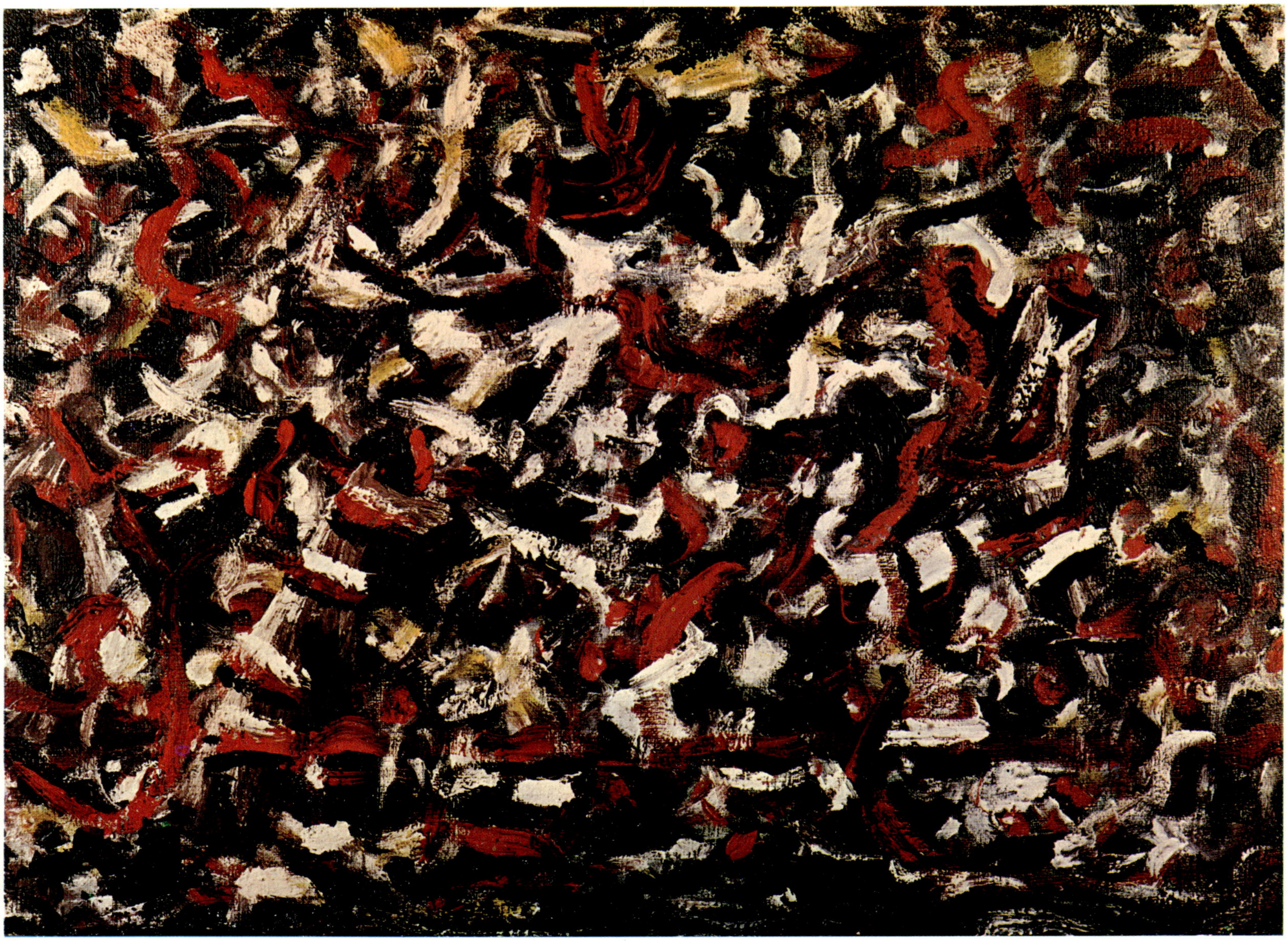

6

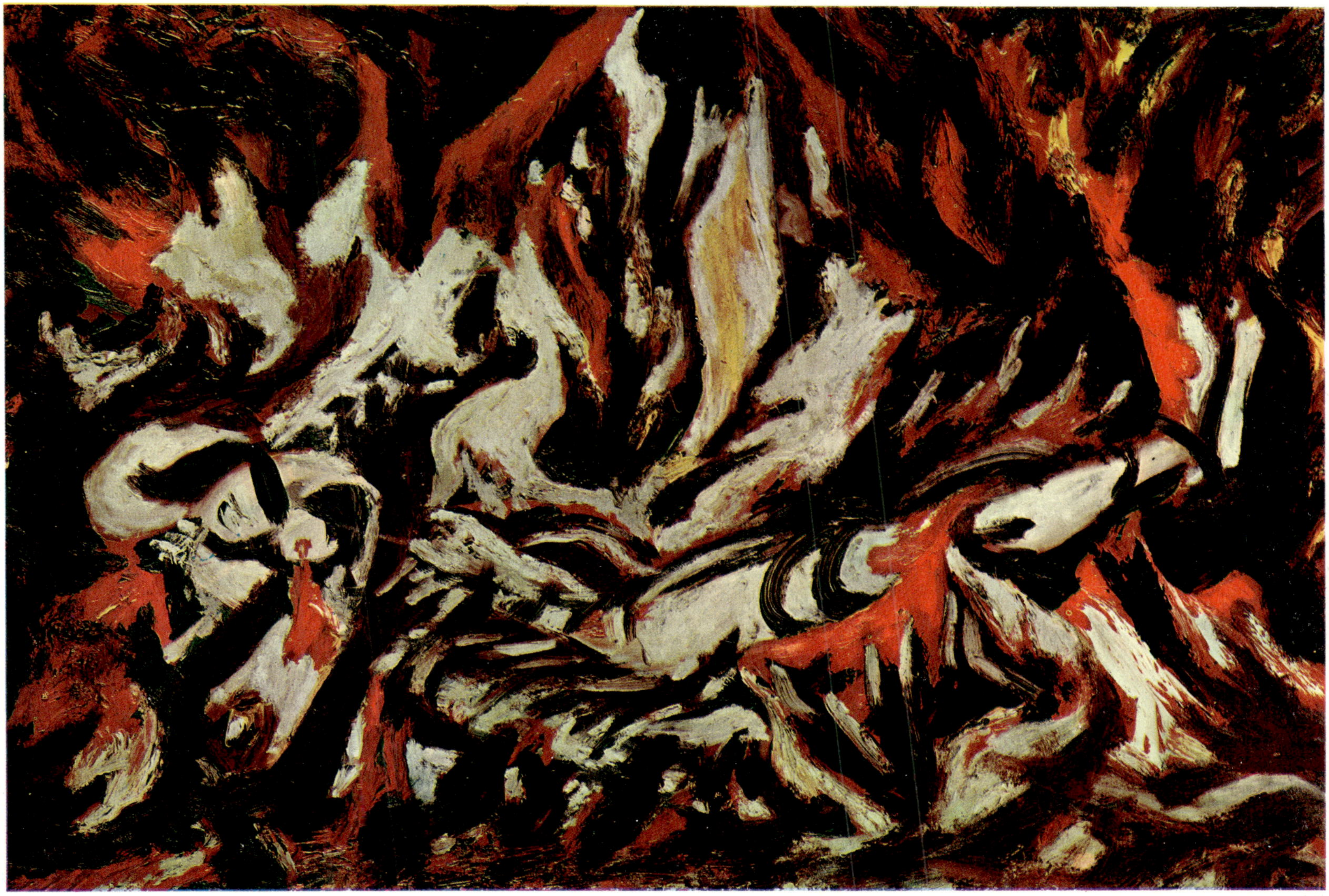

7

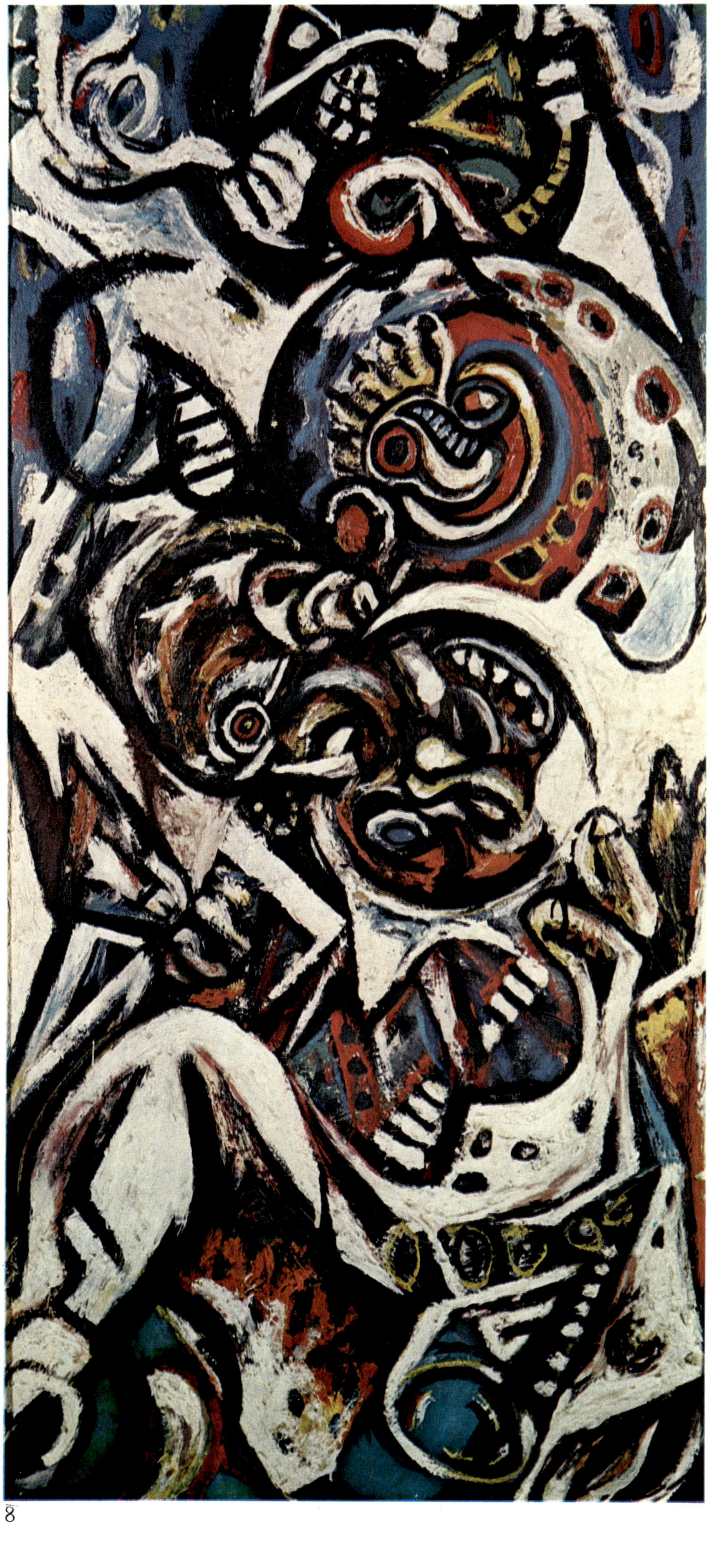

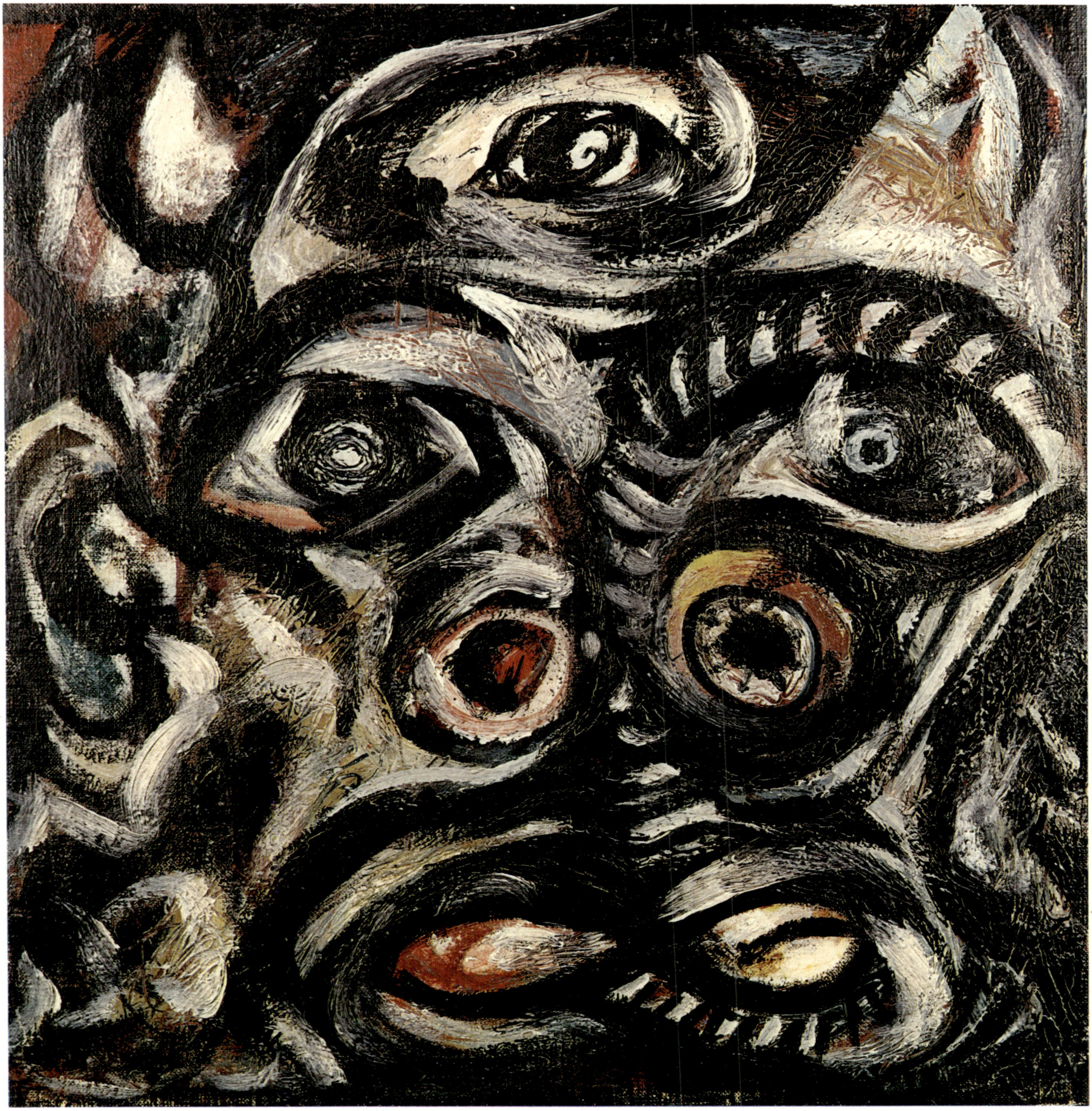

9

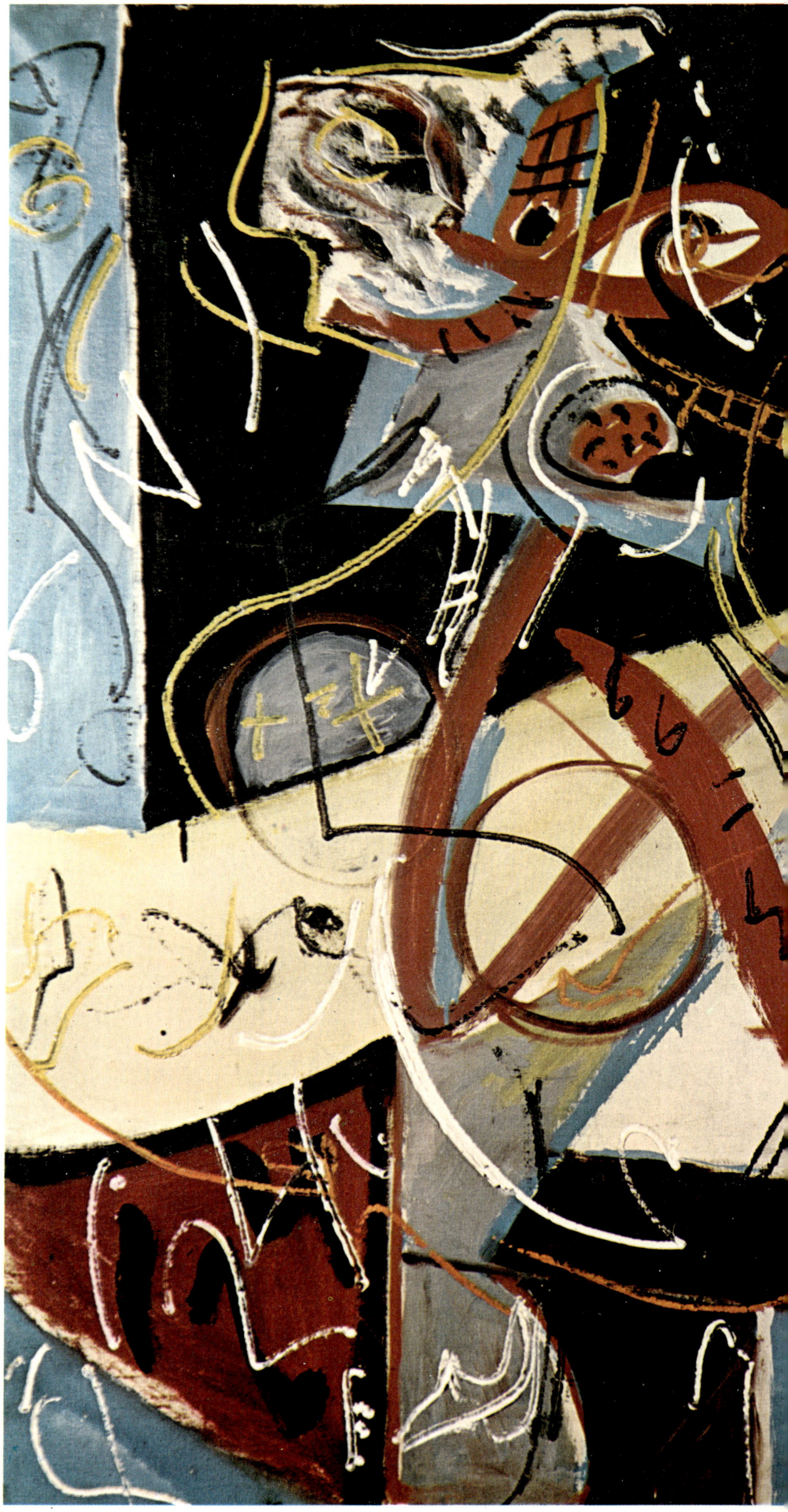

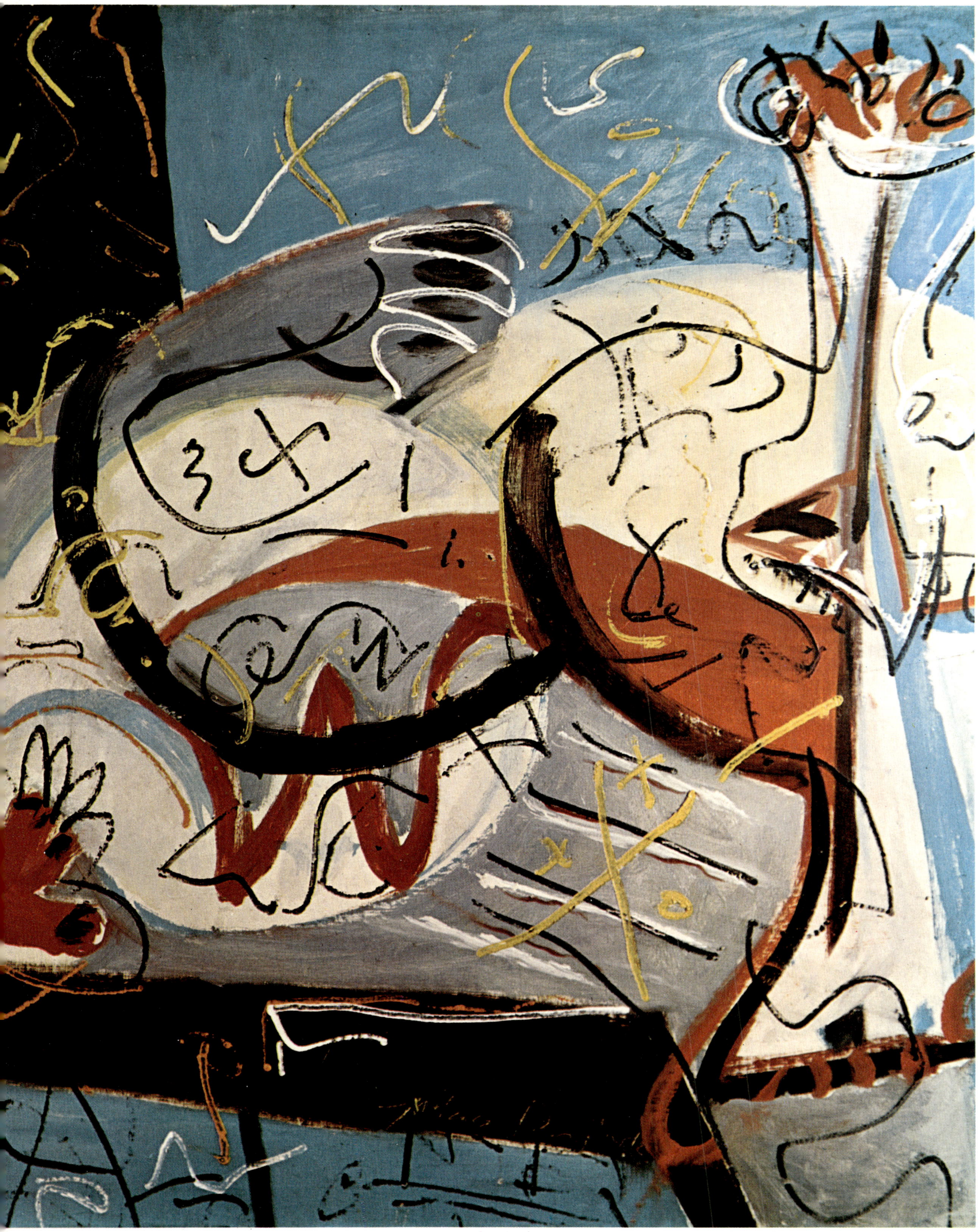

10-11

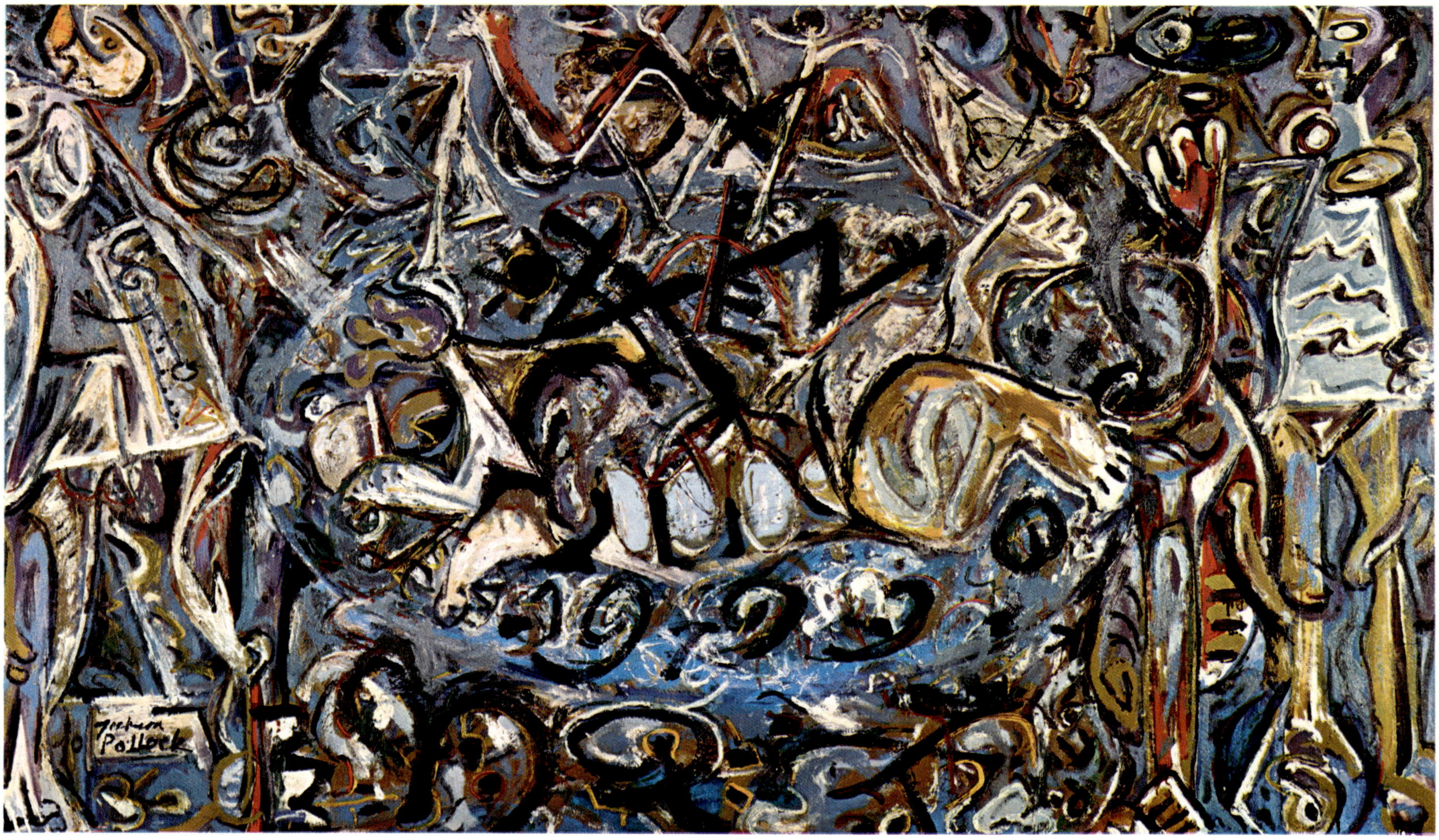

12

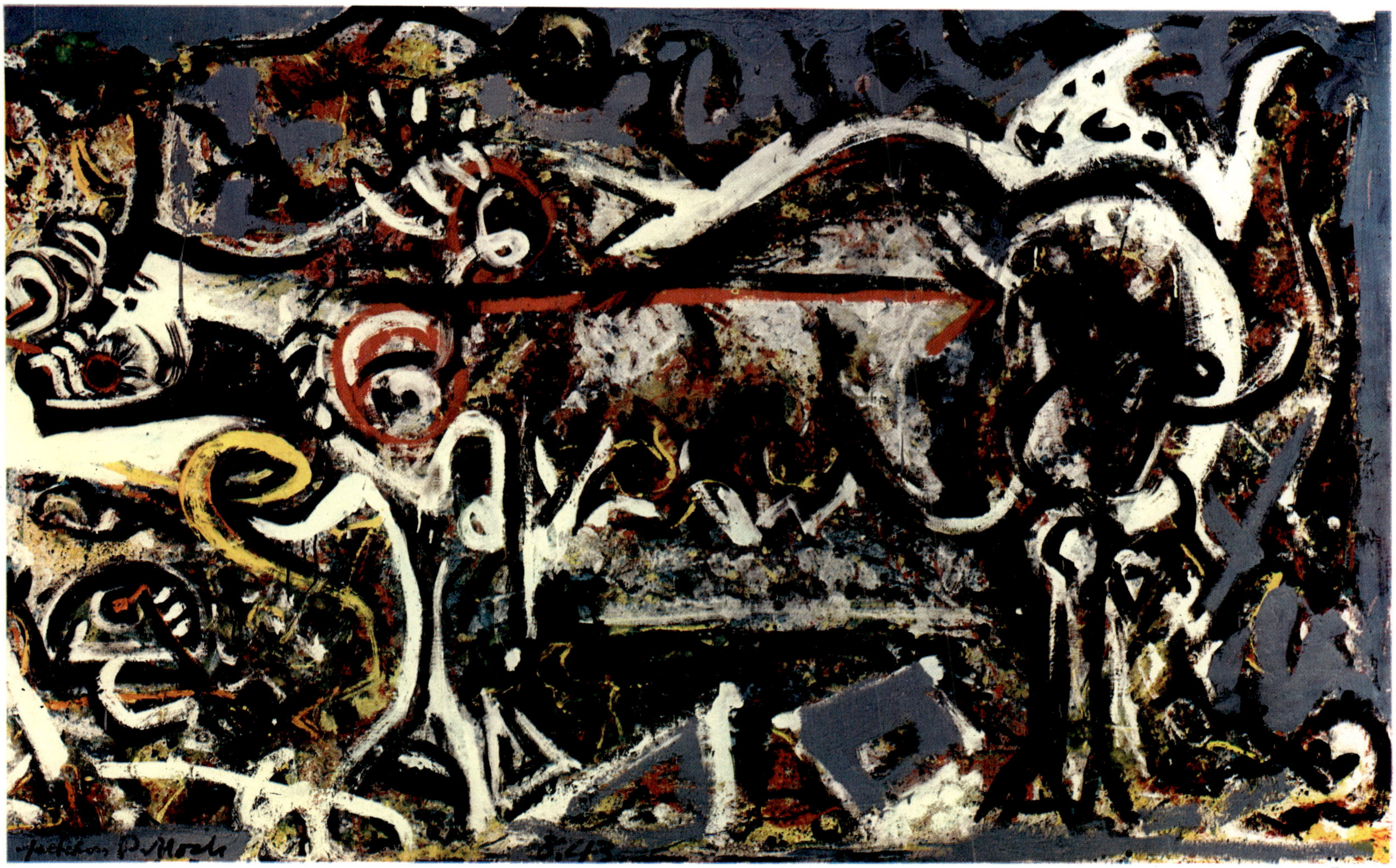

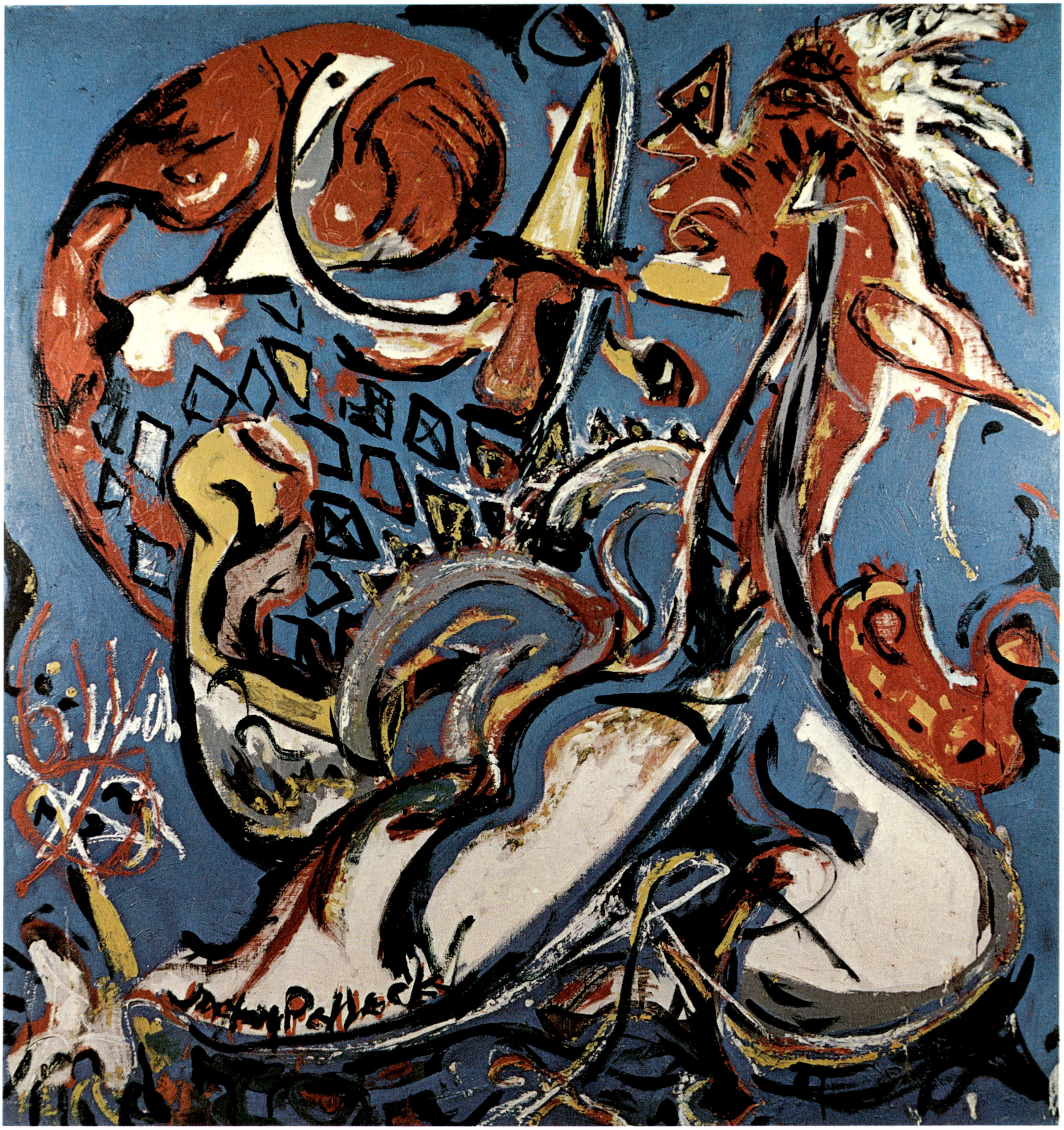

14

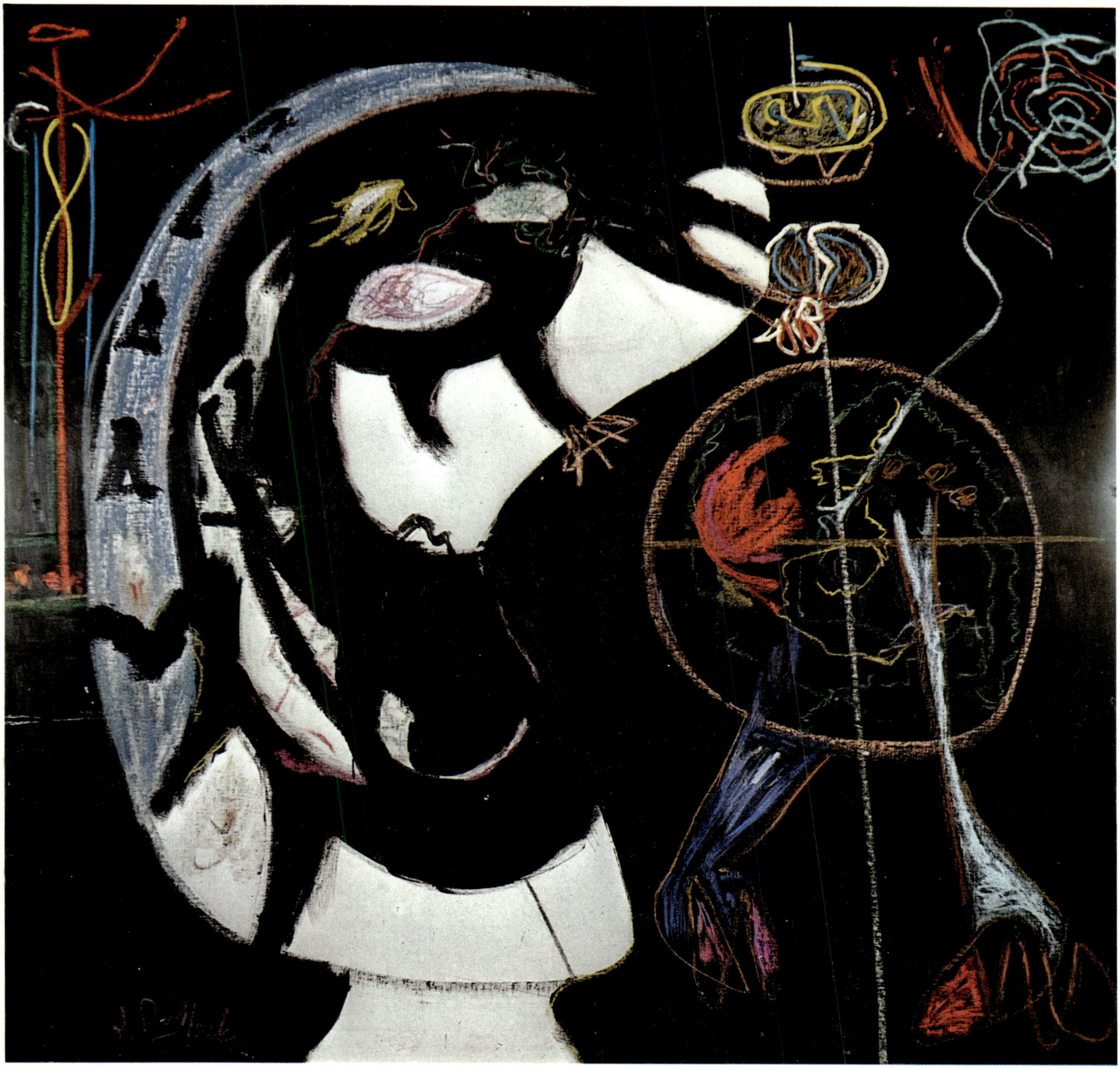

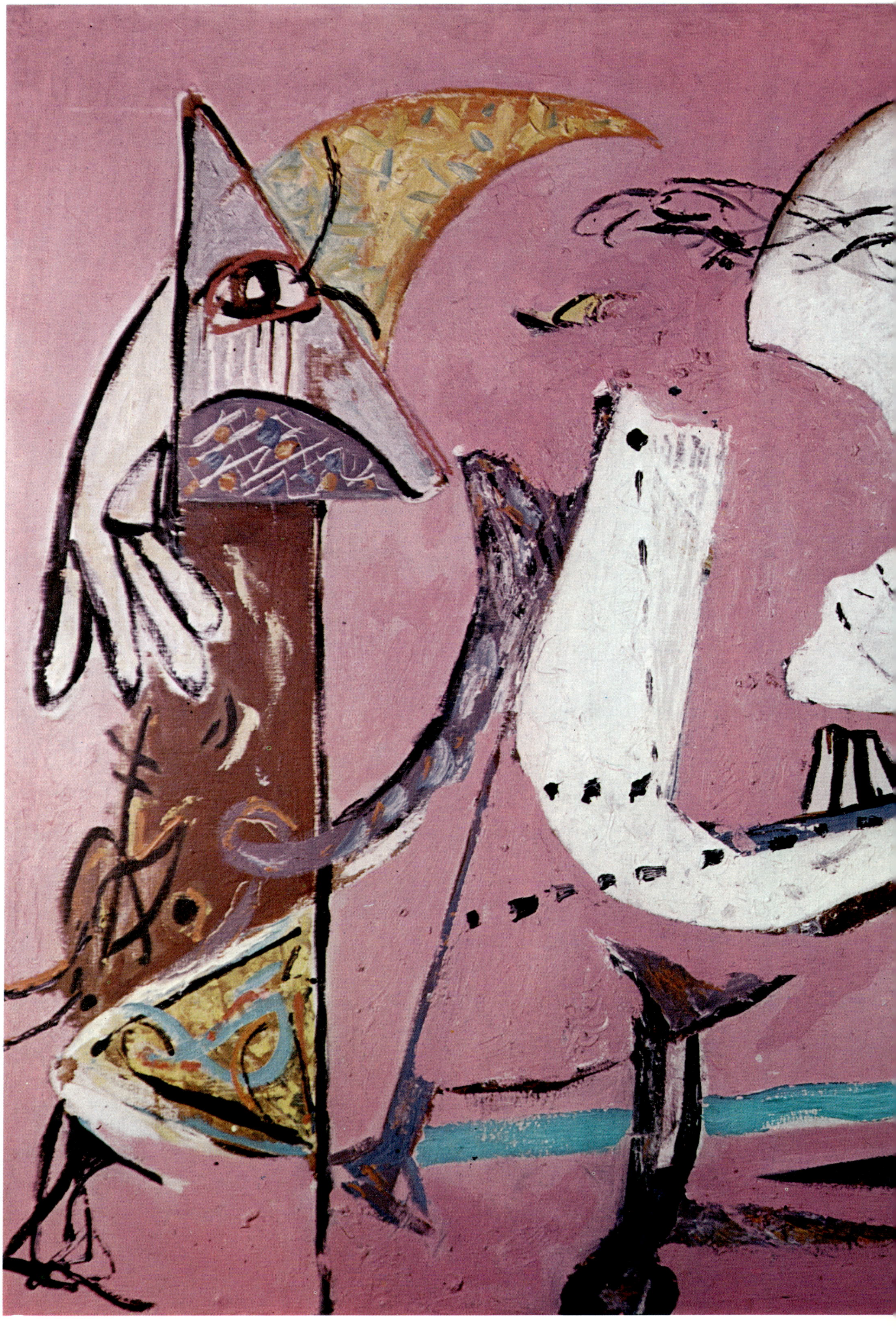

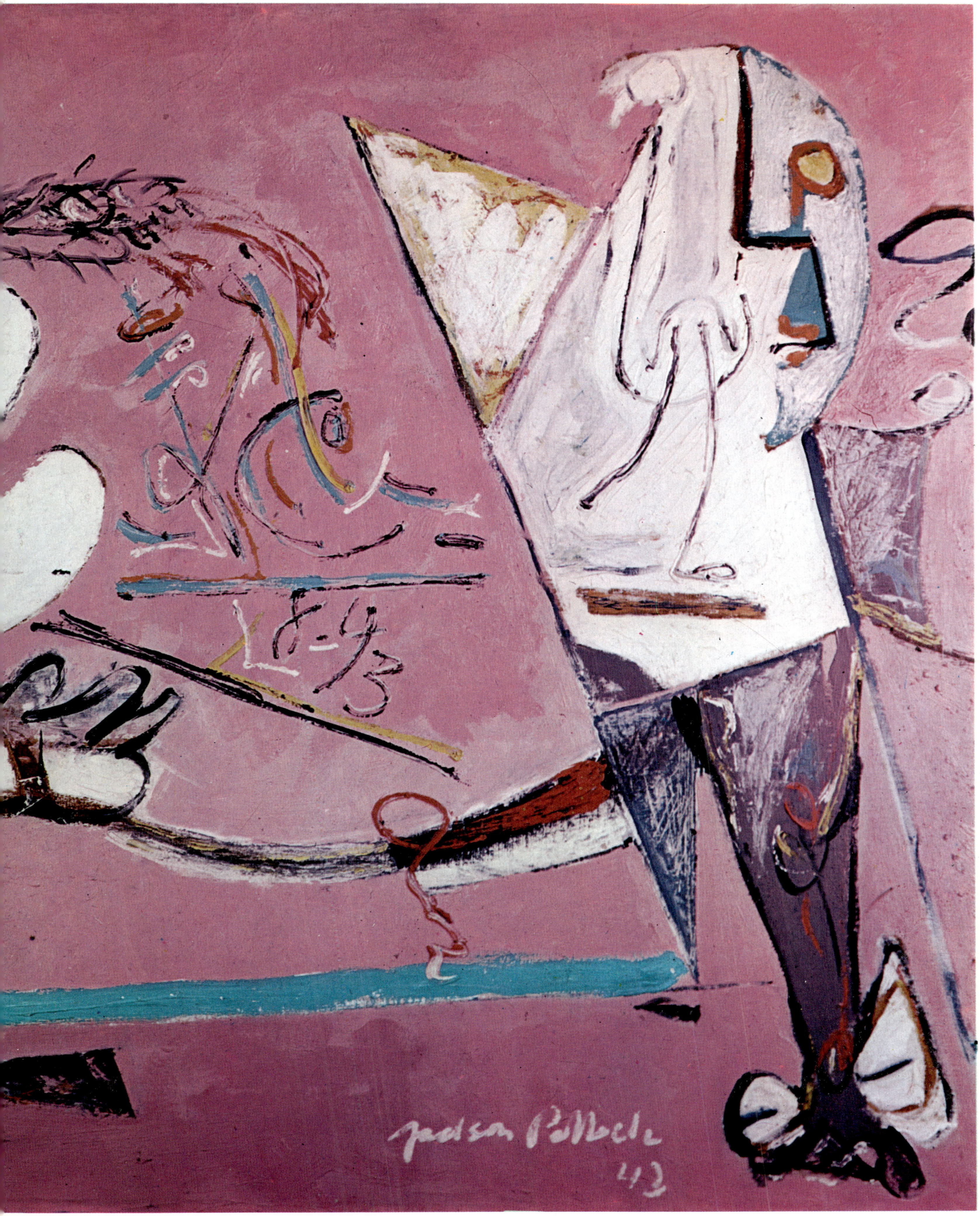

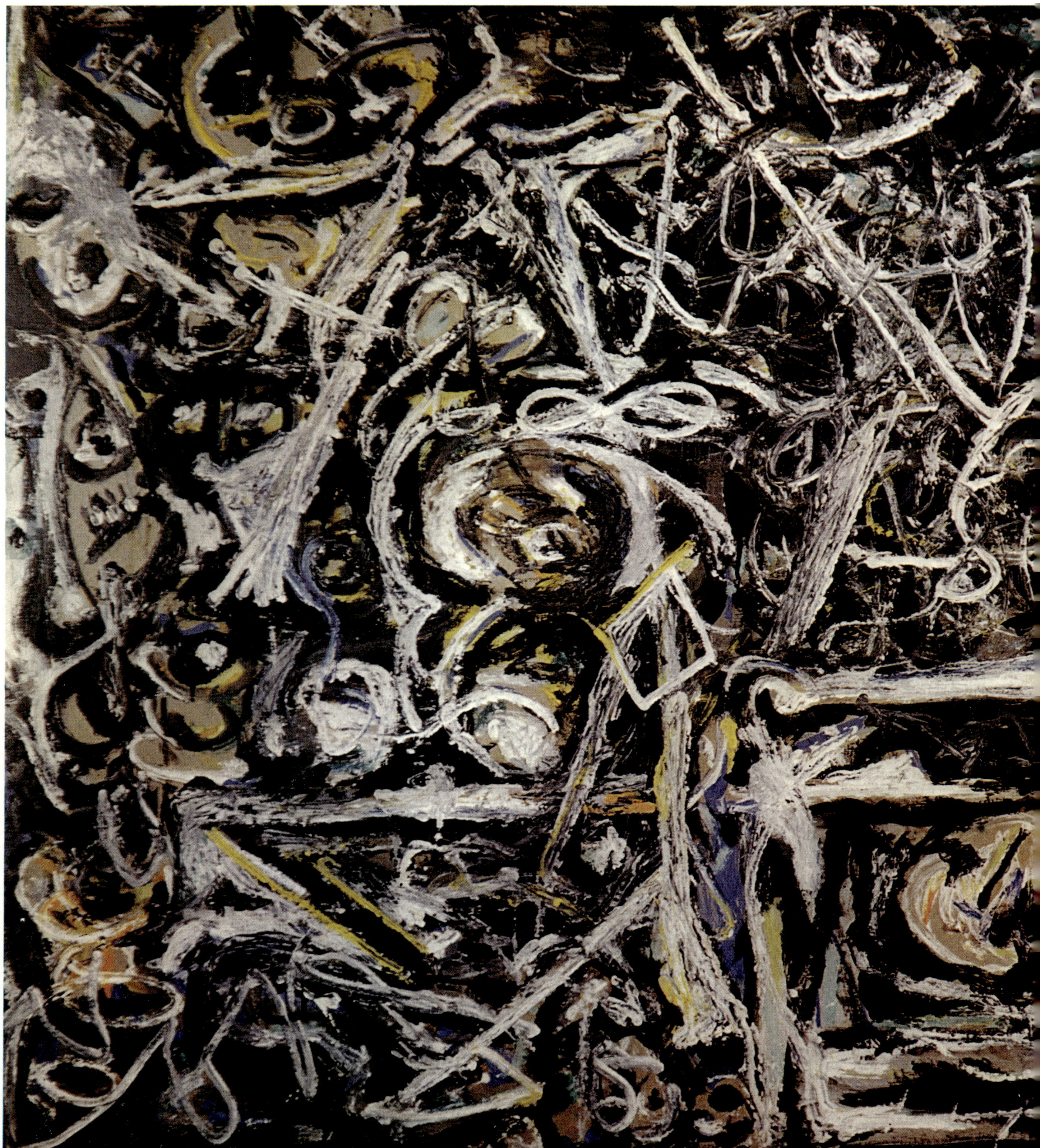

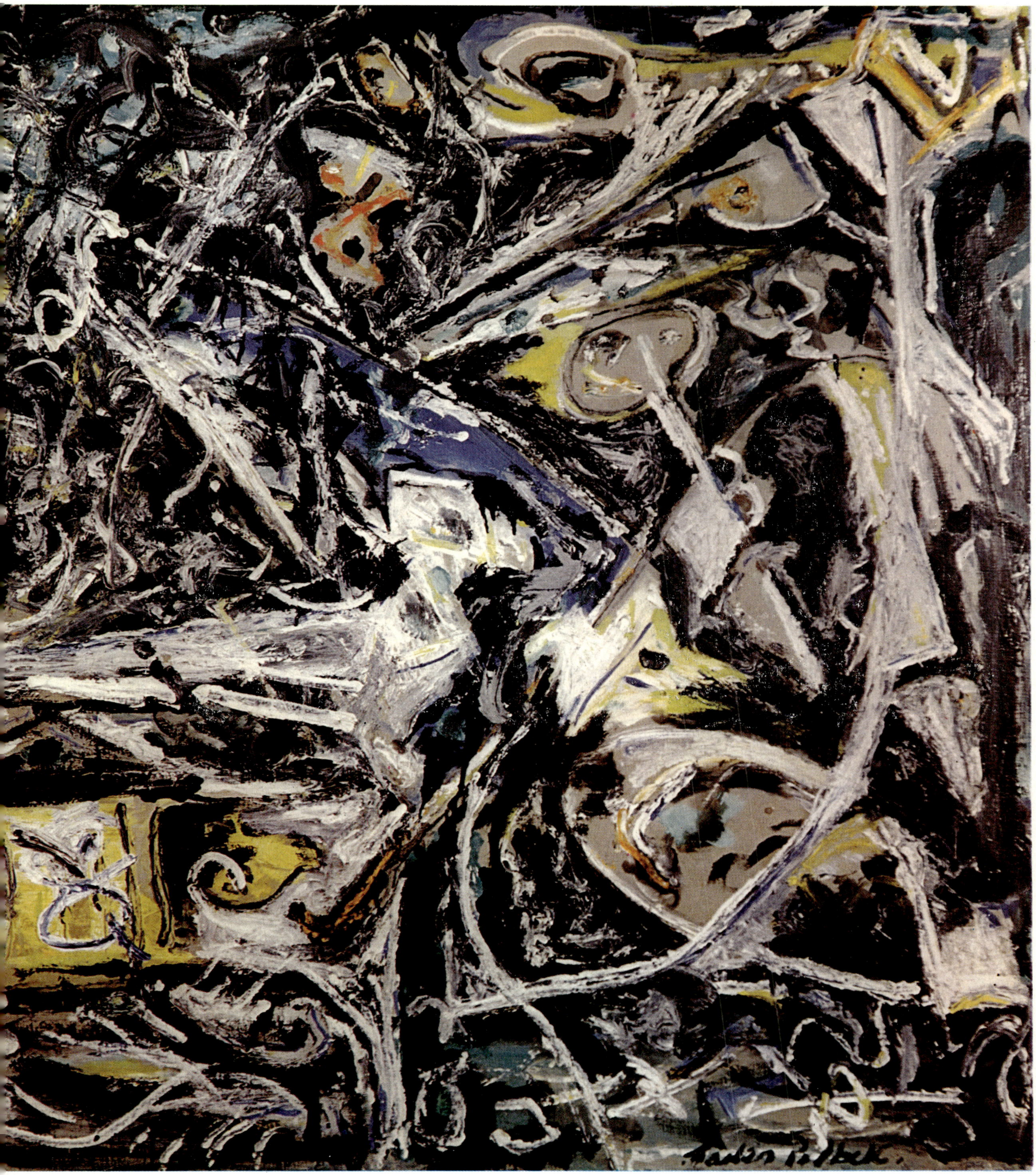

18-19

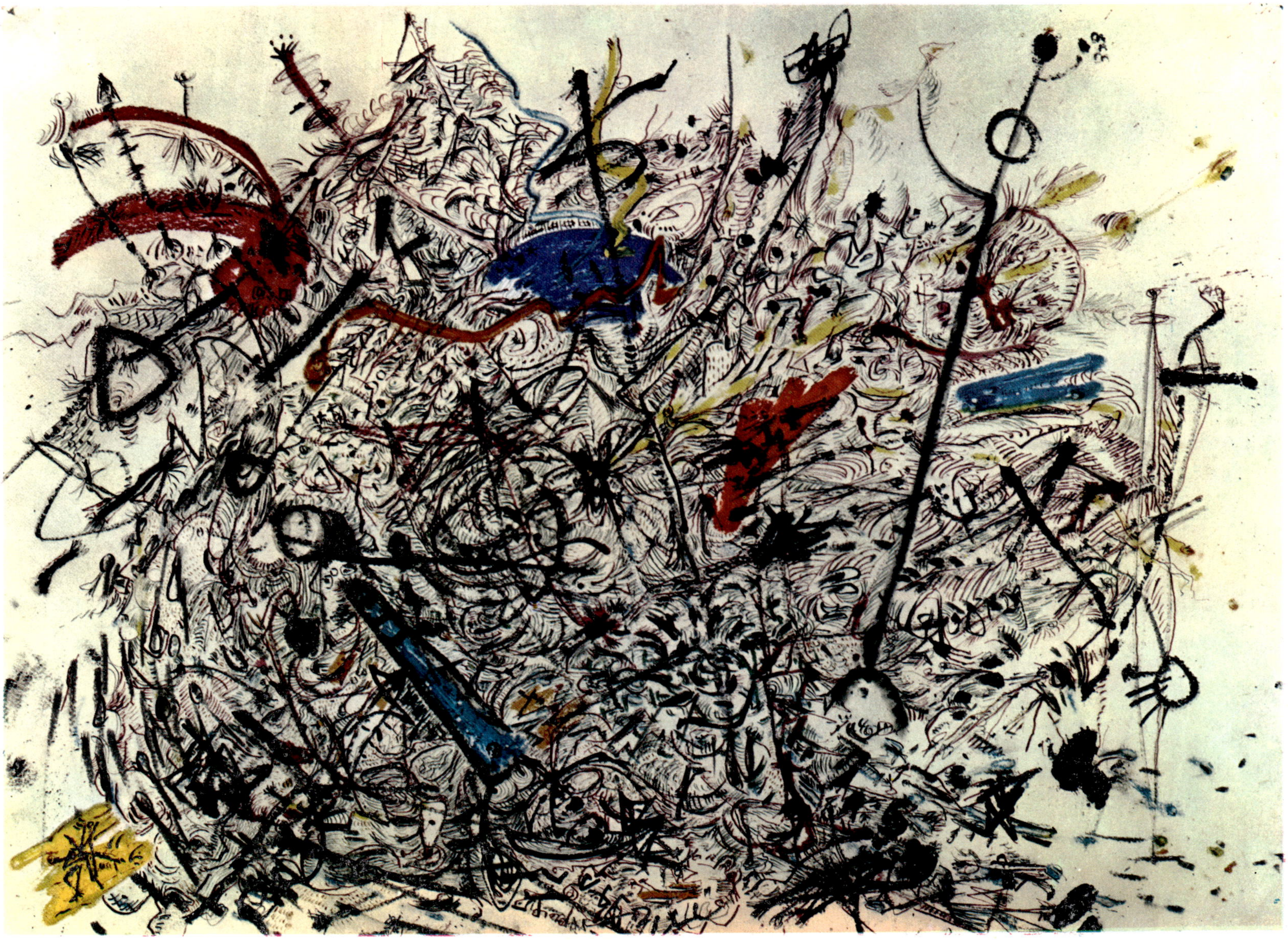

20

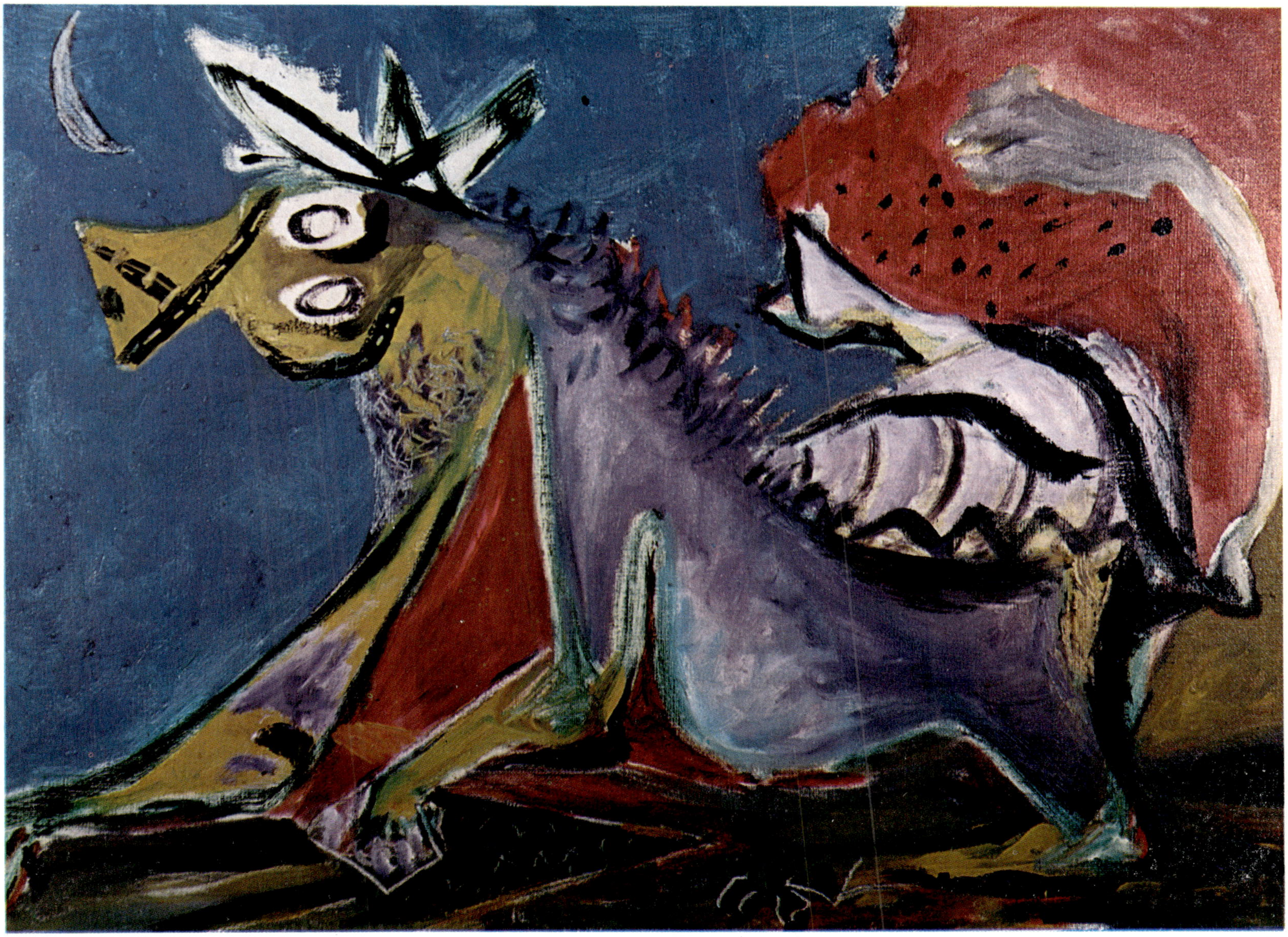

21

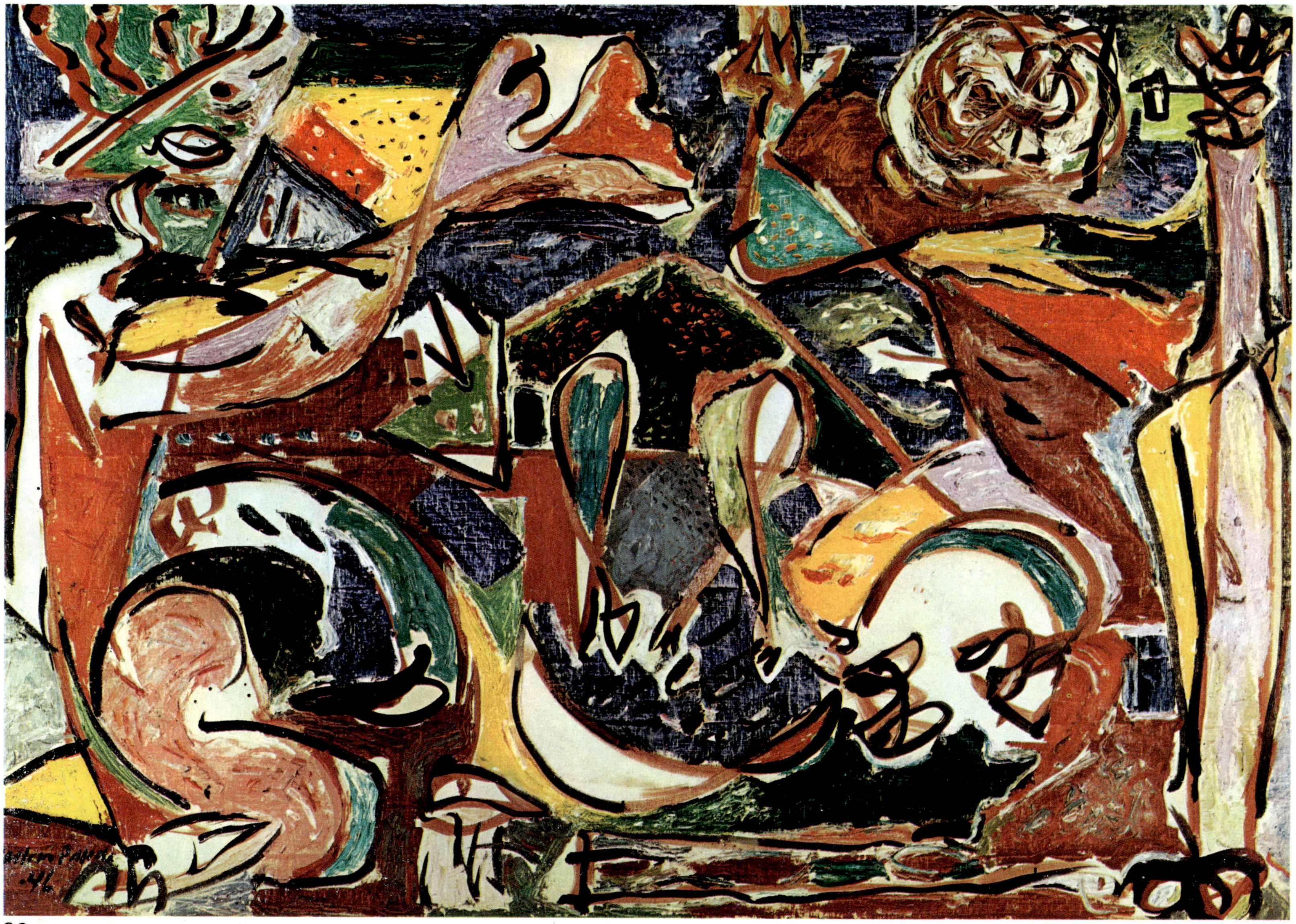

22

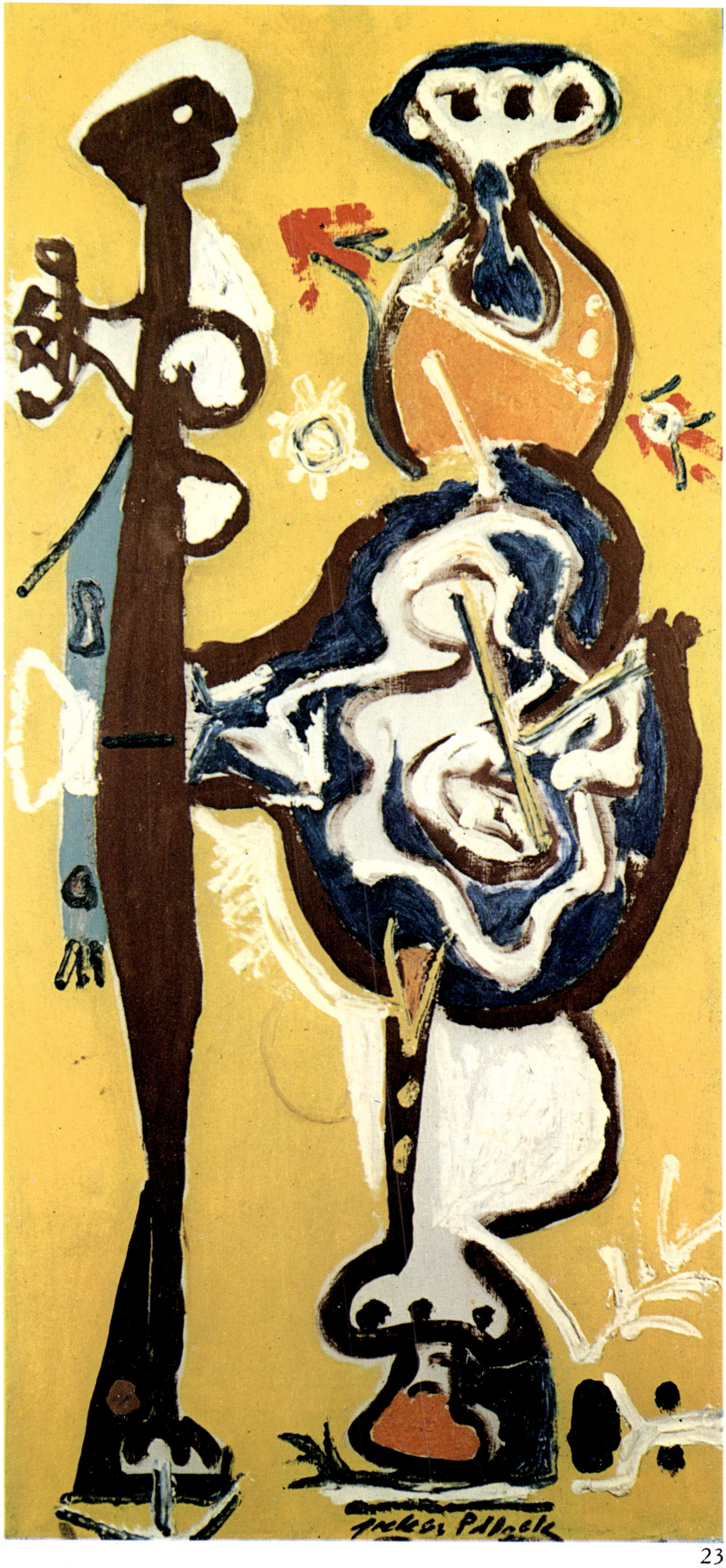
Jackson Pollock

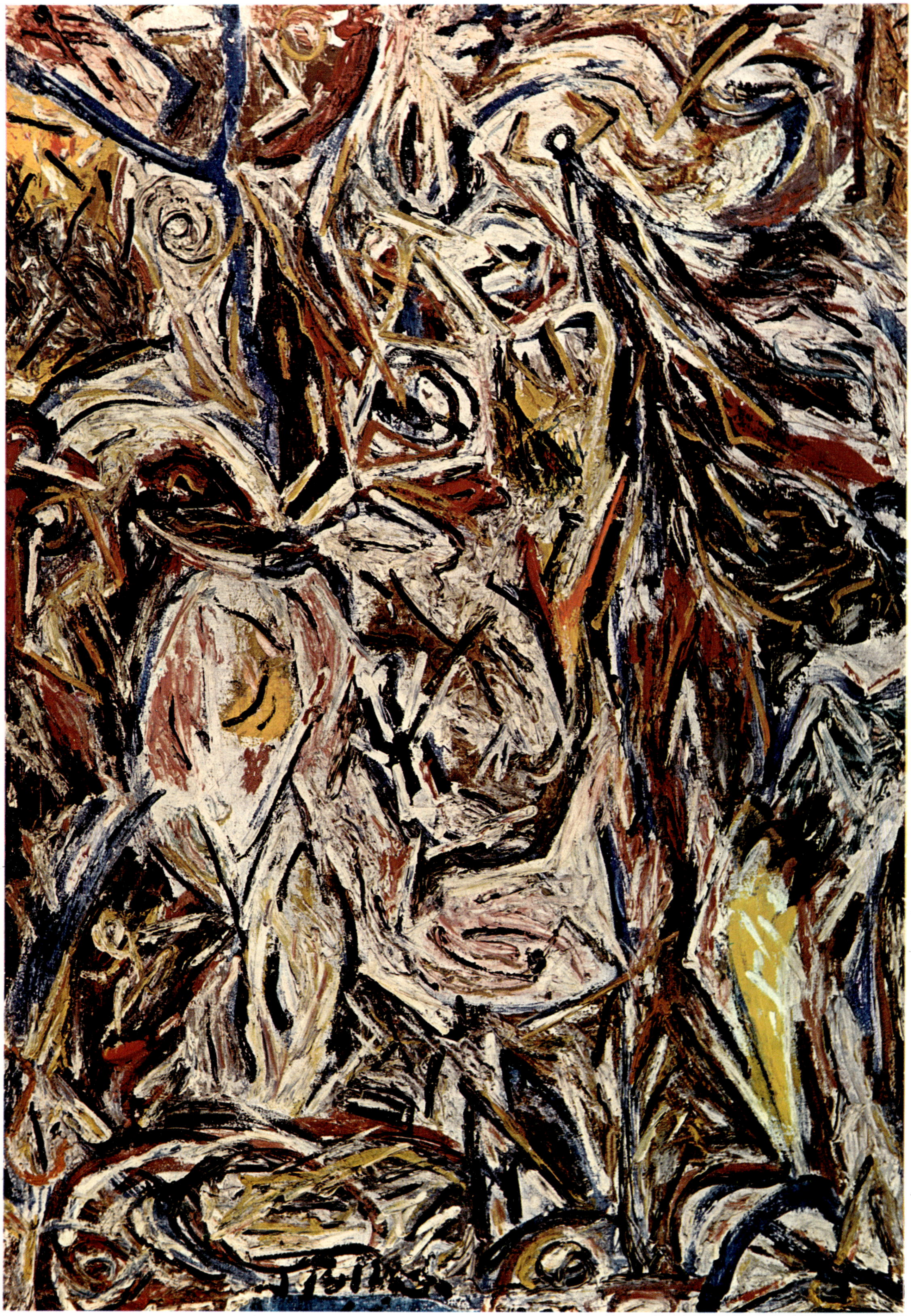

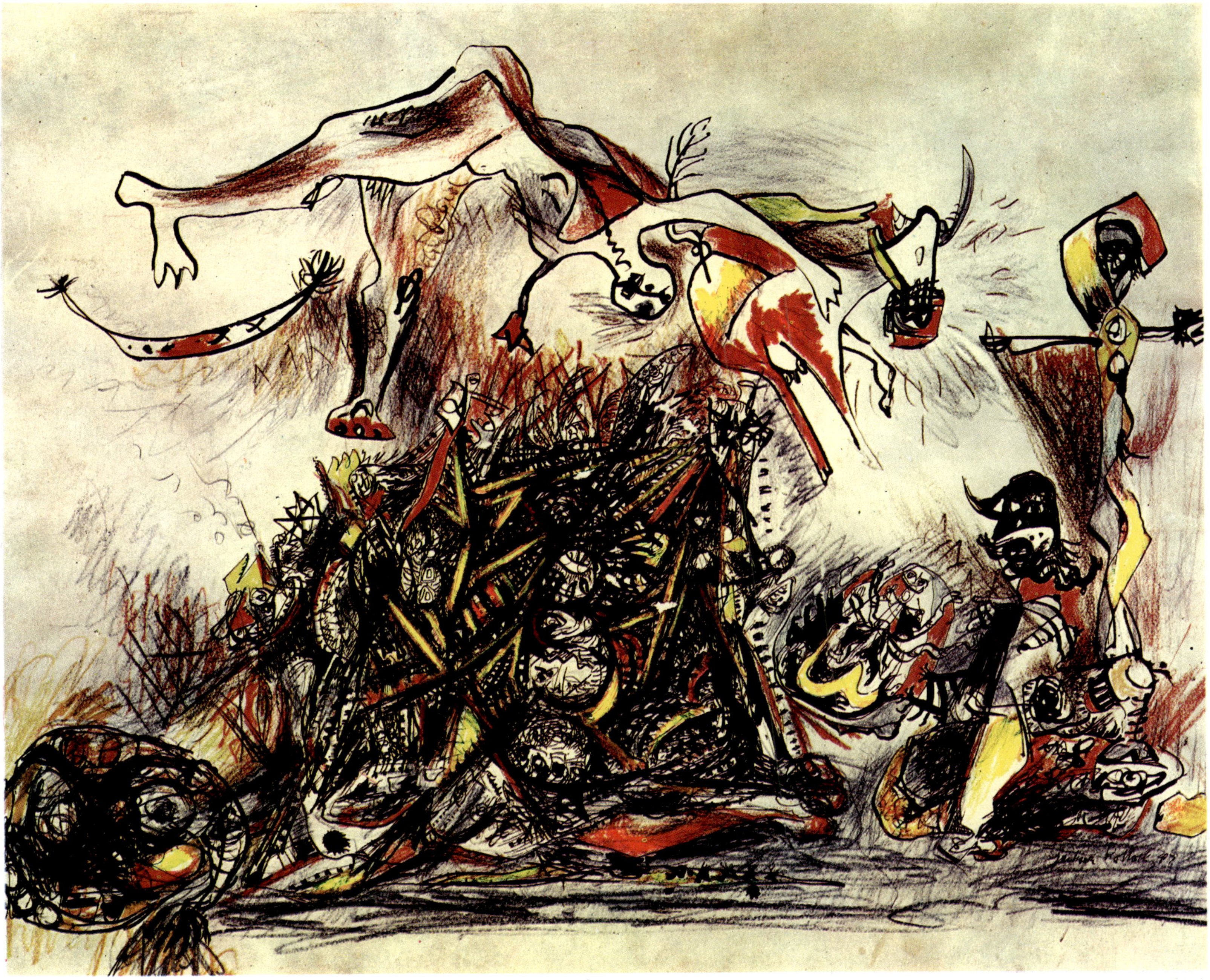

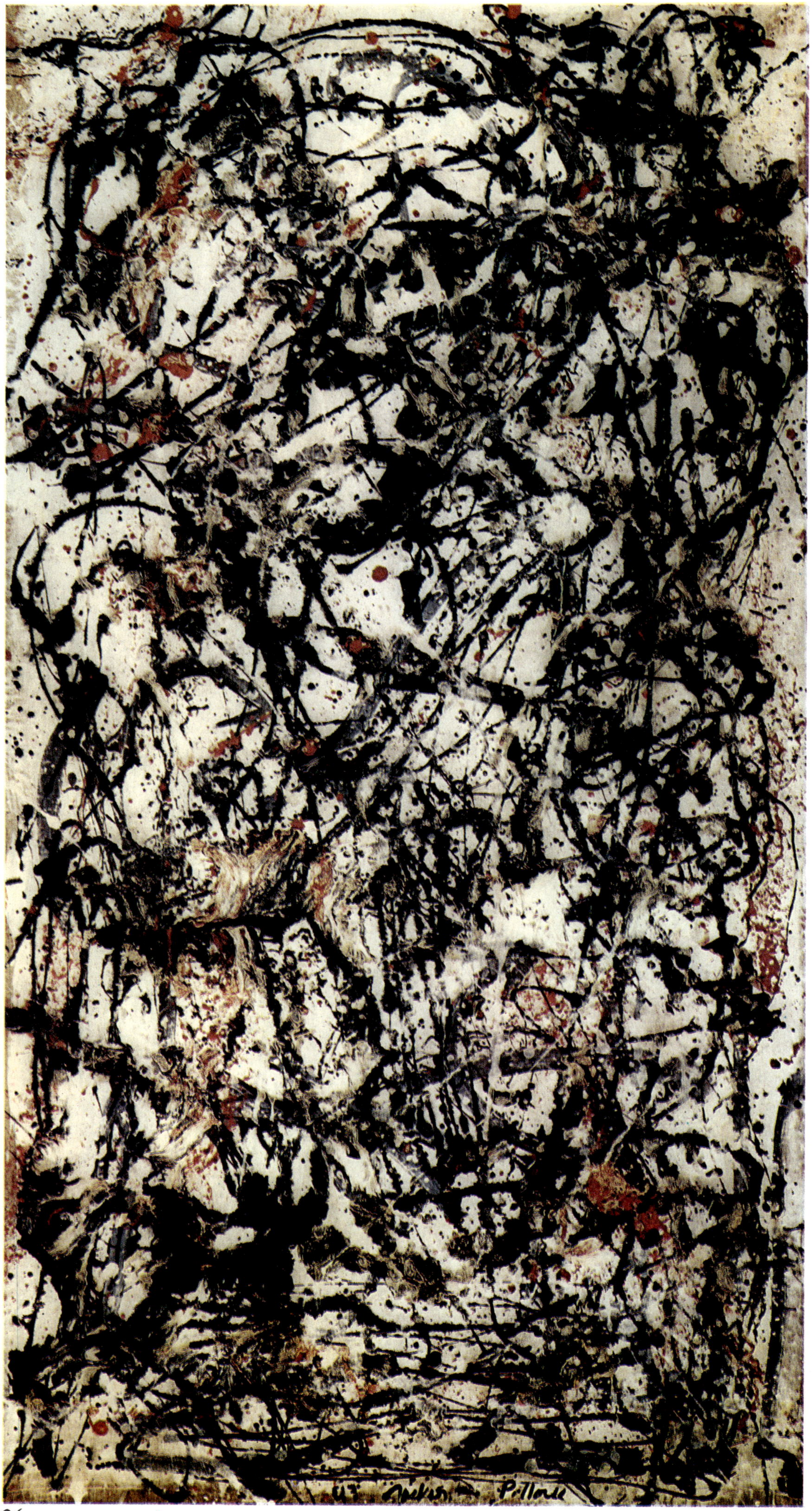

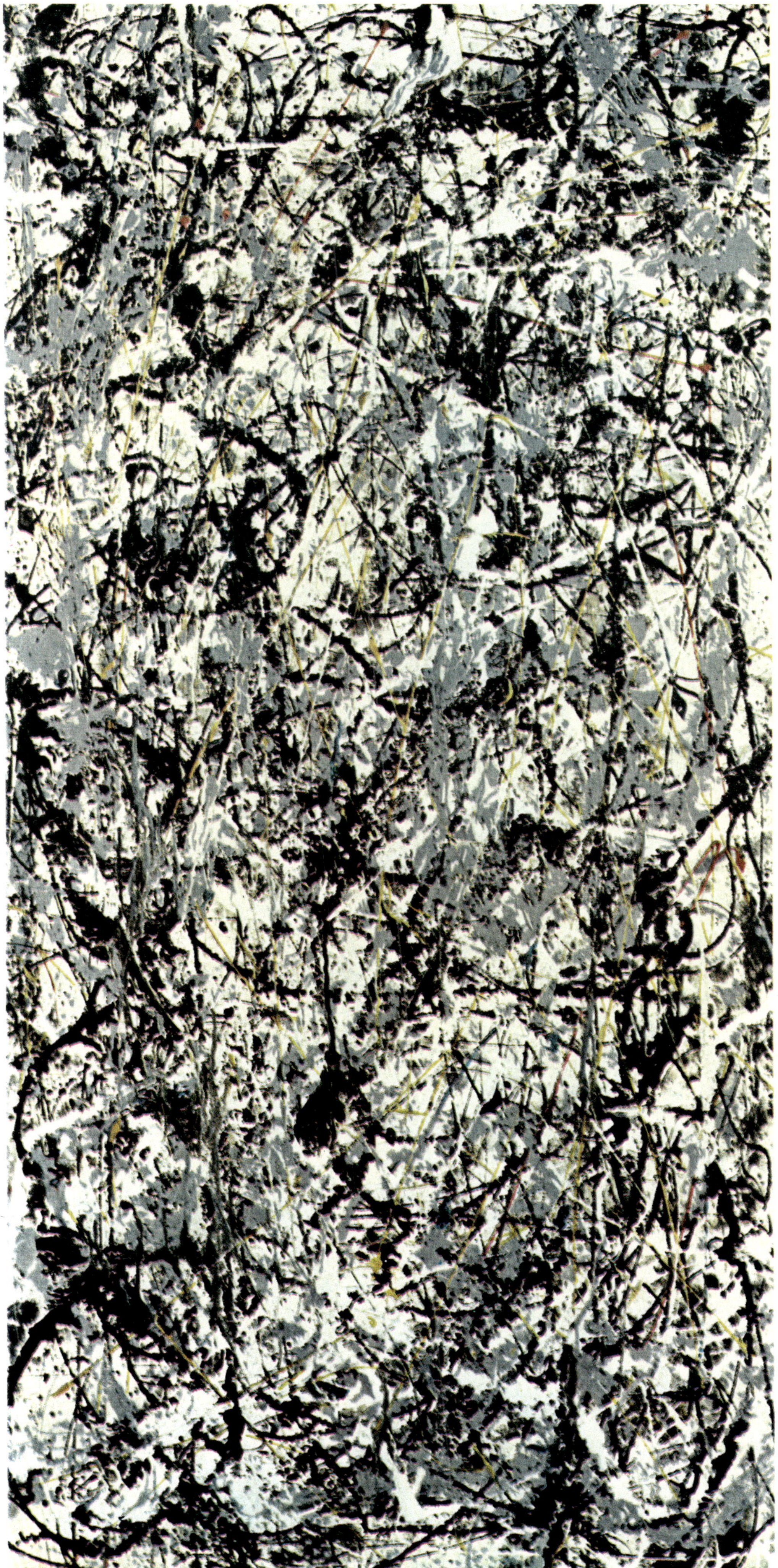

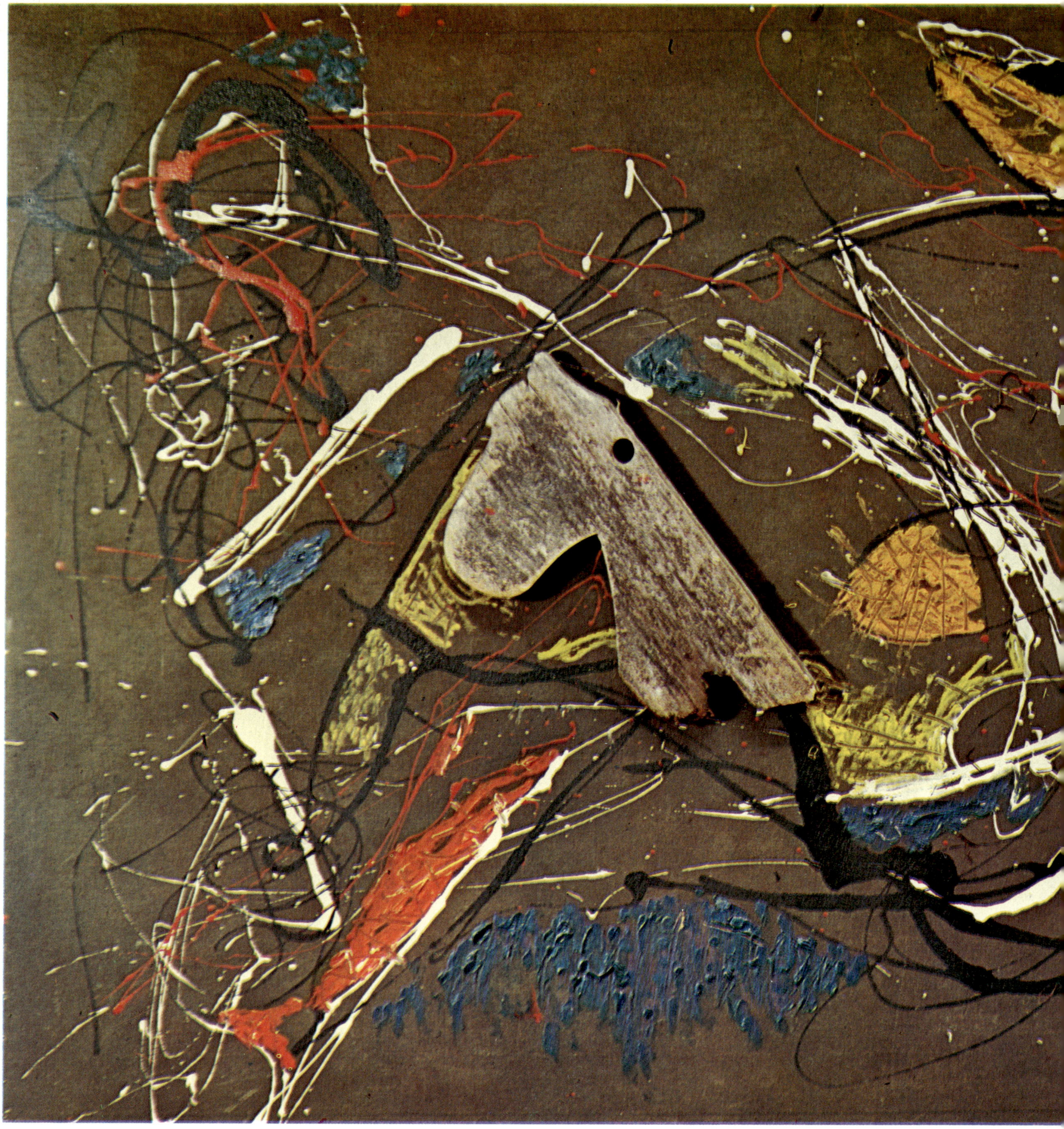

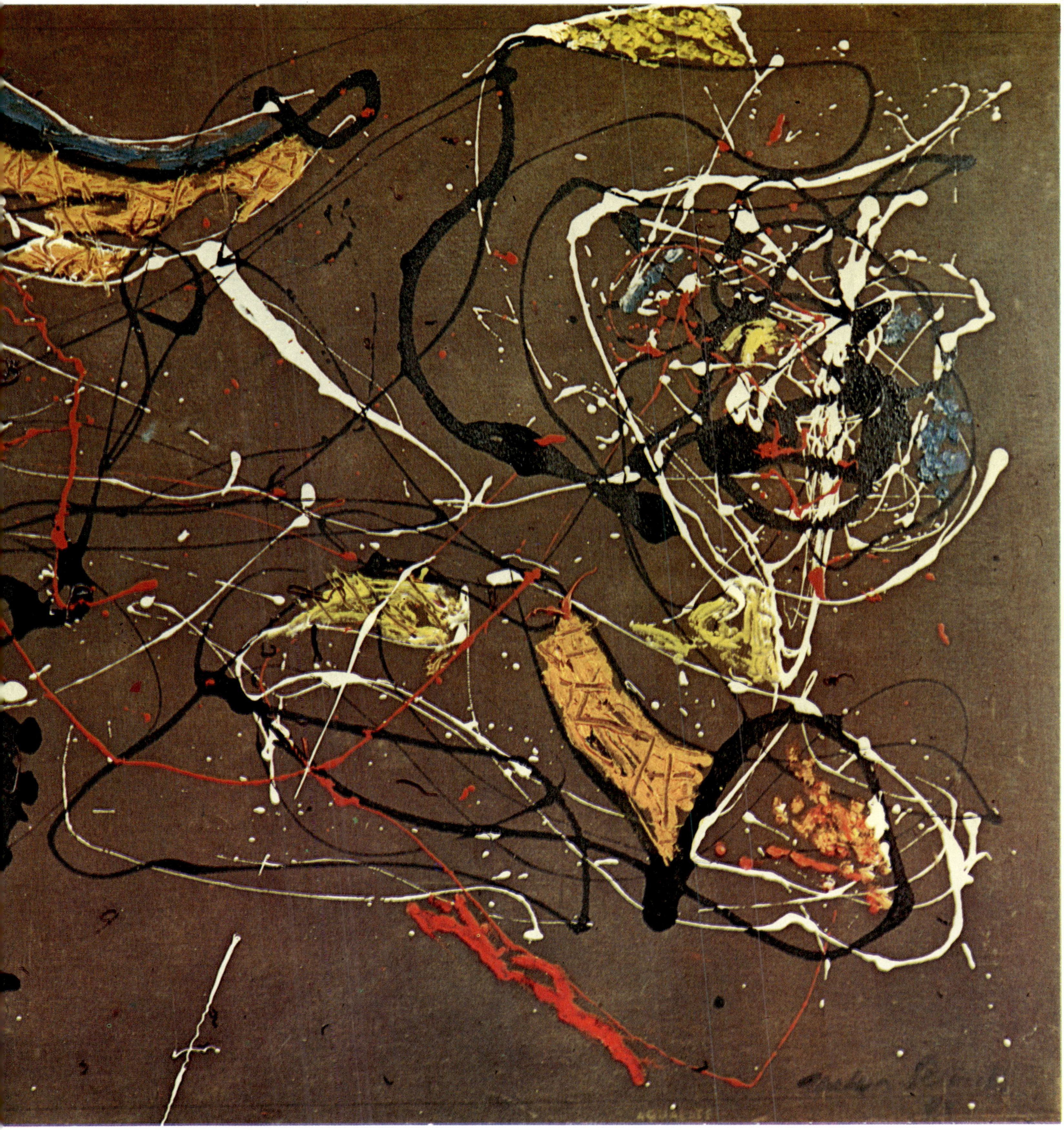

28-29

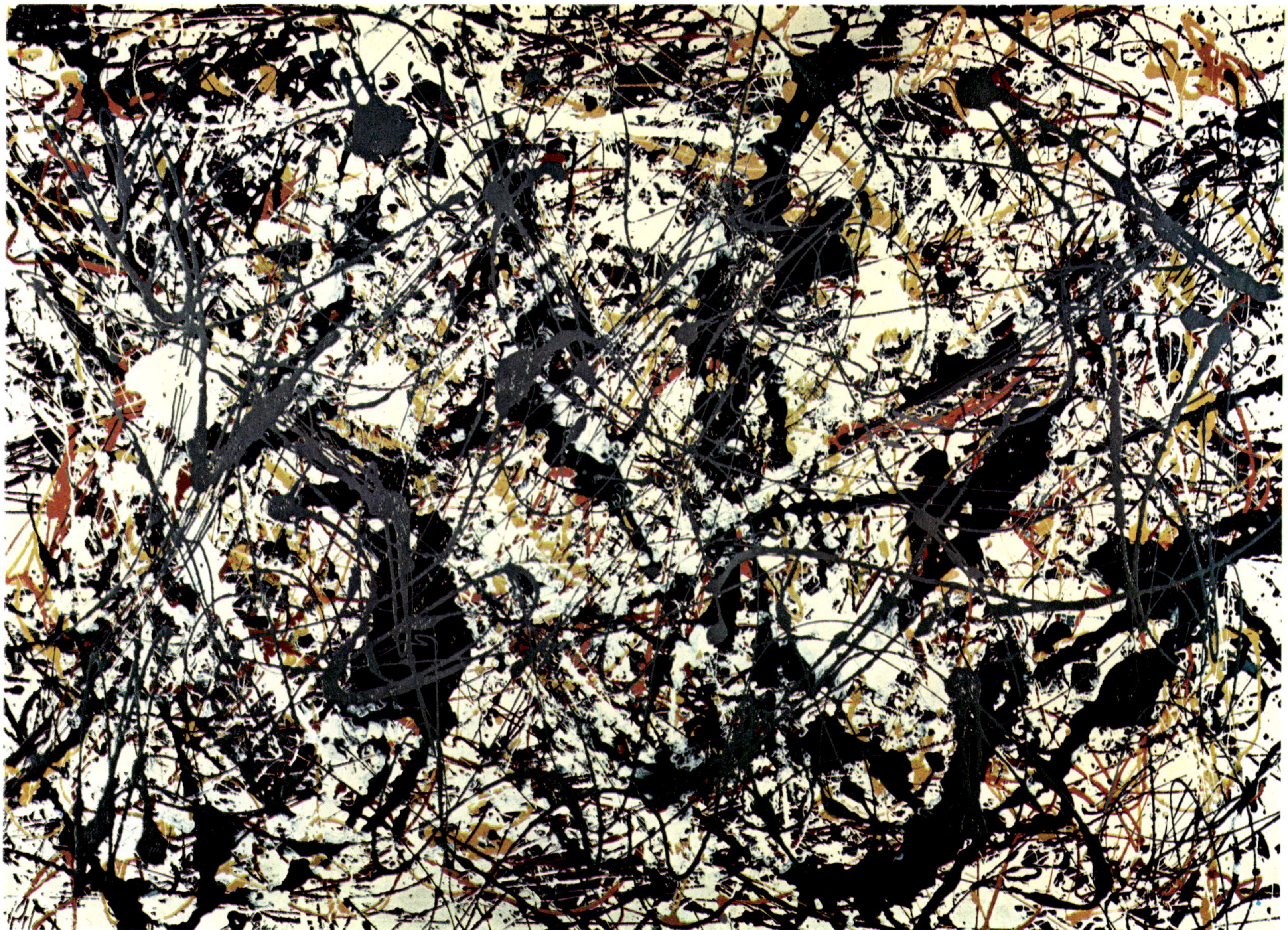

30

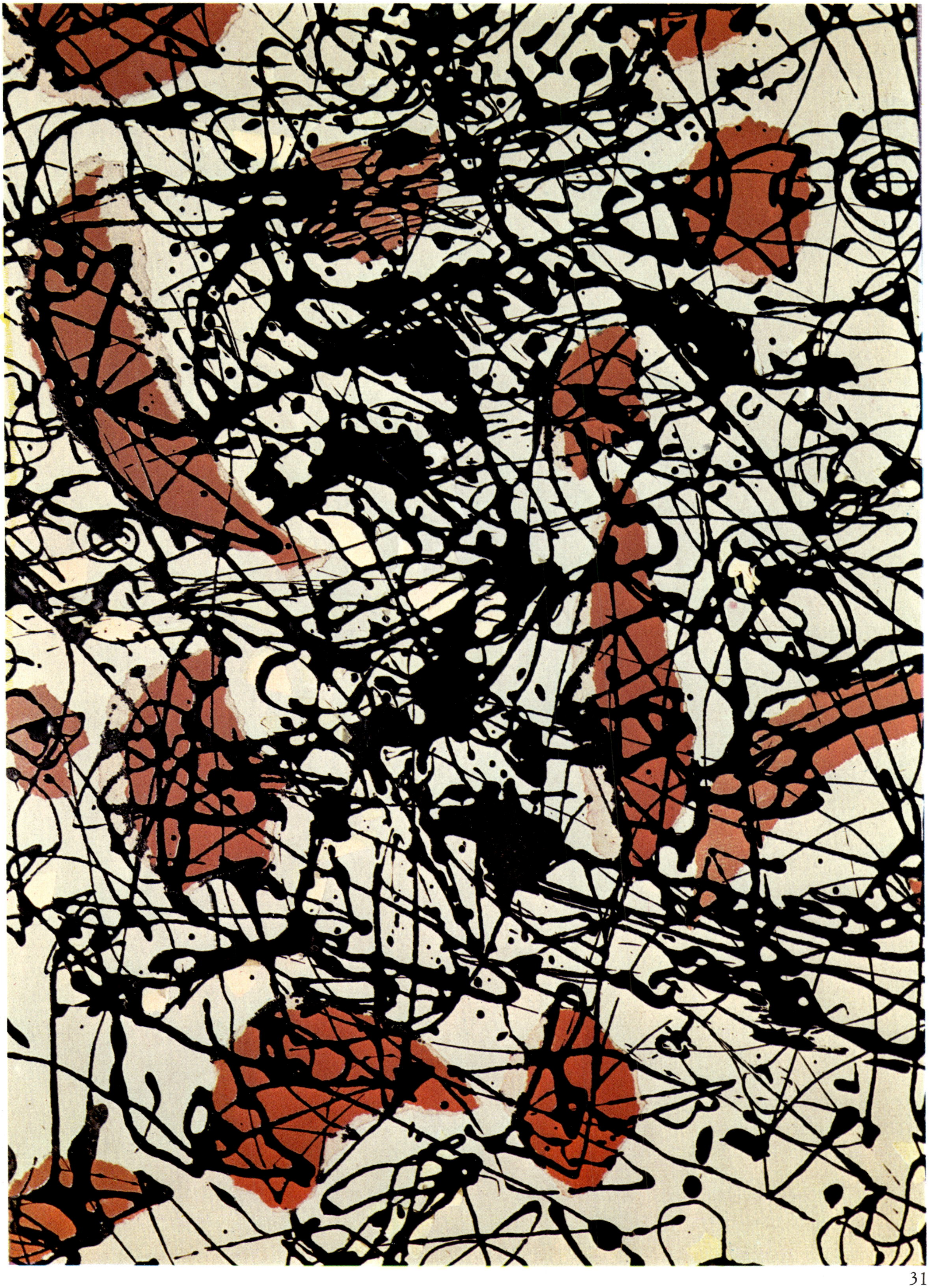

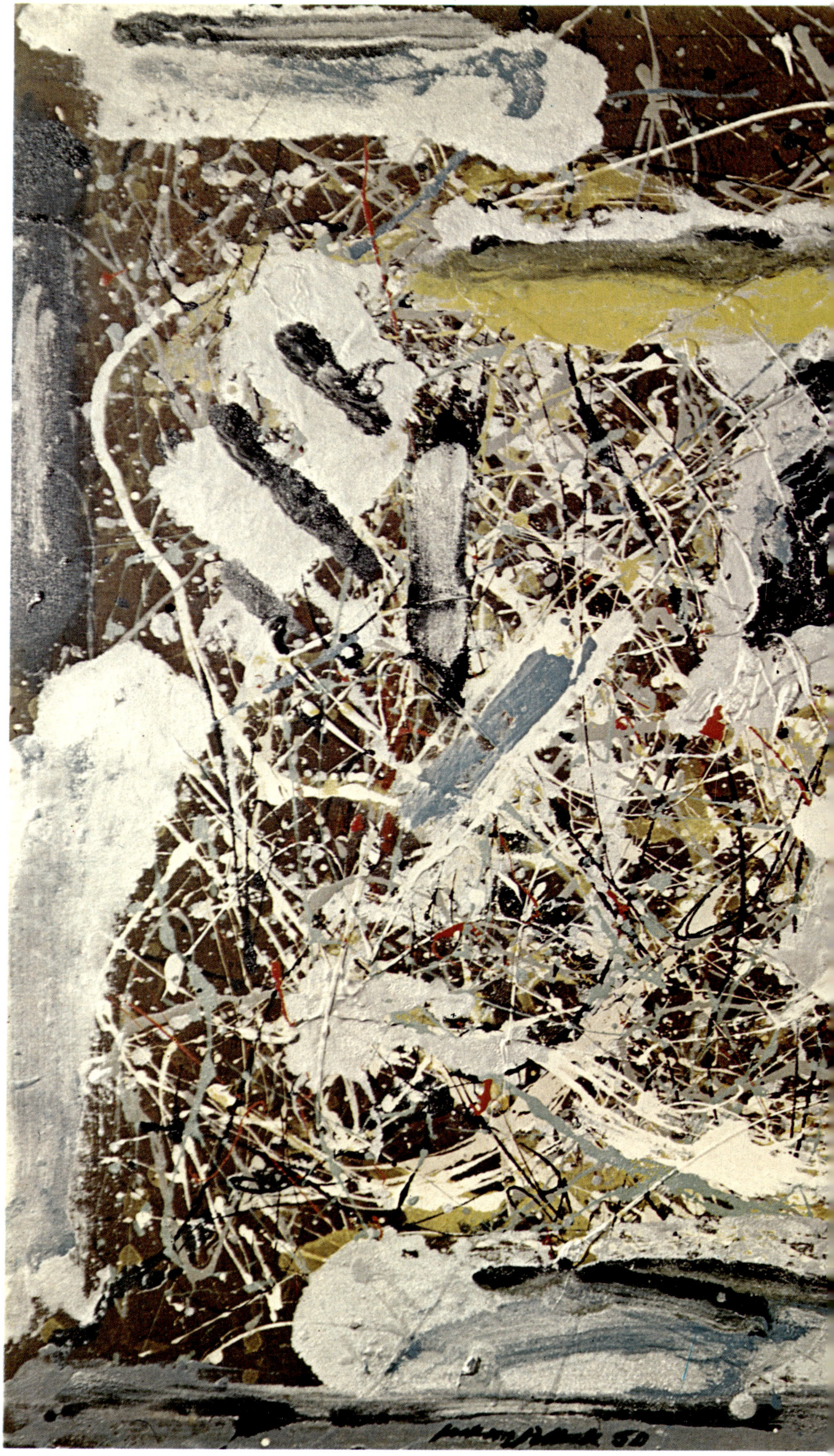

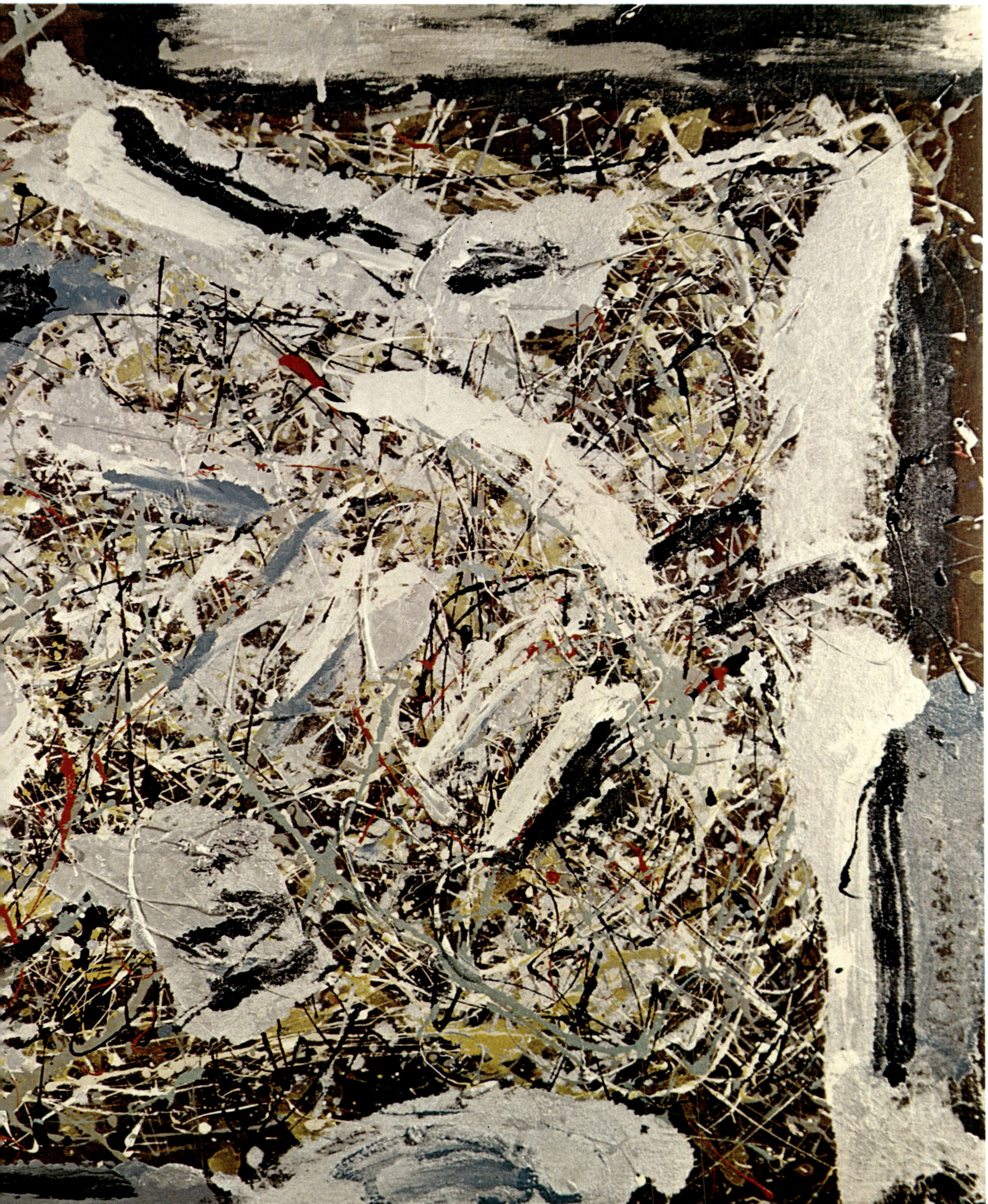

32- 33

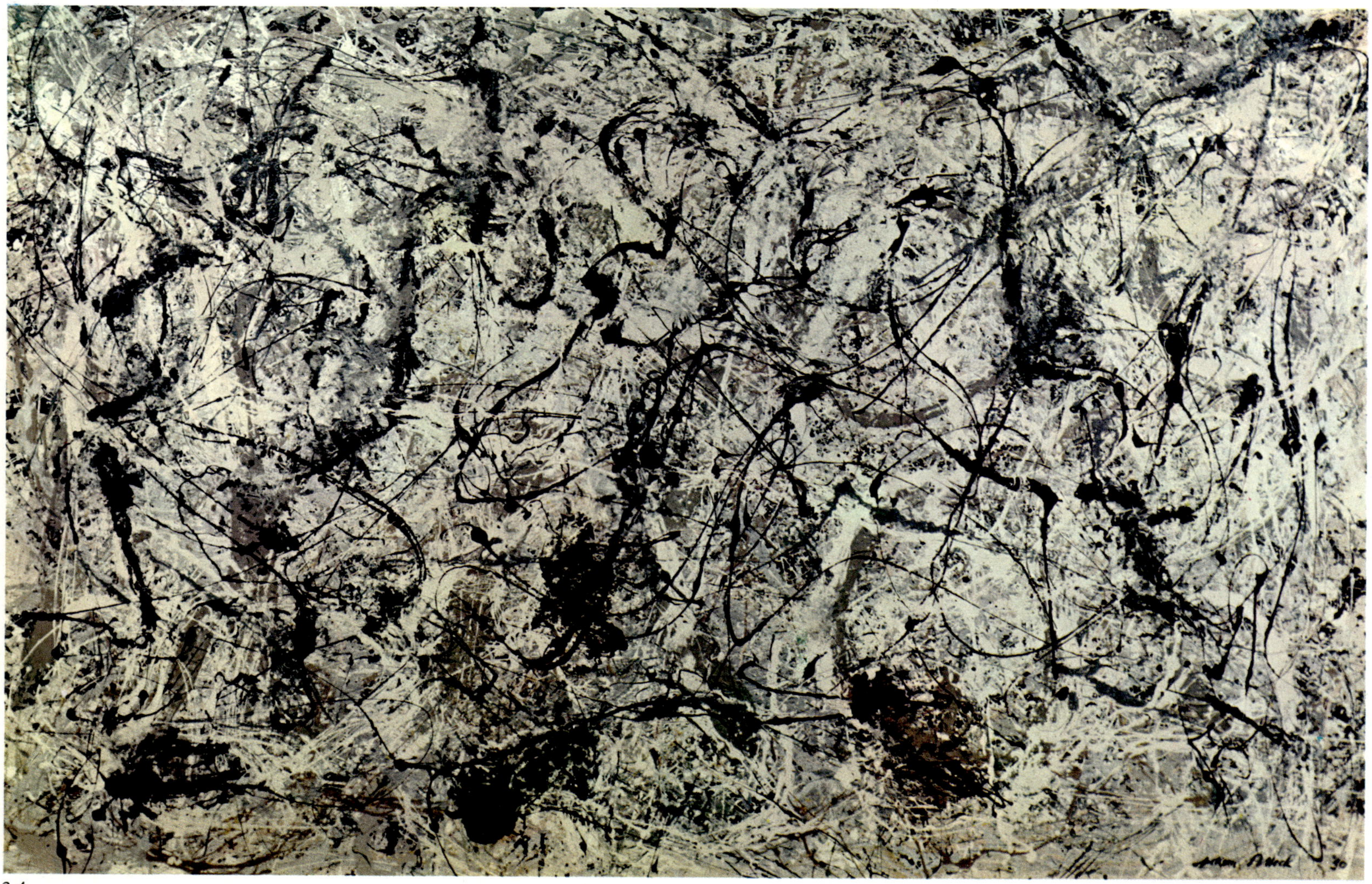

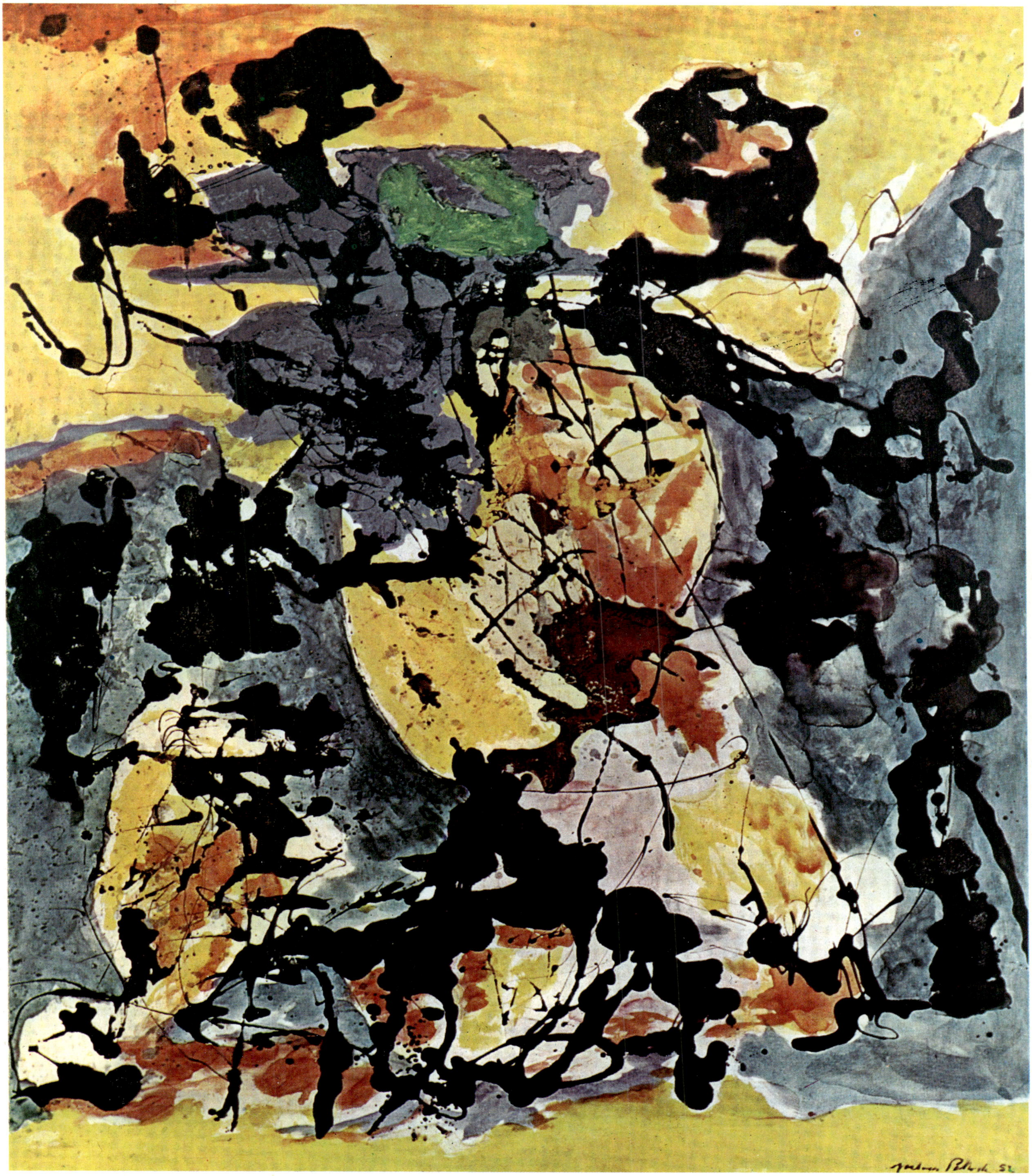

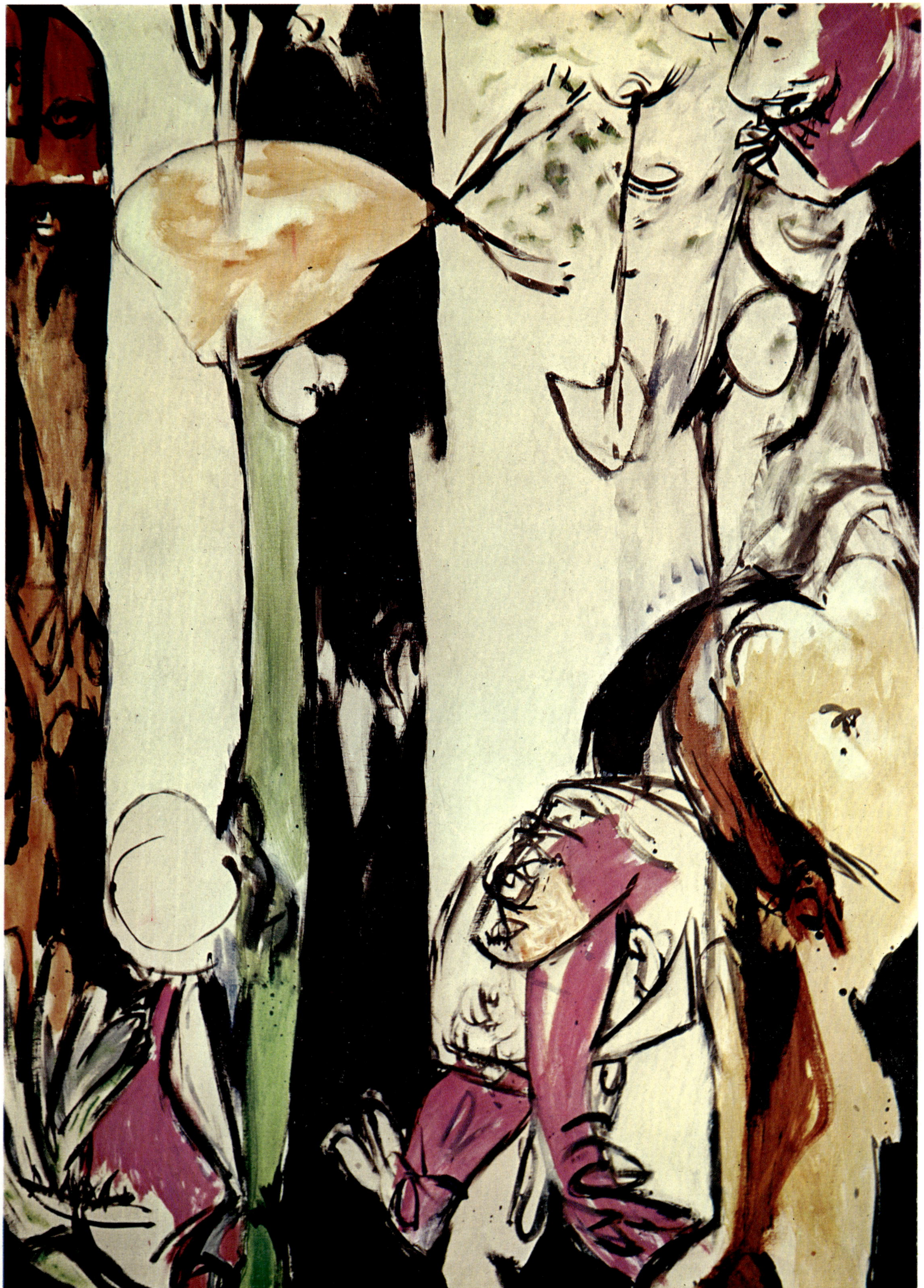

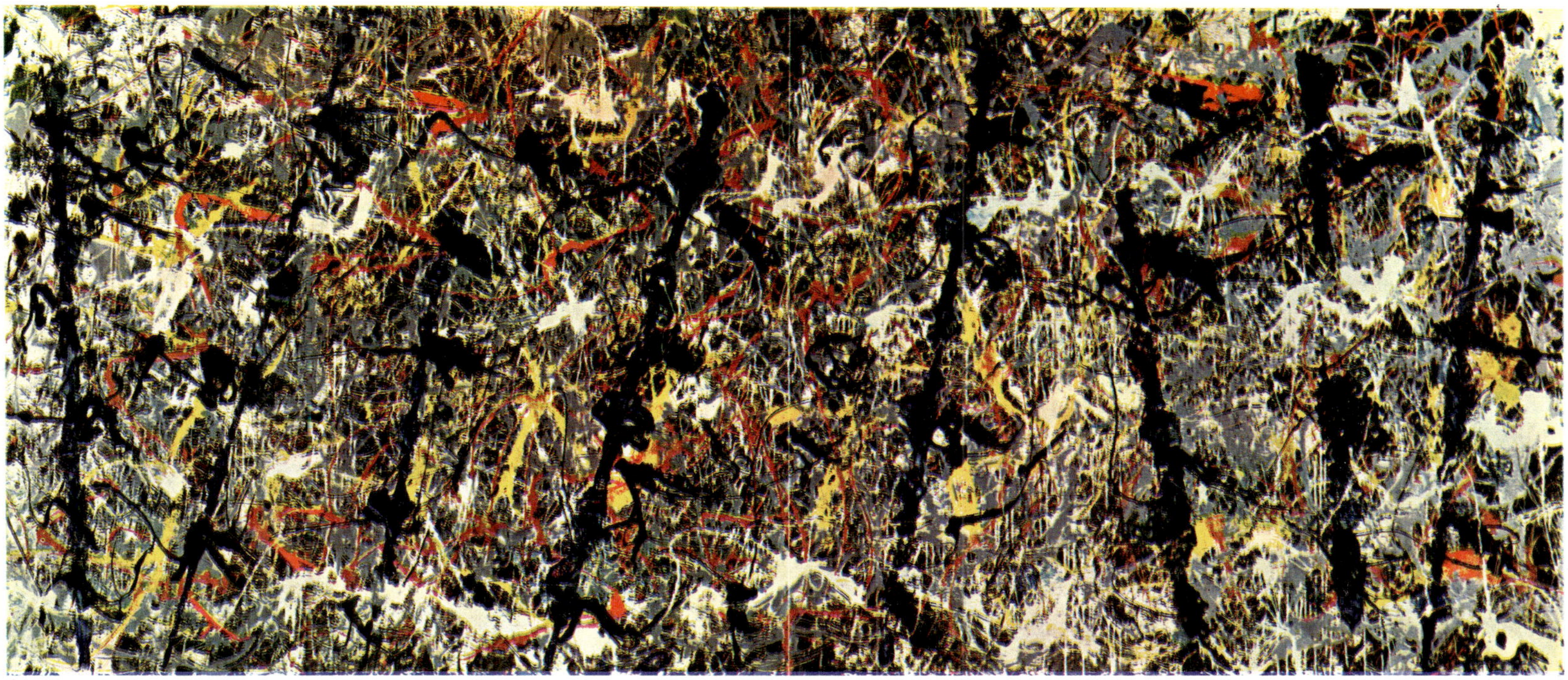

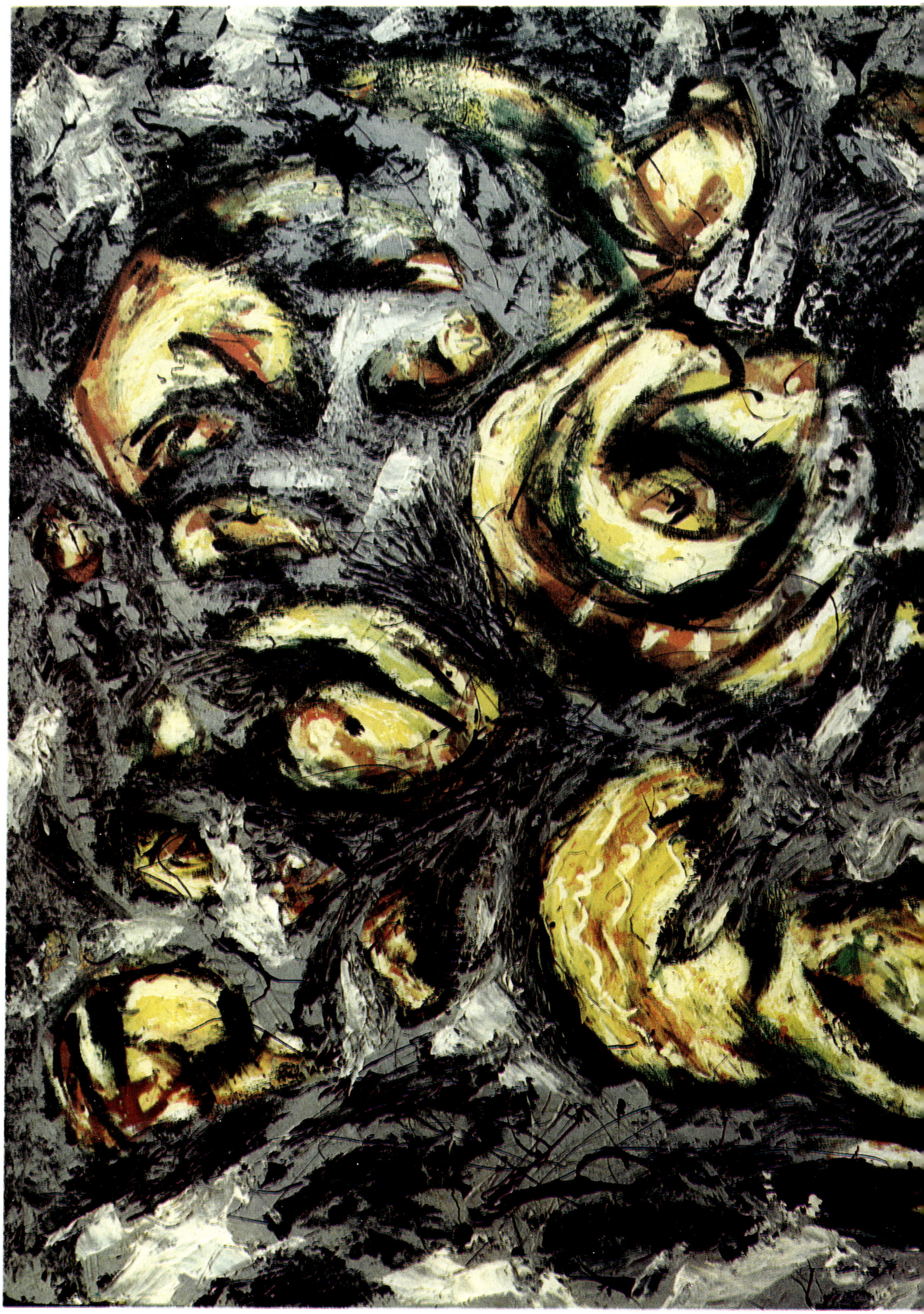

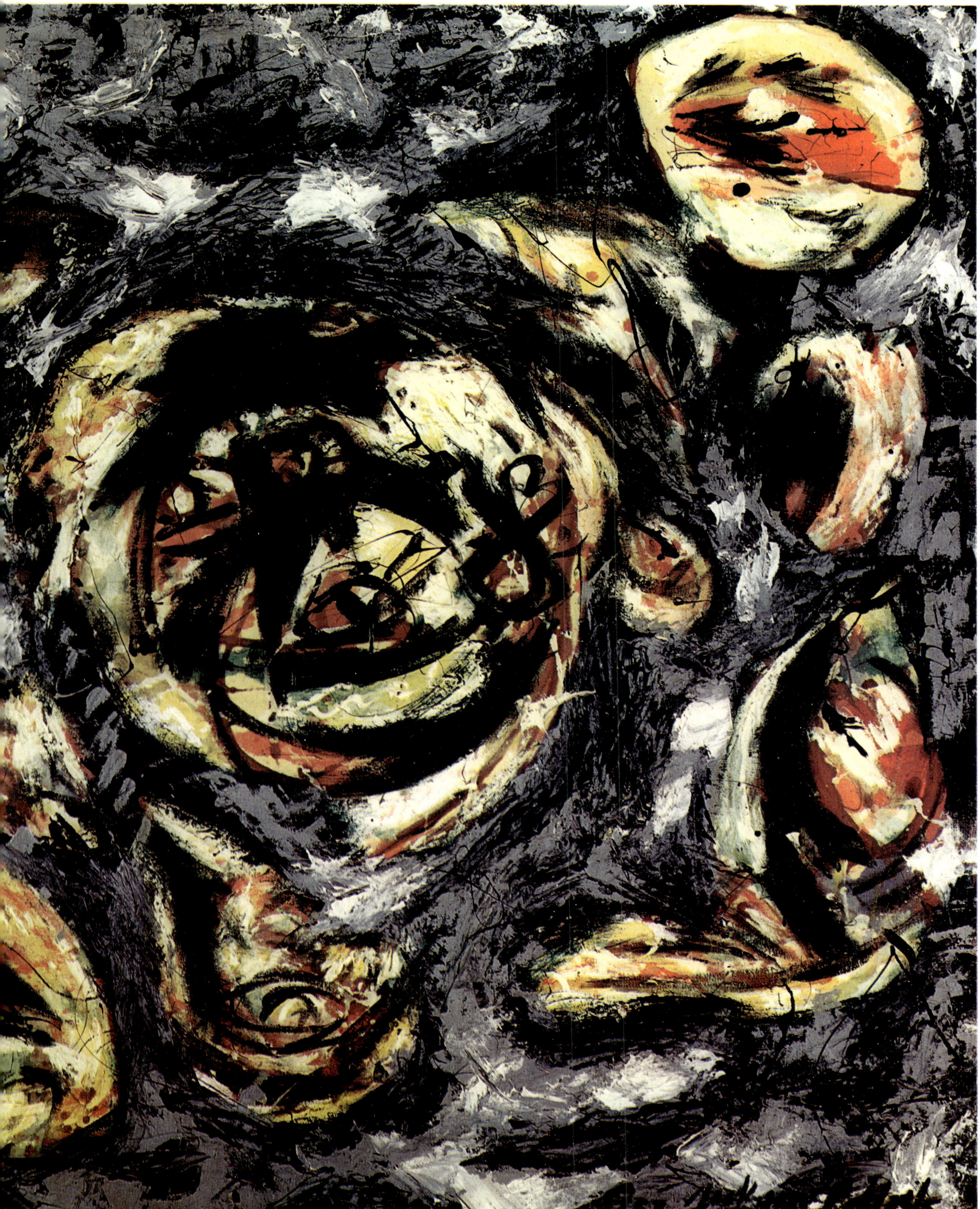

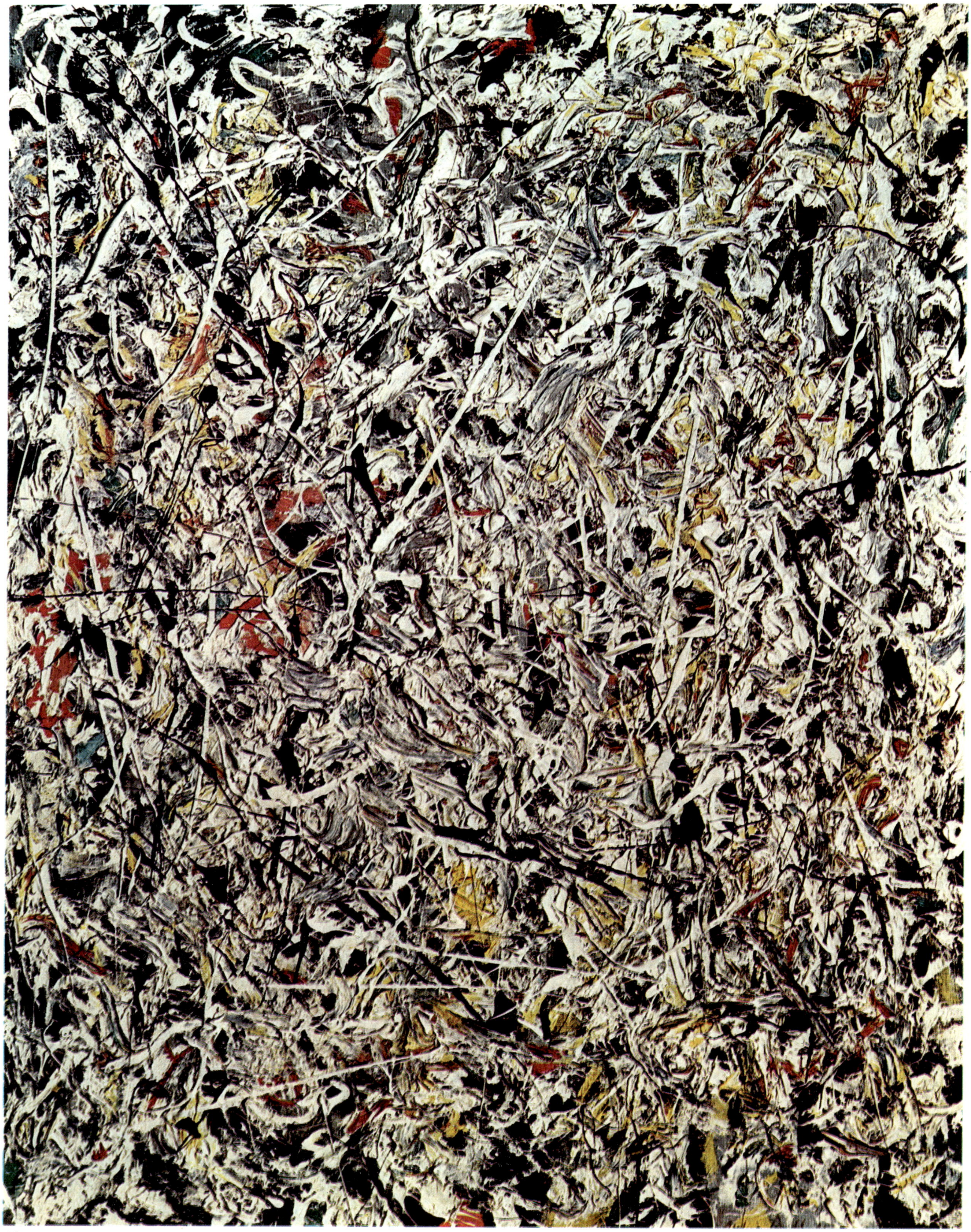

Description of colour plates

1 *Self-Portrait*
c. 1933, oil and canvas mounted on cardboard
Whereabouts unknown

2 *Seascape*
1934, oil on canvas, $12\frac{1}{4} \times 16\frac{1}{4}$ in (31×41 cm)
Lee Krasner Pollock collection, New York

3 *Woman*
c. 1936, oil on masonite
Whereabouts unknown

4 *Untitled*
c. 1936, oil on cardboard
Whereabouts unknown

5 *Untitled*
c. 1937, oil on masonite
Whereabouts unknown

6 *Untitled*
c. 1937, oil on canvas, 15×20 in ($38 \times 50{\cdot}5$ cm)
Lee Krasner Pollock collection, New York

7 *The Flame*
1937, oil on canvas, 20×30 in ($51{\cdot}2 \times 76{\cdot}4$ cm)
Lee Krasner Pollock collection, New York

8 *Birth*
c. 1938, oil on canvas, $46 \times 22\frac{1}{2}$ in ($116{\cdot}5 \times 57$ cm)
Lee Krasner Pollock collection, New York

9 *Head*
c. 1938, oil on canvas
Whereabouts unknown

10–11 *Shorthand Figure*
1942, oil on canvas
Whereabouts unknown

12 *Pasiphaë*
1943, oil on canvas, 56×96 in ($142{\cdot}6 \times 243{\cdot}8$ cm)
Lee Krasner Pollock collection, New York

13 *The She-Wolf*
1943, oil on canvas, 42×67 in ($106{\cdot}7 \times 170{\cdot}2$ cm)
Museum of Modern Art, New York

14 *The Moon Woman cuts the Circle*
c. 1943, oil on canvas, $42\frac{1}{4} \times 40$ in (107×102 cm)
Lee Krasner Pollock collection, New York

15 *Night Sounds*
c. 1944, oil and pastel on canvas, $42\frac{3}{4} \times 45\frac{3}{4}$ in ($109 \times 116{\cdot}5$ cm)
Lee Krasner Pollock collection, New York

16–17 *Search for a Symbol*
1943, oil on canvas
Marlborough Gallery, Rome

18–19 *Night Mist*
1944, oil on canvas

20 *Drawing*
c. 1943–45, water-colours, pencil and coloured inks on paper, $22\frac{1}{4} \times 30\frac{1}{2}$ in ($56{\cdot}5 \times 77$ cm)
Dwight Ripley collection, New York

21 *Horse*
c. 1945, oil on canvas
Whereabouts unknown

22 *The Key*
1946, oil on canvas, 59×84 in ($149{\cdot}9 \times 213{\cdot}4$ cm)
Lee Krasner Pollock collection, New York

23 *The Development of the Foetus*
1946, oil on canvas
Whereabouts unknown

24 *Composition*
1946, oil on canvas
Tapié de Celeyran collection, Paris

25 *War*
1947, encre de chine and coloured pencil on paper, $20\frac{1}{2} \times 26$ in (52×66 cm)
Lee Krasner Pollock collection, New York

26 *Enchanted Wood*
1947
Peggy Guggenheim collection, Venice

27 *Cathedral*
1947, Duco and aluminium paint on canvas, 71×35 in ($180{\cdot}3 \times 89$ cm)
Museum of Fine Arts (Bernard J. Reis donation), Dallas

28–29 *The Wooden Horse*
1948, oil on paper, $22\frac{1}{2} \times 30\frac{3}{4}$ in ($57{\cdot}3 \times 78{\cdot}1$ cm)
Paul Facchetti collection, Paris

30 *Painting*
1948, oil on paper, $22\frac{1}{2} \times 30\frac{3}{4}$ in ($57{\cdot}3 \times 78{\cdot}1$ cm)
Paul Fachetti collection, Paris

31 *Seven*
1950, oil on canvas
Cardazzo collection, Venice

32–33 *Silver Plaques*
1950, oils
Whereabouts unknown

34 *Number Twelve*
1952, oil, Duco and Dev-o-lac on canvas, 102×89 in (259×226 cm)
Private collection, New York

35 *Number Twenty-Eight*
1950, oil, Duco and aluminium paint on canvas, 68×105 in (173×267 cm)
Mrs Albert H. Newman collection, Chicago

36 *Easter and the Totem*
1953, oil on canvas, 82×58 in ($208{\cdot}6 \times 147{\cdot}3$ cm)
Lee Krasner Pollock collection, New York

37 *Blue Poles*
1953, oil, Duco and aluminium paint on canvas, $83 \times 192\frac{1}{2}$ in ($210{\cdot}8 \times 488{\cdot}9$ cm)
Ben Heller collection, New York

38–39 *Ocean Greyness*
1953, oil on canvas, $57\frac{3}{4} \times 94\frac{1}{2}$ in (147×240 cm)
Guggenheim Museum, New York

40 *White Light*
1954, oil on canvas, 48×38 in ($122{\cdot}5 \times 97$ cm)
Sidney Janis Gallery, New York

Biographical notes

Paul Jackson Pollock was born on January 12th, 1912, in the small town of Cody in Wyoming. He spent the years of his childhood and adolescence in close contact with the earth and the wide open spaces of the American landscape, first in Cody then in Arizona and California. His father's real name was LeRoy McCoy but he had taken the surname of Pollock from his putative father and worked unsuccessfully as a farmer until the beginning of the 1920s when he obtained state employment as a surveyor.

From what we may deduce from Jackson's childhood recollections, as told to his wife Lee Krasner, his father was a mild and melancholy man with an essentially introvert temperament. On the other hand, his mother, Stella McClure, was an energetic character (like so many women in American society) and managed all household affairs.

In 1925 Jackson, who was the last of five children, went to the Manual Arts School of Los Angeles where he attended lessons until 1929. We know that he became interested in sculpture before painting, thanks to his brother Charles' example (two or three pieces of his sculpture have survived but their quality is indifferent and their significance minute). According to Tomassoni, 'more directly than painting, this activity of his even more immediately displays the characteristics of his rough, immediate and impulsive temperament and makes it possible to verify them'.

After being expelled from the Manual Arts School for having published, together with some of his fellow students, a newspaper demolishing the ideals of the average young American, and after directing his symbols and myths towards a substantial negation of tradition and authority, Pollock moved to New York in 1929. In the meantime he had worked for two years (1928–29) with his father and his brother Sanford as a geological surveyor in the Grand Canyon, in Arizona and in California. It is probable that while he was engaged in this direct contact with the grandeur and violence of the American landscape Pollock began, if only unconsciously, to find himself as an artist (more than one of his pictures would seem to suggest a title connected in some way with the geological inferno of the Grand Canyon); it was almost certainly then that he began to be addicted to alcohol–an addiction that increased dramatically as the years went by.

We also know that when he was at Los Angeles he became interested in Far Eastern and Indian philosophy (Krishnamurti), Jung and psychoanalysis. From the little information we have, we can see Pollock as a young man objectively incapable of integrating himself in society, complex, misunderstood and perhaps somehow conditioned by the disparity in character and personality he so strongly felt between himself and his parents. In New York, Pollock joined the Art Students' League where, with his brother Charles, he studied under Thomas Hart Benton, the best-known exponent of American regional realism. Pollock not only owed to Benton his instruction but also material aids, friendship and paternal protection. Impelled by his temperament he made frequent and adventurous journeys away from New York, especially to the Far West.

From 1938 until 1942, Pollock worked for the Federal Arts Project, an organization set up by the federal government which aimed at giving artists 'public' opportunities (this was the time of Roosevelt's New Deal) but he showed little interest in the venture and his success was equally meagre.

His first important public appearance came in 1939 in an exhibition organized by John Graham at the MacMillar Gallery in New York, but it was only in 1942 that he really began to establish himself as a successful artist. It was in this year that he took part in the great exhibition 'Art of this Century' and earned the appreciation of Clement Greenberg, who made acute analyzes of the motifs and character of his paintings in various articles. Greenberg's critical intelligence was to be a support to Pollock's further career until he was at the peak of his success. At the same time, Robert Motherwell introduced him to Peggy Guggenheim, who gave him a five-year contract and commissioned him to paint a large work for her house in New York.

Pollock remained in New York for another four years. In 1946 he moved to East Hampton, Long Island, with his wife Lee Krasner, also a painter, whom he had married in 1940. The last ten years of his life were spent in a rush of violent, intense activity. After his great one-man show in 1948, he exhibited in 1950 at the Venice Biennale, in a show with De Kooning and Gorky organized by the Museum of Modern Art, and at the Milanese Galleria del Naviglio. In 1952 and 1953 he exhibited at the Studio Paul Facchetti in Paris and at the Zurich Kunsthaus.

But his addiction to alcohol had become increasingly violent and Pollock henceforth lived in a kind of daze to which alcoholism contributed as much as his creative fever. Robertson notes that in the last years of his life he habitually listened on his tape recorder to the poems of Dylan Thomas, and recordings of music by John Cage, Moreton Feldman, Varèse and Stravinsky, as a counterpoint to his own inexhaustible activity.

On December 11th, 1956, he died at the age of forty-four in a car accident, which came as the climax to the process of destruction of life that he recreated in the act and the event of painting.

38 *Jackson Pollock*
1950. Photograph by Hans Namuth

39 Jackson and Lee Krasner Pollock at East Hampton
1950. Photograph by Hans Namuth

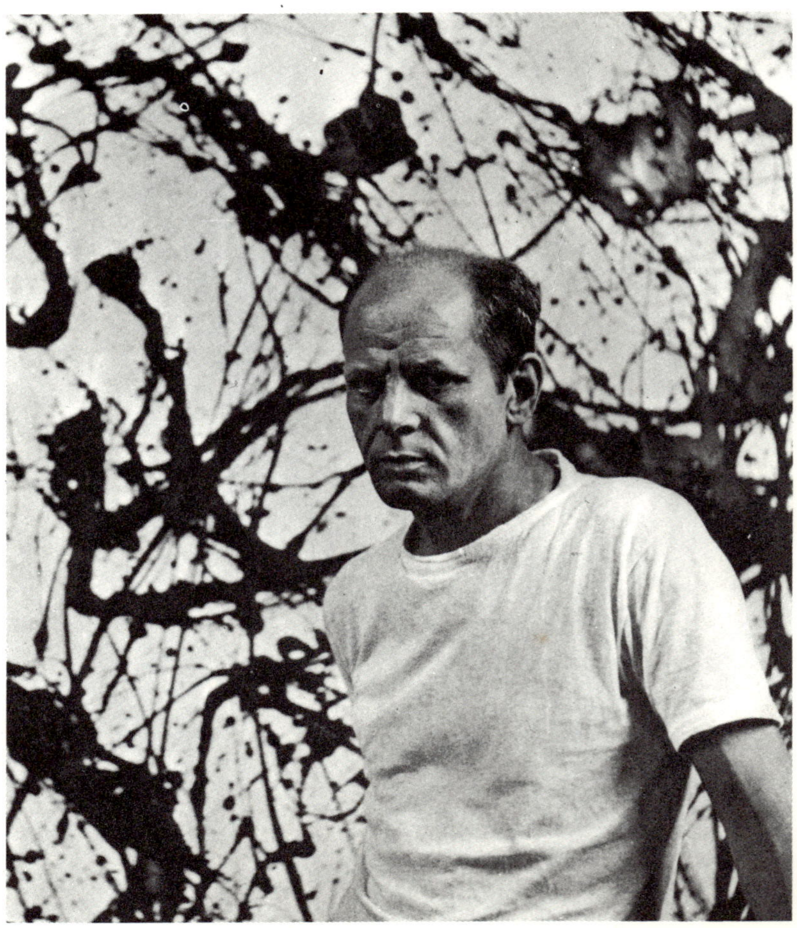

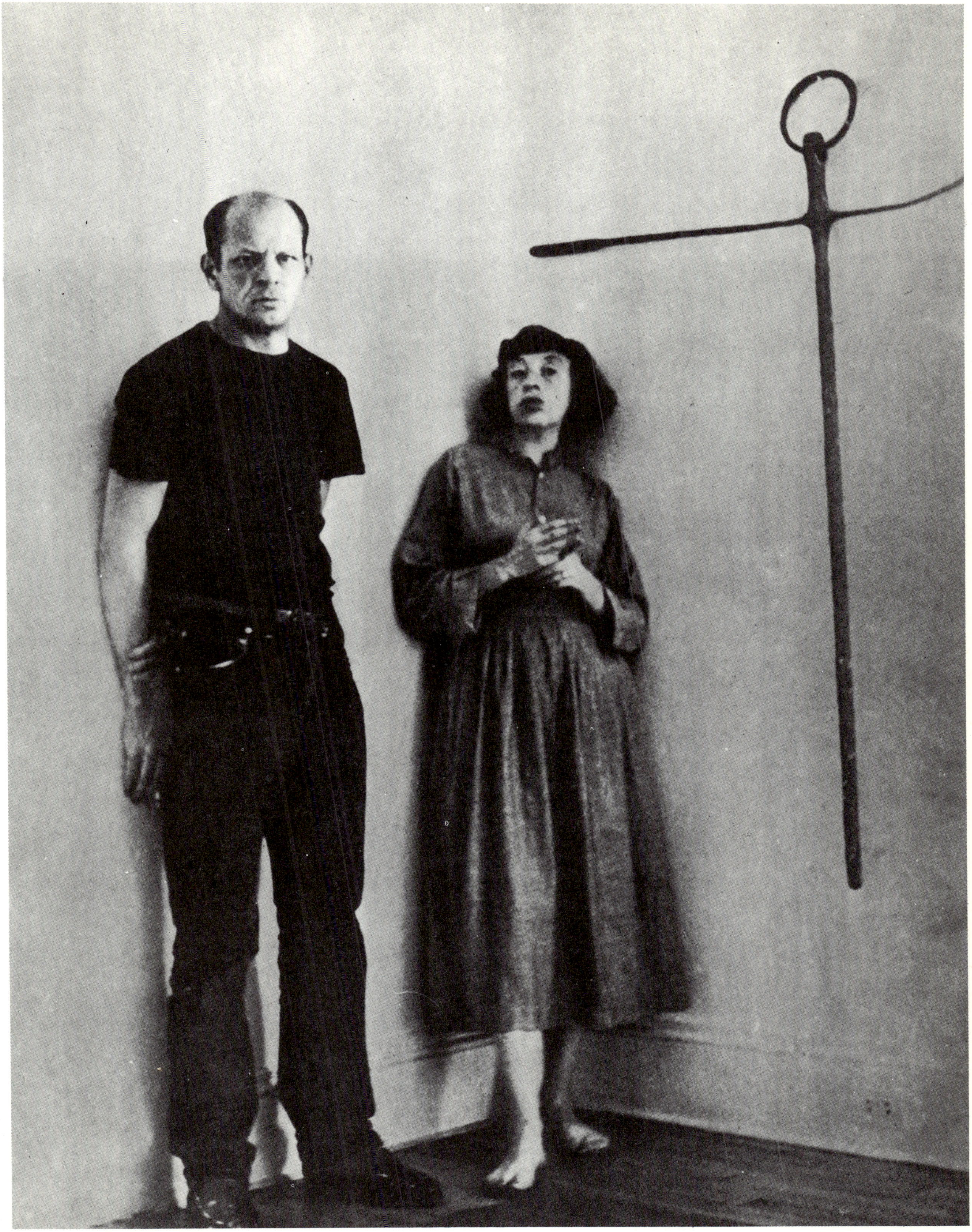

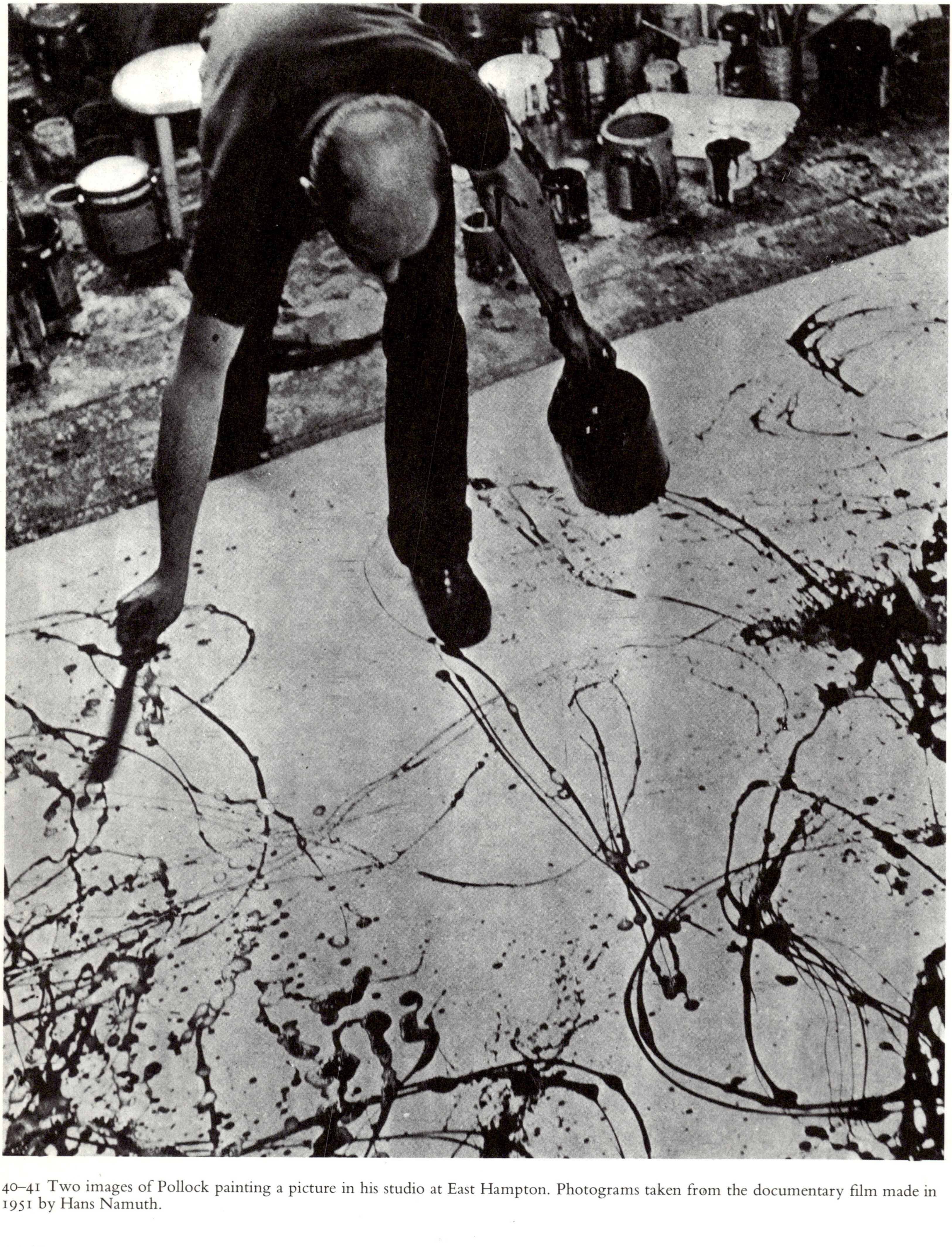

40–41 Two images of Pollock painting a picture in his studio at East Hampton. Photograms taken frøm the documentary film made in 1951 by Hans Namuth.

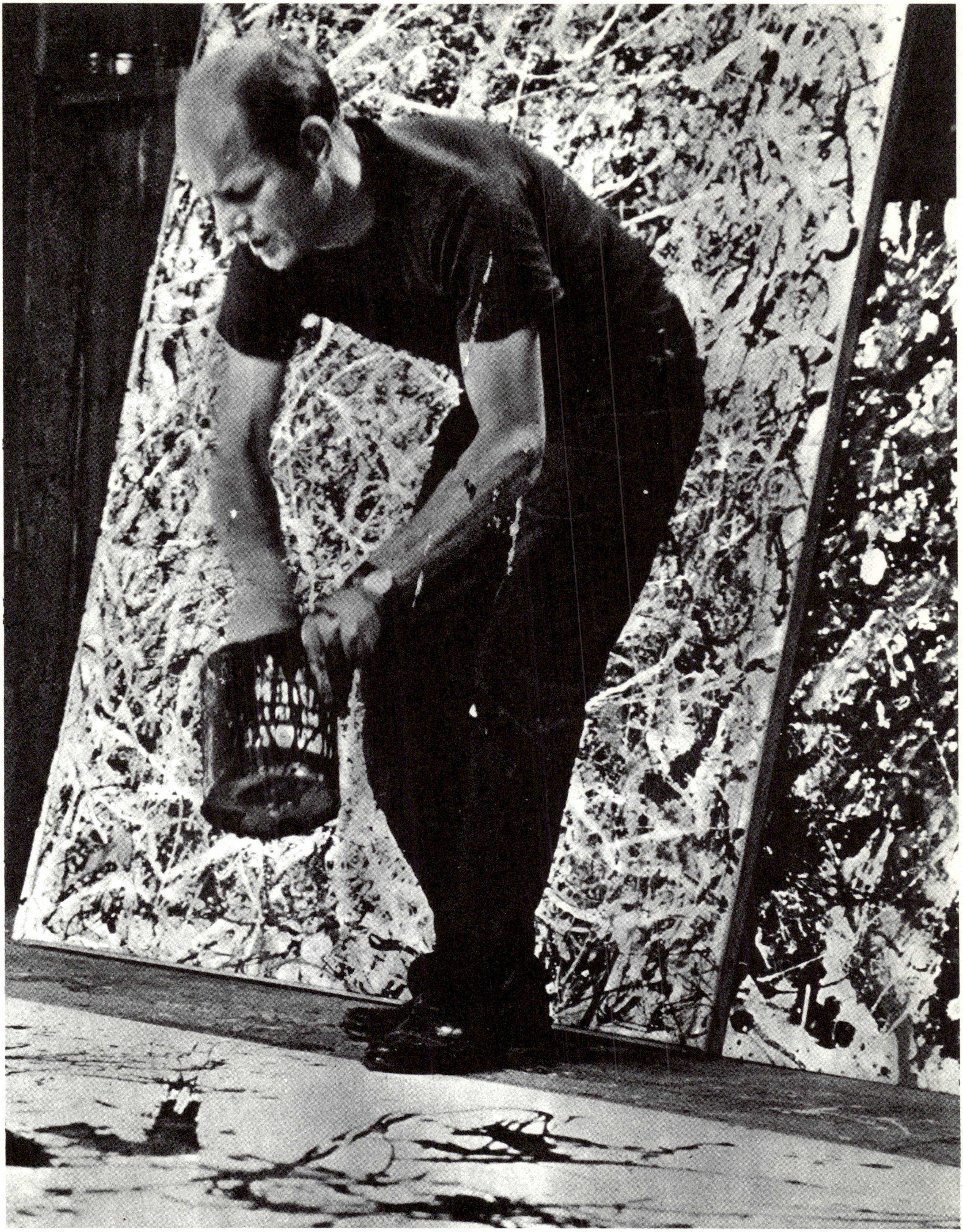

Bibliography

STATEMENTS BY THE ARTIST

'My painting', *Possibilities*, New York, 1947–48; 'A Questionnaire', *Arts and Architecture*, New York, February 1944.

BOOKS AND ARTICLES

P. BOSWELL Jr., *Modern American Painting*, New York, 1940; J. MELLQUIST, *The Emergence of an American Art*, New York, 1942; D. C. MILLER and A. H. BARR Jr., *American Realists and Magic Realists*, New York, 1943; S. M. KOOTZ, *New Frontiers in American Painting*, New York, 1943; J. J. SWEENEY, *Jackson Pollock*, catalogue of the Art of this Century exhibition, New York, November 1943; C. GREENBERG, *The Nation*, New York, November 27, 1943; R. MOTHERWELL, 'The Modern Painter's World', *Dyn*, No. 6, 1944; J. J. SWEENEY, 'Five American Painters', *Harper's Bazaar*, New York, April 1944; S. JANIS, *Abstract and Surrealist Art in America*, New York, 1944; J. J. SWEENEY, *Jackson Pollock*, catalogue of the exhibition at the Chicago Art Club, Chicago, March 1945; C. GREENBERG, *The Nation*, New York, April 7, 1945; P. GUGGENHEIM, *Out of this Century*, New York, 1946; A. D. GRUSKIN, *Painting in the U.S.A.*, New York, 1946; C. GREENBERG, *The Nation*, New York, April 13, 1946; C. GREENBERG, *The Nation*, New York, December 28, 1946; C. GREENBERG, *The Nation*, New York, February 1, 1947; C. GREENBERG, 'The Present Prospects of American Painting and Sculpture', *Horizon*, New York, October 1947; J. T. SOBY, *Contemporary Painters*, New York, 1948; C. GREENBERG, *The Nation*, New York, January 24, 1948; F. S. WIGHT, *Milestones of American Painting in our Century*, Boston, 1949; A. LEEPA, *The Challenge of Modern Art*, New York, 1949; A. HERBIN, *L'art non-figuratif, non-objectif*, Paris, 1949; P. TYLER, 'Jackson Pollock: The infinite Labyrinth', *Magazine of Art*, New York, March 1950; A. H. BARR Jr., *Gorky, Pollock, De Kooning*, catalogue of the XXV Biennale, Venice, 1950; A. H. BARR Jr., 'Gorky, De Kooning, Pollock, 7 Americans open in Venice', *Art News*, New York, June 1950; B. ALFIERI, *"Guazzabugli" di Jackson Pollock*, catalogue to the exhibition in the Ala Napoleonica in the Piazza San Marco, Venice, 1950; QUARANTOTTI-GAMBINI, 'Il quaderno veneziano di Jackson Pollock', *Il Giornale di Trieste*, September 19, 1950; R. GOODNOUGH, 'Pollock paints a Picture', *Art News*, New York, May 1951; M. SEUPHOR, 'La peinture aux Etats Unis', *Art d'Aujourd'hui*, Paris, June 1951; A. C. RITCHIE, *Abstract Painting and Sculpture in America*, catalogue to the exhibition at the Museum of Modern Art, New York, 1951; T. B. HESS, *Abstract Painting: Background and American Phase*, New York, 1951; A. OSSORIO, *Jackson Pollock*, catalogue for the exhibition at the Betty Parsons Gallery, New York, 1951; G. NICCO-FASOLA, *Ragione dell'Arte astratta*, Milan, 1951; J. I. H. BAUR, *Revolution and Tradition in Modern American Art*, Cambridge, Mass., 1951; C. GREENBERG, *Partisan Review*, New York, January–February 1952; M. TAPIE, *Jackson Pollock*, catalogue for the exhibition at the Studio Paul Fachetti, Paris, 1952; A. OSSORIO, *Jackson Pollock*, catalogue for the exhibition at the Studio Paul Fachetti, Paris, 1952; A. OSSORIO, *Jackson Pollock*, catalogue for the exhibition '15 Americans' at the Museum of Modern Art, New York, 1952; C. GREENBERG, *Harper's Bazaar*, New York, February 1952; H. ROSENBERG, *Art News*, 1952; C. GREENBERG, *Jackson Pollock*, catalogue of the retrospective Pollock exhibition at Bennington College, Vermont, 1952; *Amerikanische Malerei und Bildhauerei der Gegenwart*, catalogue of the exhibition at the Kunsthaus, Zurich, 1953; J. FITZSIMMONS, 'Jackson Pollock', *Arts and Architecture*, New York, March 1954; A. H. BARR Jr., *Masters of Modern Art*, New York, 1954; W. HAFTMANN, *Malerei im 20. Jahrhundert*, Munich, 1954; J. J. SWEENEY, *Younger Americans: A Selection*, The Solomon E. Guggenheim Museum, New York, 1954; C. GREENBERG, 'American Type Painting', *Partisan Review*, New York, 1955; B. H. FRIEDMAN, 'Profile: Jackson Pollock', *Art in America*, New York, December 1955; *15 Years of Jackson Pollock*, catalogue for the exhibition at the Sidney Janis Gallery, New York, 1955; J. T. SOBY, 'Un demi-siècle d'art aux Etats-Unis, La Peinture moderne Americaine et Paris', *Cahiers d'Art*, No. 30, Paris, 1955; C-P. BRU, *Esthétique de l'abstraction*, Toulouse, 1955; H. READ, *The Philosophy of Modern Art*, New York, 1955; S. HUNTER, 'Jackson Pollock: The Maze and the Minotaur', *New World Writing*, New York, 1956; V. WILLINGS, 'Thoughts after a car crash', *Encounter*, London, October 1956; M. SHAPIRO, 'The younger American painters of today', *The Listener*, London, January 26, 1956; R. BLESH, *Modern Art USA*, New York, 1956; M. D. CANDEE, 'Jackson Pollock', *Current Biography*, New York, April 1956 and *Current Biography Annual*, New York, 1956; D. ASHTON, 'Jackson Pollock', *Arts and Architecture*, New York, January 1956; L. VENTURI, *I pittori americani e la citta*, XXVIII Venice Biennale, 1956; K. B. SAXYER, 'Jackson Pollock 1912–1956', *Cimaise*, Paris, November–December 1956; F. ARCANGELI, 'Pollock o dell'arbitrio', *L'Europeo*, Milan, December 30, 1956; N. POUSETTE-DART, *American Painting Today*, New York, 1956; L. DEGAND, *Langage et signification de la peinture en figuration et abstraction*, Paris, 1956; P. HERON, *The Changing Forms of Art*, London, 1956; M. RAGON, *L'aventure de l'art abstrait*, Paris, 1956; G. M. POLLOCK, *XXième Siècle*, Paris, January 1956; S. HUNTER, 'Jackson Pollock', *Museum of Modern Art Bulletin*, Vol. 24, No. 2, New York, 1956–57; P. TYLER, 'Hopper/Pollock', *Art News*, No. 26, 1957; J. I. H. BAUR, *New Art in America*, New York, 1957; E. CRISPOLTI, 'Appunti su Jackson Pollock', *I Quattro Soli*, Turin, January–February 1957; C. GREENBERG, 'Jackson Pollock', *Evergreen Review*, Vol. 1 No. 3, New York, 1957; P. RESTANY, 'L'art aux Etats Unis: Pollock l'eclabousseur', *Prisme des Arts*, No. 15, Paris, 1957; S. HUNTER, 'Contributo alla conoscenza di Pollock', *I Quattro Soli*, Turin, January–February 1957; S. RODMAR, *Conversations with the Artists*, New York, 1957; M. SEUPHOR, 'Jackson Pollock', *Dictionnaire de l'Art Abstrait*, Paris, 1957; S. HUNTER, 'Jackson Pollock', catalogue of the IV Biennale, São Paolo, Brazil, 1957; *Capolavori del Museo Solomon R. Guggenheim di New York*, introduction by P. BUCARELLI, catalogue by G. CARANDENTE, Rome, 1957–58; J. I. H. BAUR, *Nature in Abstraction*, New York, 1958; W. GROHMANN, *Neue Kunst nach 1945*, Cologne, 1958; G. POENSGEN and C. ZAHN, *Abstrakte Kunst: ein Weltsprache*, Baden-Baden, 1958; G. RIETVELD, 'A View of Life', *Delta*, 1958; F. A. WILSON, *Art into Life*, 1958; L. ALLOWAY, 'The Art of Jackson Pollock: 1912–1956', *The Listener*, London, November 27, 1958; J. BERGER, 'La colla bianca', *The New Statesman*, London, November 22, 1958; M. MCCLURE, 'Ode to Jackson Pollock', *Evergreen Review*, Vol. 2, No. 6, New York, 1958; R. SMITH, 'Jackson Pollock: 1912–56', *Art News and Review*, London, November 22, 1958; D. SUTTON, 'Jackson Pollock', *Financial Times*, London, November 25, 1958; M. CALVESI, 'Il genio di Pollock', *I Quattro Soli*, Turin, April 1958; S. HUNTER, catalogue of the exhibition at the Galleria Nazionale d'Art Moderna, Rome, 1958; E. CRISPOLTI, *Pollock*, Milan, 1958; S. HUNTER, *Modern American Painting and Sculpture*, New York, 1959; F. O'HARA, *Jackson Pollock*, New York, 1959; H. ROSENBERG, *The Tradition of the New*, New York, 1959; A. CHASTEL, *Le Monde*, January 17, 1959; M. DE MICHELI, *Le avanguardie artistiche del Novecento*, Milan, 1959; H. KRAMER, 'Jackson Pollock and Nicolas de Staël', *Arts Yearbook*, New York, 1959; M. MIDDLETON, 'Pollock', *Motif*, London, February 1959; W. RUBIN, 'Notes on Masson and Pollock', *Arts*, New York, November 1959; J. RUSSEL, *Horizon*, New York, 1959; H. READ, *A Concise History of Modern Painting*, London, 1959; B. ROBERTSON, *Jackson Pollock*, London 1960; N. PONENTE, *La peinture moderne: Tendences contemporaines*, Geneva, 1960; E. B. HENNING, *Paths of Abstract Art*, Cleveland, 1960; H. READ, 'Social Significance of Abstract Art', *Quadrum*, No. 9, 1960; B. H. FRIEDMAN, *New York School: Some Young Artists*, New York, 1960; M. SEUPHOR, *Abstract Painting*, New York, 1961; M. WALLIS, 'Origin and Foundation of Non-objective Painting', *Journal of Aesthetics*, No. 19, 1961; L. TRUCCHI, *Qualche Ritratto da Cézanne a Pollock*, Rome, 1961; G. DORFLES, *Ultime tendenze nell'arte d'oggi*, Milan, 1961; I. TOMASSONI, *Per una ipotesi barocca*, Rome, 1963; J. CLAUS, *Theorien zur zeitgenossischer Malerei*, Hamburg, 1963; A. FERMIGIER, 'Paris–New York, 1940–45', *Art de France*, No. 4, 1964; G. C. ARGAN, *Salvezza e caduta nell'arte moderna*, Milan, 1964; H. ROSENBERG, *New York Magazine*, May 6, 1967; W. RUBIN, 'Jackson Pollock and the Modern Tradition', *Art Forum*, February–March 1967; F. V. O'CONNOR, 'The Genesis of Jackson Pollock', *Art Forum*, May 1967; F. V. O'CONNOR, *Jackson Pollock*, The Museum of Modern Art, New York, 1967; I. TOMASSONI, *Pollock*, London 1968; D. H. ROBBINS and H. ZERNER, 'A propos de la rétrospective Jackson Pollock', *Revue de l'Art*, No. 3, 1969.